LIFE IN CHRIST

LIFE IN CHRIST

Lessons from Our Lord's Miracles and Parables

The Miracles of Our Lord
Volume 11

Charles H. Spurgeon

We love hearing from our readers. Please contact us at www.anekopress.com/questions-comments with any questions, comments, or suggestions.

Life in Christ, Vol. 11
© 2023 by Aneko Press
All rights reserved. First edition 1891.
Revisions copyright 2023

Cover Design: Natalia Hawthorne
Cover Painting: Matt Philleo
Editors: Ruth Clark and J. Martin

Aneko Press
www.anekopress.com
Aneko Press, Life Sentence Publishing, and our logos are trademarks of
Life Sentence Publishing, Inc.
203 E. Birch Street
P.O. Box 652
Abbotsford, WI 54405

RELIGION / Christian Life / Spiritual Growth
Paperback ISBN: 979-8-88936-260-9
eBook ISBN: 979-8-88936-261-6
10 9 8 7 6 5 4 3 2 1
Available where books are sold

Contents

Chapter 1

The Prodigal's Return

But when he was yet a great way off, his father saw him,
and had compassion, and ran, and fell on his neck, and
kissed him. (Luke 15:20)

All persons engaged in education will tell you that they find it far more difficult to make the mind unlearn its errors than to make it receive truth. If we could suppose a man is totally ignorant of anything, we would have a fairer chance of instructing him quickly and effectively than we would have had if his mind had been previously stored with falsehood. I have no doubt that you, each of you, find it harder to unlearn than to learn.

To get rid of old prejudices and preconceived notions is a very hard struggle indeed. It has been well said that those few words, "I am mistaken," are the hardest in all the English language to pronounce, and certainly it takes very much force to compel us to pronounce them; and after having done so, it is even then difficult to wipe away the slime that an old serpentine error has left upon the heart. Better for us not to have known at all than to have known the wrong thing.

Now, I am sure that this truth is never more true than when it applies to God. If I had been let alone to form my notion of God, entirely from Holy Scripture, I feel that with the assistance of his Holy Spirit, it would have been far easier for me to understand what he is, and how he governs the world, than to learn even the truths of his own Word, after the mind had become perverted by the opinions of others. Why, brethren, who is it that gives a fair representation of God?

The Arminian slanders God by accusing him (not in his own intention, but really so) of unfaithfulness; for he teaches that God may promise what he never performs; that he may give eternal life, and promise that those who have it shall never perish, and yet they may perish after all. He speaks of God as if he were a changeable being, for he talks of his loving men one day, and hating them the next; of his writing their names in the Book of Life one hour, and then erasing their names in the next.

Many children of God, who have imbibed these errors in early youth, have had to drag along their poor wearied and broken frames for many a day, whereas they might have walked joyfully to heaven if they had known the truth from the beginning. On the other hand, those who hear the Calvinistic preacher are very apt to misinterpret God. Although we trust we would never speak of God in any other sense than that in which we find him represented in sacred Scripture, yet are we well aware that many of our hearers, even through our assertions, when most guarded, are apt to get a caricature of God rather than a true picture of him.

They imagine that God is a severe being, angry and fierce, very easily to be moved to wrath, but not so easily to be induced to love. They are apt to think of him as one who sits in a supreme and lofty state, either totally indifferent to the wishes of his creatures, or else determined to have his own way with them, as an arbitrary Sovereign, never listening to their desires, or showing compassion to their woes.

Oh, that we could unlearn all these fallacies, and believe God to be what he is! Oh, that we could come to Scripture, and there look into that glass that reflects his sacred image, and then receive him as he is, the all-wise, the all-just, and yet the all-gracious and all-loving Jehovah! I shall endeavor this morning, by the help of God's Holy Spirit, to represent the lovely character of Christ; and if I shall be happy enough to have some in my audience who are in the position of the Prodigal Son in the parable – coming to Christ, and yet a great way off from him – I shall trust that they will be led by the same divine Spirit, to believe in the loving-kindness of Jehovah, and so may find peace with God now, before they leave this house of prayer.

When he was yet a great way off, his father saw him, and had compassion, and ran, and fell on his neck, and kissed him. First, I shall notice the *position* intended in the words, *a great way off;* secondly, I shall notice the *peculiar troubles* that agitate the minds of those who are in this condition; and then, thirdly, I shall endeavor to teach *the great loving-kindness of our own adorable God,* inasmuch as when we are *a great way off,* he runs to us, and embraces us in the arms of his love.

First, then, what is the position signified by being *a great way off?* I must just notice what is *not* that position. It is not the position of the man who is careless and entirely regardless of God; for you notice that the prodigal is represented now as having come to himself, and as returning to his father's house. Though it be true that all sinners are *a great way off* from God, whether they know it or not, yet in this particular instance, the position of the poor prodigal is intended to signify the character of one who has been aroused by conviction, who has been led to abhor his former life, and who sincerely desires to return to God.

I shall not, then, this morning, specially address the blasphemer and the profane. To him, there may be some incidental warning heard, but I shall not specially address such a character. It is another person for whom this text is intended: the man who has been a blasphemer, if you please, who may have been a drunkard, and a swearer, and what not, but who has now renounced these things, and is steadfastly seeking after Christ, that he may obtain eternal life. That is the man who is here said to be, though coming to the Lord, *a great way off.*

Once again, there is another person who is not intended by this description, namely, the very great man, the Pharisee who thinks himself extremely righteous, and has never learned to confess his sin. You, sir, in your understanding, are not *a great way off,* but you are so really in the sight of God. You are as far from him as light is from darkness, as the east is from the west; but you are not spoken of here. You are like the Prodigal Son, only that instead of spending your life righteously, you have run away from your Father, and hidden in the earth the gold that he gave you, and are able to feed upon the husks that swine do eat, while by a miserable economy of good works you are hoping to save enough of your fortune to support yourself here and in eternity. Your hope of self-salvation is a fallacy, and you are not addressed in the words of the text. It is the man who knows himself lost but desires to be saved, who is here declared to be met by God, and is received with affectionate embraces.

And now we come to the question, Who is the man, and why is he said to be a great way off? For he seems to be very near the kingdom, now that he knows his need and is seeking the Savior. I reply, in the first place, he is a great way off in his own understandings. You are here this morning, and you have an idea that never was man so far from God as you are.

You look back upon your past life, and you recollect how you have offended God, despised his Sabbath, neglected his Book, trampled upon the blood of sprinkling, and rejected all the invitations of his mercy. You turn over the pages of your history, and you remember the sins that you have committed – the sins of your youth and your former transgressions, the crimes of your manhood, and the riper sins of your older years – like black waves dashing upon a dark shore, they roll in wave upon wave, upon your poor troubled memory.

There comes a little wave of your childish folly, and over that there leaps one of your youthful transgressions, and over the head of this there comes a very Atlantic billow of your manhood's transgressions. At the sight of them you stand astonished and amazed. "O Lord, my God, how deep is the gulf that divides me from you, and where is the power that can bridge it? I am separated from you by leagues of sin; whole mountains of my guilt are piled upwards between me and you. O God, should you destroy me now, you would be just; and if you ever bring me to yourself, it must be nothing less than a power as omnipotent as that which made the world, which can ever do it. Oh! how far am I from God!"

Some of you would be startled this morning if your neighbors were to give you revelations of their own feelings. If yonder man standing there in the crowd could come into this pulpit, and reveal what he now feels, you might perhaps be horrified at his description of his own heart. How many of you have no notion of the way in which a soul is cut and hacked about, when it is under the convictions of the law? If you would hear the man reveal what he feels, you would say, "Ah! he is a poor deluded enthusiast; men are not so bad as that"; or else you would be apt to think he had committed some nameless crime that he dare not mention, that was preying on his conscience.

No sir, he has been as moral and as upright as you have been; but should he describe himself as he now discovers himself to be, he would shock you utterly. And yet you are the same, though you feel it not, and would indignantly deny it.

When the light of God's grace comes into your heart, it is something like the opening of the windows of an old cellar that has been shut up for many days. Down in that cellar, which has not been opened for many months, are all kinds of loathsome creatures, and a few sickly plants dulled by the darkness. The walls are dark and damp with the trail of reptiles; it is a horrid, filthy place in which no one would willingly enter. You may walk there in the dark very securely, and except now and then for the touch of some slimy creature, you would not believe the place was so bad and filthy.

Open those shutters, clean a pane of glass, let a little light in, and now see how a thousand noxious things have made this place their habitation. Sure, 'twas not the light that made this place so horrible, but it was the light that showed how horrible it was before. So, let God's grace just open a window and let the light into a man's soul, and he will stand astonished to see at what a distance he is from God.

Yes sir, today you think yourself second to none but the Eternal. You imagine that you can approach his throne with a steady step; it is but a little that you have to do to be saved; you imagine that you can accomplish it at any hour, and save yourself upon your dying bed as well as now. Ah! sir, if you could but be touched by Ithuriel's wand, and made to be in appearance what you are in reality, then you would see that you are far enough from God even now, and so far from him, that unless the arms of his grace were stretched out to bring you to himself, you would perish in your sin.

Now I turn my eye again with hope, and trust I have not a few in this large assembly who can say, "Sir, I feel I am far from God, and sometimes I fear I am so far from him that he will never have mercy upon me. I dare not lift so much as my eyes towards heaven; I strike my breast, and say, 'Lord have mercy upon me, a sinner.'" Oh! poor heart; here is a comforting passage for you: *When he was yet a great way off, his father saw him, and had compassion [on him]*.

But again, there is a second sense in which some now present feel themselves to be far off from God. Conscience tells every man that if he would be saved, he must get rid of his sin. The Antinomian may possibly pretend to believe that men can be saved while they live in sin; but conscience will never allow any man to swallow so flagrant a lie as that. I have not one person in this congregation who is not perfectly assured that if he is to be saved, he must cease his drunkenness and his depravity. Surely there is not one here so stunned with the laudanum of hellish indifference as to imagine that he can revel in his lusts, and afterwards wear the white robe of the redeemed in paradise.

If you imagine that you can be partakers of the blood of Christ, and yet drink the cup of Belial; if you imagine that you can be members of Satan and members of Christ at the same time, then you have less sense than one would give you credit for. No, you know that right arms must be cut off, and right eyes plucked out – that the most darling sins must be renounced, if you would enter into the kingdom of God.

And I have a man here who is convinced of the unholiness of his life, and he has endeavored to reform, not because he thinks reformation would save him, for he knows better than that, but because he knows that this is one of the first fruits of grace – reformation from sin. Well, poor man, he has for many years been a hard-core drunkard, and he struggles now to overcome the passion. He has almost accomplished it; but he never had such a Herculean labor to attempt before, for now some temptation comes upon him so strongly that it is as much as he can do to stand against it; and perhaps sometimes since his first conviction of sin he has even fallen into it.

Or perhaps it is another sin, and you, my brother, have set your face against it; but there are many bonds and fetters that bind us to our sins, and you find that though it was easy enough to spin the warp and woof of sin together; it is not so easy to unravel that which you have spun. You cannot purge your house of your idols; you do not yet know how to give up all your lustful pleasures. Not yet can you renounce the company of the ungodly. You have cut off one by one your most intimate acquaintances, but it is very hard to do it completely, and you are struggling to accomplish it, and you often fall on your knees and cry, "O Lord, how far I am from you! what high steps these are which I have to climb! Oh! how can I be saved? Surely, if I cannot purge myself from my old sins,

I shall never be able to hold on my way; and even should I get rid of them, I should plunge into them once more." You are crying out, "Oh, how great my distance from God! Lord, bring me near!"

Let me present you with one other aspect of our distance from God. You have read your Bibles, and you believe that faith alone can unite the soul to Christ. You feel that unless you can believe in him who died upon the cross for your sins, you can never see the kingdom of God; but you can say this morning, "Sir, I have endeavored to believe; I have searched the Scriptures, not hours, but days together, to find a promise upon which my weary foot might rest. I have been upon my knees many and many a time earnestly pleading for a divine blessing; but though I have pleaded, all in vain have I urged my plea, for until now no whisper have I had of grace, no token for good, no sign of mercy. Sir, I have endeavored to believe, and I have said,

'O could I but believe!
    Then all would easy be;
I would, but cannot – Lord, relieve,
    My help must come from thee!'

"I have used all the power I have and have desperately endeavored to cast myself at the Savior's feet and see my sins washed away in his blood. I have not been indifferent to the story of the cross; I have read it a hundred times, and even wept over it; but when I endeavor to put my hand upon the scapegoat's head, and labor to believe that my sins are transferred to him, some demon seems to stop the breath that would breathe itself forth in adoration, and something checks the hand that would lay itself upon the head that died for me."

Well, poor soul, you are indeed far from God. I will repeat the words of the text to you. May the Holy Spirit repeat them in your ear! *When he was yet a great way off, his father saw him, and had compassion, and ran, and fell on his neck, and kissed him.* So shall it be with you if you have come thus far, though great may be the distance, your feet shall not have to travel it; but God the Eternal One shall from his throne look down and visit your poor heart, though now you wait by the way, afraid to approach him.

Our second point is the peculiar troubles that agitate the breasts of those who are in this position. Let us introduce to you the poor ragged prodigal. After a life of ease, he is by his own sin plunged into poverty and labor. After feeding swine for a time, and being almost starved, he sets about returning to his father's house. It is a long and weary journey. He walks many a mile until his feet are sore, and at last from the summit of a mountain he views his father's house far away in the plain.

There are yet many miles between him and his father whom he has neglected. Can you imagine his emotions when for the first time after so long an absence he sees the old house at home? He remembers it well in the distance; for though it is long since he walked its floors, he has never ceased to recollect it; and the remembrance of his father's kindness, and of his own prosperity when he was with him, has never yet been erased from his consciousness. You would imagine that for one moment he feels a flash of joy, like some flash of lightning in the midst of the tempest, but then immediately a black darkness comes over his spirit.

In the first place, it is probable that he will think, "Oh! suppose I could reach my home, will my father receive me? Will he not shut the door in my face and tell me to depart and spend the rest of my life where I have been spending the first of it?"

Then another suggestion might arise: "Surely, the demon that led me first astray may lead me back again, before I salute my parent." "Or perhaps," thought he, "I may even die upon the road, and so before I have received my father's blessing my soul may stand before its God." I doubt not each of these three thoughts has crossed your mind if you are now in the position of one who is seeking Christ, but mourns to feel himself far away from him.

First, you have been afraid lest you should die before Christ has appeared to you. You have been for months seeking the Savior without finding him, and now the dark thought comes: "And what if I should die with all these prayers unanswered? Oh! if he would but hear me before I departed this world, I would be content, though he should keep me waiting in anguish for many years. But what if before tomorrow morning I should be a corpse? At my bed I kneel tonight and cry for mercy. Oh! if he should not send the pardon before tomorrow morning, and in the night my spirit should stand before his bar! – What then?" It is peculiar that other men think they shall live forever, but men convinced of sin, who seek a Savior, are afraid they shall not live another moment.

You have known the time, dear Christian brethren, when you dared not shut your eyes for fear you would not open them again on earth; when you dreaded the shadows of the night lest they would darken forever the light of the sun, and you would dwell in outer darkness throughout eternity. You have mourned as each day has entered, and you have wept as it has departed, because you imagined that your next step might hurl you into your eternal doom. I have known what it is to tread the earth and fear lest every tuft of grass should but cover a door to hell; trembling, lest every particle, and every atom, and every stone, should be so allied with God against me as to destroy me.

John Bunyan says that at one time in his experience, he felt that he would rather have been born a dog or a toad than a man; he felt so unutterably wretched on account of sin; and his great point of wretchedness was the fact that though he had been three years seeking Christ, he might after all die without finding him.

And in truth, this is no needless alarm. It may be perhaps too alarming to some who already feel their need for Christ, but the mass of us need perpetually to be startled with the thought of death. How few of you ever indulge that thought! Because you live and are in good health, and eat, and drink, and sleep, you think you shall not die. Do you ever soberly look at your last end? Do you ever, when you come to your beds at night, think how one day you shall undress for the last slumber?

And when you wake in the morning, do you never think that the trump of the archangel shall startle you to appear before God in the last day of the great judicial inquest, where a universe shall stand before the judge? No. "All men think all men mortal but themselves"; and thoughts of death we still push off, until at last we shall find ourselves waking up in torment, where to wake up is to wake up too late. But you to whom I specially speak this morning, you who feel that you are a great way off from Christ, you shall never die, but live, and declare the works of the Lord; if you have really sought him, you shall never die until you have found him.

There was never a soul yet, that sincerely sought the Savior, who perished before he found him. No; the gates of death shall never shut on you until the gates of grace have opened for you; until Christ has washed your sins away you shall never be baptized in Jordan's flood. Your life is secure, for this is God's constant plan – he keeps his own elect alive until the day of his grace, and then he takes them to himself. And inasmuch as you know your need of a Savior, you are one of his, and you shall never die until you have found him.

Your second fear is: "Ah, sir! I am not afraid of dying before I find Christ, I have a worse fear than that. I have had convictions before, and they have often passed away; my greatest fear today is that these will be the same." I have heard of a poor coal miner who, on one occasion, having been deeply impressed by a sermon, was led to repent of sin and forsake his former life; but he felt so great a horror of ever returning to his former behavior, that one day he knelt down and cried thus unto God: "O Lord, let me die on this spot, rather than ever deny the religion which I have embraced, and turn back to my former conduct." And we are credibly told that he died on that very spot, and so his prayer was answered. God preferred to take him home to heaven than permit him to bear the brunt of temptation on earth.

Now, when men come to Christ, they feel that they would rather suffer anything than lose their convictions. Scores of times have you and I been drawn to Christ under the preaching of the Word. We can look back upon dozens of occasions on which it seemed just the turning point with us. Something said in our hearts, "Now, believe in Christ, now is the accepted time, now is the day of salvation." But we said, "Tomorrow, tomorrow," and when tomorrow came, our convictions were gone. We thought what we said yesterday would be the deed for today; but instead of it, the procrastination of yesterday became the hardened wickedness of today: we wandered farther from God and forgot him. Now you are crying to him out of fear, lest he should give you up again. You have this morning prayed before you came here, and you said, "Father, permit not my companions to laugh me out of my religion; let not my worldly business so engross my thoughts as to prevent my due attention to the matters of another world. Oh, let not the trifles of today so absorb my thoughts that I may not be preparing myself to meet my God –

> Deeply on my thoughtful heart,
>   Eternal things impress –

and make this a real saving work that shall never die out, nor be taken from me." Is that your earnest prayer? O poor prodigal, it shall be heard, it shall be answered. You shall not have time to go back. Today your Father views you from his throne in heaven; today he runs to you in the message of his gospel; today he falls upon your neck and weeps for joy; today he says to you, *[Your] sins, which are many, are forgiven* (Luke 7:47); today, by the preaching of the Word, he bids you to come and reason with him, for *though your sins be as scarlet, they shall be as white as snow; though they be red like crimson, they shall be as wool* (Isaiah 1:18).

But the last and the most prominent thought which I suppose the prodigal would have, would be that when he did get to his father, he would say to him, "Get on with you, I will have nothing more to do with you."

"Ah!" thought he to himself, "I recollect the morning when I rose up before daybreak, since I knew I could not stand my mother's tears, I remember how I crept down the back staircase and took all the money with me, how I stole down the yard and ran away into the land where I spent my all. Oh! what will the old gentleman say of me when I come back? Why, there he is! He is running to me. But he has got a horsewhip with him, to be sure, to whip me away. It is not at all possible that if he comes, he will have a kind word for me. The most I can expect is that he will say, 'Well, John, you have wasted all your money, you cannot expect me to do anything for you again. I won't let you starve; you shall be one of my servants; there, come, I will take you as a servant'; and if he will do that, I will be obliged to him; no, that is the very thing I will ask of him. I will say, *'Make me as one of thy hired servants.'*"

"Oh," said the devil within him, "your father will never speak comfortably to you; you had better run away again. I tell you if he gets near you, you will have such a dressing as you never received in your life. You will die with a broken heart; you will very likely fall dead here; the old man will never bury you; the carrion crows will eat you. There is no hope for you: see how you have treated him. Put yourself in his place. What would you do if you had a son that had run away with half your living, and spent it on harlots?" And the son thought that if he were in his father's place, he would be very harsh and severe; and possibly, he would almost turn upon his heel to run away. But he had not time to do that. When he was just thinking about running away, all of a sudden, his father's arms were around his neck, and he had received the paternal kiss. No, before he could get his whole prayer finished, he was arrayed in a white robe, the best in the house; and they had brought him to the table, and the fatted calf was being killed for his meal.

And poor soul, it shall be so with you. You say, "If I go to God, he will never receive me. I am too vile and wretched; others he may have pressed to his heart, but he will not do so to me. If my brother should go, he might be saved, but there are such aggravations in my crime. I have grown so old since; I have done such a deal of mischief; I have so often blasphemed him, so frequently broken his Sabbaths. Ah! and I have so often deceived him; I have promised I would repent, and when I have gotten well, I have lied to God, and gone back to my old sin. Oh, if he would but let me creep inside the door of heaven! I will not ask to be one of his children; I will only ask that he will let me be where the Syrophenician woman desired to be – to be a dog, to eat the crumbs that fall from the Master's table. That is all I ask; and oh! if he will but grant it to me, he shall never hear the last of it, for as long as I live, I will sing his praise; and when the world fades away, and the sun grows dim with age, my gratitude, immortal as my soul, shall never cease to sing his love, who pardoned my grossest sins and washed me in his blood." It shall be so. Come and try. Now, sinners, dry your tears; let hopeless sorrows cease; look to the wounds of Christ, who died; let all your griefs now be removed, there is no further cause for them. Your Father loves you; he accepts you and receives you to his heart.

Now, in conclusion, I may notice how these fears were met in the prodigal's case, and how they shall be met in ours if we are in the same condition.

The text says, *His father saw him.* Yes, and God saw you just now. That tear that was wiped away so hastily – as if you were ashamed of it – God saw it, and he stored it in his bottle. That prayer that you did breathe just a few moments ago, so faintly, and with such little faith – God heard it. The other day you were in your chamber, where no ear heard you; but God was there. Sinner, let this be your comfort, that God sees you when you begin to repent. He does not see you with his usual gaze, with which he looks on all men; but he sees you with an eye of intense interest. He has been looking on you in all your sin, and in all your sorrow, hoping that you would repent; and now he sees the first gleam of grace, and he beholds it with joy.

Never a watchman on the lonely castle top saw the first gray light of morning with more joy than that with which God beholds the first desire in your heart. Never a physician rejoiced more when he saw the first heaving of the lungs in one that was supposed to be dead, than God does rejoice over you, now that he sees the first token for good. Think not that you are despised, and unknown, and forgotten. He is observing you from his high throne in glory and rejoicing in what he sees. He saw you pray, he heard you groan, he observed your tear; he looked upon you and rejoiced to see that these were the first seeds of grace in your heart.

And then the text says he *had compassion* on him. He did not merely see him, but he also wept within himself to think he should be in such a condition. The old father had a very long range of eyesight; and though the prodigal could not see him in the distance, he could see the prodigal. And the father's first thought when he saw him was this – "O my poor son, O my poor boy! that ever he should have brought himself into such a state as this!" He looked through his telescope of love, and he saw him and said, "Ah! he did not go out of my house in such an appearance as that. Poor creature, his feet are bleeding; he has come a long way, I'll be ready. Look at his face; he doesn't look like the same boy that he was when he left me. His eye that was so bright is now sunken in its socket; his cheeks that once stood out with fatness have now become hollow with famine. Poor wretch, I can count all his bones, he is so emaciated."

Instead of feeling any anger in his heart, he felt just the contrary: he felt such pity for his poor son. And that is how the Lord feels for you – you who are groaning and moaning on account of sin. He forgets your sins; he only weeps to think you have brought yourself to be what you are: "Why did you rebel against me, and bring yourself into such a state as this?"

It was just like that day when Adam sinned. God walked in the garden, and he missed Adam. He did not cry out, "Adam, come here and be judged!" No; with a soft, sorrowful, and grieving voice, he said,

"Adam, where are you? Oh, my fair Adam, you whom I made so happy, where are you now? Oh Adam! you did think to become a God; where are you now? You have walked with me; do you hide yourself from your friend? Little do you know, oh Adam, what woes you have brought on yourself, and your offspring. Adam, where are you?"

And the Lord's bowels yearn today for you. He is not angry with you; his anger is passed away, and his hands are stretched out still. Inasmuch as he has brought you to feel that you have sinned against him, and to desire reconciliation with him, there is now no wrath in his heart. The only sorrow that he feels is sorrow that you should have brought yourself into a state so mournful as that in which you now are found.

But he did not stop at mere compassion. Having had compassion, he *ran, and fell on his neck, and kissed him.* This you do not understand yet, but you will. As sure as God is God, if you this day are seeking him correctly through Christ, the day shall come when the kiss of full assurance shall be on your lips, when the arms of sovereign love shall embrace you, and you shall know it to be so. You may have despised him, but you shall know him yet to be your Father and your Friend. You may have scoffed at his name; you shall one day come to rejoice in it as being better than pure gold. You may have broken his Sabbaths and despised his Word; the day is coming when the Sabbath shall be your delight, and his Word your treasure.

Yes, marvel not. You may have plunged into the kennel of sin and made your clothes black with iniquity; but you shall one day stand before his throne as white as the angels are; and that tongue that once cursed him shall yet sing his praise. If you are a real seeker, the hands that have been stained with lust shall one day grasp the harp of gold, and the head that has plotted against the Most High shall yet be girded with gold. Does it not seem a strange thing that God should do so much for sinners? But strange though it seems, it shall be strangely true.

Look at the staggering drunkard in the alehouse. Is there a possibility that one day he shall stand among the fairest sons of light? A possibility! alas, a certainty, if he repents and turns from the error of his ways. Hear you yonder curser and swearer? See you the man who labels himself as a servant of hell, and is not ashamed to do so? Is it possible that he shall one day share the bliss of the redeemed? It is possible! alas, more, it is sure, if he turns from his evil ways. O sovereign grace, turn men that they may repent! *Turn ye, turn ye from your evil ways; for why will ye die, O house of Israel?*

> Lord do thou the sinner turn,
>   For thy tender mercies' sake!

One word or so, and I will be done. If any of you today are under conviction of sin, let me solemnly warn you not to frequent places where those convictions are likely to be destroyed.

A correspondent of the *New York Christian Advocate* furnishes the following poignant narrative:

"When I was traveling in the state of Massachusetts, twenty-six years ago, after preaching one evening in the town of——, a very serious-looking young man arose and wished to address the assembly. After obtaining permission, he spoke as follows: 'My friends, about one year ago, I set out in company with a young man of my intimate acquaintance, to seek the salvation of my soul. For several weeks we went on together, we labored together, and often renewed our covenant never to give over seeking until we obtained the religion of Jesus. But all at once, the young man neglected attending meetings, appeared to turn his back on all the means of grace, and grew so shy of me that I could scarcely get an opportunity to speak with him.

"His strange conduct gave me much painful anxiety of mind; but still I felt resolved to obtain the salvation of my soul, or perish, making the publican's plea. After a few days, a friend informed me that my young companion had received an invitation to attend a ball and was determined to go. I went immediately to him, and, with tears in my eyes, endeavored to persuade him to change his mind, and to go with me on that evening to a prayer meeting. I pleaded with him in vain. He told me, when we parted, that I must not give him up as lost, for after he had attended that ball, he intended to make a business of seeking religion.

"The appointed evening came, and he went to the ball, and I went to the prayer meeting. Soon after the meeting opened, it pleased God, in answer to my prayer, to make my soul rejoice in his justifying love. Soon after the ball opened, my young friend was standing at the head of the ballroom, with the hand of a young lady in his hand, preparing to lead down the dance; and, while the musician was turning his violin, without one moment's warning, the young man sallied back, and fell dead on the floor. I was immediately sent for, to assist in conveying his remains to his father's house. You will be better able to judge what were the emotions of my heart when I tell you that that young man was my own brother."

Trifle not, then, with your soul, for eternity shall be too short for you to utter your lamentations over such trifling.

Chapter 2

The Prodigal's Reception

*And he arose, and came to his father. But when he was yet
a great way off, his father saw him, and had compassion,
and ran, and fell on his neck, and kissed him.* (Luke 15:20)

There he is! He is as wretched as misery itself; as filthy as his brute
associates who could satisfy themselves with husks, while he could
not. His clothes hang upon him in rags, and what he is without, that
he is within. He is disgraced in the eyes of the good, and the virtuous
remember him with indignation. He has some desires to go back to
his father's house; but *these desires are not sufficient to alter his condition.* Mere desires have not scraped the filth from him, nor have they
so much as patched his rags. Whatever he may or may not desire, he
is still filthy, still disgraced, still an alien from his father's house, and
he knows it, for he has come to himself. He would have been angry if
we had said as much as this before, but now we cannot describe him
in words too gloomy.

With many tears and sighs he assures us that he is even worse than
he appears to be, and that no man can know all the depth of the vileness
of his conduct. He has spent his living with harlots; he has despised a
generous parent's love and broken loose from his wise control; he has
done evil with both his hands to the utmost of his strength and opportunity. There he stands, notwithstanding this confession, just what I

have described him to be; for even though he has said within himself, *I have sinned*, yet *that confession has not removed his griefs.*

He acknowledges that he is not worthy to be called a son – and it is true he is not; but his unworthiness is not removed by his consciousness of it, nor by his confession of it. He has no claims to a father's love. If that father shuts the door in his face, he acts with justice toward him; if he shall refuse so much as to speak a single word, except words of rebuke, no one can blame the father, for the son has so sadly erred. To this the son utters no protest; he confesses that if he be cast away forever, he well deserves it.

This picture, I know, is the photograph of some who are now present. You feel your vileness and sinfulness, but you cannot look upon that sense of vileness as in any way excusing or altering your condition. You feel, but you cannot plead your feelings. You confess this morning that you have desires towards God, but that you have no rights to him – you cannot demand anything at his hands. If your soul were sent to hell, his righteous law approves it, and so does your own conscience. You can see your rags, you can observe your filthiness, you can long for something better, but you *are* no better; you have no more claims than you used to have upon God's mercy; you stand here today, a self-convicted offender against the loving-kindness and holiness of God. I pray that to such of you as are in this case, I may be the bearer of a message from God to your soul this morning.

O you who know the Lord, put up earnest and silent prayers just now, that my message may come home with power to troubled consciences; and I beg you, for your own profit, look back to the hole of the pit from where you were dug, and to the miry clay from where you were drawn, and remember how God received you. And while we talk of what he is willing and able to do to the far-off sinners, let your souls leap with joyous gratitude at the recollection of how he received you into his love, and made you partakers of his grace in days gone by.

There are two things in the text: the first is *the condition of many a seeker – he is yet a great way off*; and then, secondly, *the matchless kindness of the father towards him.*

First, dear friends, the condition of such a seeker – he is *yet a great way off.*

He is a great way off if you consider one or two things. Remember *his lack of strength*. This poor young man had for some time been without food – being brought so very low that the husks upon which the swine fed would have seemed a delicacy to him if he could have eaten them. He is so hungry that he has become emaciated, and to him every mile has the weariness of leagues within it. It costs him many pains and sore griefs to drag himself along, even though it be but an inch. So, the sinner is a long way off from God when you consider his utter lack of strength to come to God. Even such strength as God has given him is very painfully used. God has given him strength enough to desire salvation, but that desire is always accompanied with deep and sincere grief for sin. The point that he has already reached has exhausted all his power, and all he can do is fall down before Jesus and say,

> Oh! for this no strength have I,
> My strength is at thy feet to lie.

He is a great way off again, if you consider *his lack of courage*. He longs to see his father, but yet the probabilities are that if his father should come, he would run away; the very sound of his father's footsteps would act upon him as they did on Adam in the garden – he would hide himself among the trees so that instead of crying after his father, the great Father would have to cry after him – "Where are you, poor fallen creature? Where are you?" His lack of courage, therefore, makes the distance long, for every step up to this time has been taken as though into the jaws of death. "Ah!" says the sinner, "it must be long before I can dare to hope, *for mine iniquities are gone over mine head* so that I cannot look up" (Psalm 38:4). Are you then in alarm and dread this morning?

Your prayers seem to yourself to have been no prayers at all. When you think of God, terror comes over your mind, and you feel that you are a long, long way from him. You imagine that it is not likely that he will hear your cries nor give heed to your words. You are *yet a great way off*.

You are a great way off when we consider *the difficulty of the way of repentance*. John Bunyan tells us that Christian found, when he went back to the arbor after his lost roll, that it was very hard work going back.

Every backslider finds it so, and every repentant sinner knows that there is a bitterness in mourning for sin comparable to the loss of one's only son. A drowning man feels no great pain: the sensations of drowning are even said to be pleasant. It is only when the man is being restored to life, when the blood begins to make the veins tingle because life leaps there, when once again the nerves are sensible, then we are told that the whole body is full of many agonies, but then they are the agonies of life. So the poor repentant one feels the goal must be a great way off, for if he had to feel as he now feels, even for a month, it would be a great time; and if he had to journey many miles as he now journeys, so painfully, with such bleeding feet, it would indeed be a great way off.

Let us look into this matter and show that while the road seems long on this account, *it really is long* if we view it in certain lights. There are many seeking sinners who are a great way off in *their life*. I think I see the man now, and hear him thus grieve himself, saying, "I have left off my drunkenness. I could not sit where I used to sit by the hour. I thank God I shall never be seen reeling through the streets again, for that groveling lust I detest. I have given up Sabbath breaking, and I am found in God's house; and I have endeavored, as much as I can, to renounce the habit of swearing, but still I am a great way off. I do not feel as if I could yet lay hold of Christ, for I cannot master my own passions yet. An old companion stopped me this week, and he had not long been talking before I found the old man was in me, and the old lustings came up into my face again. Why, sir, the other day a swear word came suddenly out of my mouth. I thought I had gotten over it, but I had not – I am a great way off. When I read of what saints are, and observe what true Christians are, I do feel that my conduct is so inconsistent and so widely apart from what it ought to be, that I am a great way off."

Ah! dear friend, you are; and if you had to come to God by the way of your own righteousness you would never reach him, for he is not thus to be found. Christ Jesus is the way. He is the safe, sure, and perfect road to God. He who sees Jesus has seen the Father; but he who looks to himself will only see despair. The road to heaven by Mount Sinai is impassable by mortal man, but Calvary leads to glory; the secret places of the stairs are in the wounds of Jesus.

Again, you feel yourself a great way off as to *knowledge*. "Why," say you, "before I felt thus, I considered myself a master of all theology: I could twist the doctrines around my fingers. When I listened to a sermon, I felt quite able to criticize it, and to give my judgment. Now I see that my judgment was about as valuable as the criticism of a blind man upon a picture, for I was without spiritual sight. Now I feel myself to be a fool. I do know what sin means, but only to a degree. Even here I feel that I am not conscious of the heinousness of human guilt. I have heard the doctrine of the atonement of Christ, and I thank God I know it to some degree, but the excellence and glory of the substitutionary sacrifice that Christ offered I confess I do not fully comprehend."

The sinner's confession now is that instead of understanding Scripture, he finds he needs to go like a child to school to learn the ABCs of it. "O sir," says he, "I am a great way off from God, for I am so ignorant, so foolish; I seem to be but as a beast when I think of the deep things of God." Ah! poor soul, poor young wandering brother, I wonder not that it seems so to you, for the ignorance of the carnal man is indeed fearful, and only God can give you light. But he can give it to you in a moment, and the distance between you and him upon the score of ignorance can be bridged at once, and you may comprehend even today, *with all saints what is the breadth, and length, and depth, and height; and to know the love of Christ, which passeth knowledge* (Ephesians 3:18-19).

In another point also many an earnest seeker is a great way off, and I mean in *his repentance.* "Alas!" says he, "I cannot repent as I ought. If I could feel the brokenness of heart that I have heard and seen in some! Oh! what would I give for repentant sighs; how thankful would I be if my head were waters, and my eyes fountains of tears' if I could even feel that I was as humble as the poor publican, and could stand with downcast eyes and beat upon my breast and say, '*God be merciful to me a sinner.*' But alas! I have been a hearer of the Word for years, and all the progress I have made is so little, that while I know the gospel to be true, I do not feel it. I know myself to be a sinner, and sometimes I mourn over it, but my mourning is so superficial, and my repentance is a repentance that needs to be repented of. O sir, if God would use the heaviest hammer that he had, if he would but break my heart, every broken fragment would bless his name. I wish I had a genuine repentance. Oh! how I pant to be brought to feel that I am lost, and to desire Christ with that vehement desire that will not take a denial; but in this point my heart seems as hard as hell-hardened steel, cold as a rock of ice; it will not, cannot yield, though wooed by love divine. A stone itself may run in liquid torrents, but my soul yields to nothing. Lord, break it! Lord, break it!!" Ah! poor heart, I see you are a great way off, but do you know that if my Lord would appear to you this morning, and say to you, *I have loved thee with an everlasting love,* your heart would break in a moment?

> Law and terrors do but harden,
>> All the while they work alone;
> But a sense of blood-bought pardon,
>> Can dissolve a heart of stone.

Great way off as you are, if the Lord pardons you, while you are yet callous and consciously hard of heart, will you not then fall at his feet and commend that great love with which he loved you, even when you were dead in trespasses and sins?

Yes, but I think I hear one say, "There is another point in which I feel a great way off, for I have little or no *faith.* I have heard faith preached every Sabbath day; I know what it is, I think I do, but I cannot reach it. I know that if I cast myself wholly upon Christ I shall be saved. I quite comprehend that he does not ask anything of me, any willings, or doings, or feelings; I know that Christ is willing to receive the greatest sinner out of hell if that sinner will but come and simply trust him. I have tried to do it; sometimes I have thought I had faith, but then again when I have looked at my sins, I have doubted so dreadfully, that I perceive I have no faith at all. There are sunshiny moments with me when I think I can say,

> My faith is built on nothing less,
>> Than Jesus' blood and righteousness,

but oh! when I feel my corruptions within rising upon me, I hear a voice saying, *The Philistines be upon thee, Samson* (Judges 16:9), and immediately I discover my own weakness. I do not have the faith that I want; I am a great way off from it, and I fear that I shall never possess it." Yes, my brethren, I perceive your difficulty, for I have felt the sorrow of it myself; but oh! my Lord, who is the Giver of faith, who is exalted on high to give repentance and remission of sins, can give you the faith you so much desire, and can cause you this morning to rest with perfect confidence upon the work that he has finished for you.

To gather up all things in one word, the truly repentant sinner feels that he is yet a great way off *in everything.* There is no point upon which you can talk with him, but that it will be sure to lead to a confession of his deficiency. Begin to put him in the scales of the sanctuary, and he cries, "Alas! before you put in the weights, I can tell you I shall be found lacking." Bring him to the touchstone, and he shrinks from it. "No," says he, "but I cannot endure any sort of trial –

> 'All unholy and unclean,
> I am nothing else but sin.'"

See, see, how well my Master has pictured your case in this parable – *yet a great way off –* yet covered with rags, yet polluted with filth, yet in disgrace, yet a stranger to your Father's house. There is only this one point about you: you have your face towards your Father, you have a desire towards God, and you would, oh! you would if you could, lay hold upon eternal life. But you feel too far off for anything like comfortable hope. Now I must confess that I feel many fears about you who are in this state; I am afraid lest you should come so far and yet go back; for there are many whom we thought had come as far as this, and yet they have gone back after all. Oh! remember that desires for God will not change you so as to save you. You must find Christ.

Remember that to *say* "I will arise" is not enough, nor even *to arise;* you must never rest until your Father has given you the kiss, until he has put on you the best robe. I am afraid lest you should rest satisfied and say, "I am in a good state; the minister tells us that many are brought to such a state before they are saved. I will stop here."

My dear friend, it is a good state *to pass through,* but it is a bad state *to rest in.* I pray you never be content with a sense of sin, never be satisfied with merely knowing that you are not what you ought to be. It never cures the fever for a man to know he has it; his knowledge is in some degree a good sign, for it proves that the fever has not yet driven him to delirium; but it never gives a man perfect health to know that he is sick. It is a good thing for him to know it, for he will not otherwise send for the physician; but unless it leads to that, he will die whether he feels himself to be sick or not.

A mere consciousness that you are hungry while your father's hired servants have *bread enough and to spare,* will not stop your hunger; you need more than this. You are a great way off, and I implore you to remember that the danger is lest you should stop here or should lose what sensibility you already have. Perhaps despair may come upon you. Some have committed suicide while under a sense of the greatness of their distance from God, because they dared not look to the Savior.

Our prayers shall go up to God that the second part of our text may come true to you, and that backsliding and despair alike may be prevented by the speedy coming of God dressed in the robes of grace to meet your guilty soul, and give you joy and peace through believing.

Secondly – and O may the Master give us his help – we have to consider the matchless kindness of the heavenly Father. We must take each word and dwell upon it.

First of all, we have here *divine observation. When he was yet a great way off,* **his father saw him** (emphasis added). It is true he has always seen him. God sees the sinner in every state and in every position. Alas, and he sees him with an eye of love too – such a chosen sinner as is described in this text – not with complacency, but still with affection.

God looks upon his wandering chosen ones. I say that father saw his son when he spent his living with harlots, saw him with deep sorrow, when *he would fain have filled his belly with the husks that the swine did eat;* but now, if there can be such a thing as for divine omniscience to become more exact, the father sees him with an eye full of a more tender love, and a greater care. *His father* **saw him**. Oh! what a sight it was for a father to see! His son, it is true, but his reprobate son who had dishonored his father's name, and had brought down the name of an honorable house to be mentioned among the dregs and scum of the earth.

There he is! What a sight for a father's eye! He is filthy, as though he had been rolling in the mire; and his bright clothing has long ago lost its fine colors, and hangs upon him in wretched rags. The father does not turn away and try to forget him, he fixes his full gaze upon him. Sinner, you know that God sees you this morning; sitting in this house you are observed by the God of heaven. There is not a desire in your heart left unexamined by him, nor a tear in your eye that he does not observe. I tell you he has seen your midnight singing, he has heard your cursings and your blasphemies, and yet he has loved you notwithstanding all that you have done.

You could hardly have been a worse rebel against him, and yet he has noted you in his book of love, and determined to save you, and the eye of his love has followed you to whatever place you have gone. Is there not some comfort here? Why could he not see his father? Was it the effect of the tears in his eyes that he could not see? Or was it that his father was of quicker sight than he? Sinner, you cannot see God, for you are unbelieving, and carnal, and blind; but he can see you. Your tears of repentance block your sight, but your Father is quick of eye, and he beholds you and loves you now; in every glance there is love. *His father saw him.*

Observe that this was a loving observation, for it is written, **His father** *saw him.* He did not see him as a mere casual observer; he did not note him as a man might note his friend's child with some pity and benevolence, but he observed him as a father alone can do. What a quick eye a parent has! Why, I have known a young man to come home, perhaps for a short holiday; the mother has heard nothing, not even a whisper, as to her son's conduct, and yet she cannot help observing to her husband, "There is a something about John that makes me suspect that he is not going on as he should do. I do not know, my husband," she says, "what it is, but yet I am sure he is getting among bad companions."

She will read his character at once. And the father notes something too; he cannot precisely say what, but cause for anxiety he knows it to be. But here we have a Father who can see everything, and who has as much of the quickness of love as he has of the certainty of knowledge. He can, therefore, see from every spot and bruise, and note every putrefying sore. He sees his poor son right through as though he were a vase of crystal; he reads his heart, not merely the telltale garments, not merely the sorrowful tale of the unwashed face and those raggedy shoes, but he can also read his soul; he understands the whole of his miserable plight.

O poor sinner, there is no need for you to give information to your God, for he knows it already. You need not pick your words in prayer in order to make your case plain and clear, for God can see it, and all you have to do is uncover your wounds, your bruises, and your putrefying sores, and say, "My Father, you see it all, the wicked tale you read in a moment; my Father, have pity on me."

The next thought to be well considered is *divine compassion.* When he saw him, he had compassion on him. Does not the word *compassion* mean "suffering with" or "fellow suffering"? What is compassion, then, but putting yourself into the place of the sufferer and feeling his grief. If I may so say, the father put himself into the son's rags, and then felt as much pity for him as that poor ragged prodigal could have felt for himself. I do not know how to bring up your compassion this morning, except it is by supposing that it is your own case. I will suppose, father, it is a son of yours. I saw, not many hours ago, a young man who brought to my mind the prodigal in this case: his face marked with innumerable lines of sin and wretchedness, his body lean and emaciated, his clothes close-buttoned, his whole appearance the very mirror of woe.

He knocked at my door. I knew his case; I cannot hurt him by telling it. He had disgraced his family, not once nor twice, but many times. At last he drew out what money he had in the business of a respectable family, came up to London with four hundred pounds, and in about five weeks spent it all; and, without a single farthing to help himself, he often lacks bread, and I fear that he has often crept at night into the parks to sleep, and thus has brought aches and pains into his bones that will hold by him until he dies. He wanders the streets by day as a vagabond and a reprobate.

I have written to his friends, so the case has been put before them; however, they will not acknowledge him; and considering his shameful conduct, I do not wonder at it. He has no father and no mother left. If he were helped beyond mere food and lodging, as far as we can judge, it would be money thrown away. If he were helped at all, he seems so desperately set on wickedness, that he would do the same again.

Yet, as I think, I can but desire to see him have one more trial at least, and he would have it, I doubt not, if *his father* was still living; but others feel the fountains of their love have stopped. As I think of him, I cannot but feel that if he were a son of mine and I were his father, and I saw him in such a case come to my door, whatever the crime was that he had committed, I must fall upon his neck and kiss him; the hugest sin could not put out forever the sparks of paternal love. I might condemn the sin in the sharpest and most severe terms; I might regret that he had ever been born, and cry with David, *O my son Absalom, my son, my son Absalom! would God I had died for thee!* (2 Samuel 18:33), but I could not shut him out of my house, nor refuse to call him my child. My child he is, and my child he shall be until he dies.

You feel just now that if it were your child you would do the same. That is how God feels towards you, his chosen, his repentant child. You *are* his child; I hope so, I trust so. Those desires that you have in your soul towards him make me feel that you are one of his children, and as God looks out of heaven, he knows what you mean. What is it? What shall I say? No, I need not describe it, but, *like as a father pitieth his children, so the Lord pitieth them that fear him* (Psalm 103:13). He will have compassion on you; he will receive you to his bosom now. Be of good courage, for the text says he *had compassion* on him.

Notice and observe carefully *the swiftness of this divine love:* He *ran.* Probably he was walking on the top of his house and looking out for his son, when one morning he just caught a glimpse of a poor, sorry figure in the distance. If he had been anything but the father, he would not have known it to be his son, because he was so changed; but he looked and looked again, until at last he said, "It is he! Oh! what marks of famine are upon him, and of suffering too!"

And down comes the old gentleman – I think I see him running downstairs, and the servants come to the windows and the doors, and say, "Where is master going? I have not seen him run at that rate for many a day." See, there he goes. He does not take the road, for that is a little round about. But there is a gap through the hedge, and he is jumping over it; the straightest way that he can find he chooses; and before the son has had time to notice who it is, he is on him, and has his arms around him, falling upon his neck and kissing him.

I recollect a young prodigal who was received in the same way. Here he stands, it is I, myself. I sat in a little chapel, little dreaming that *my Father* saw me; certainly, I was a great way off. I felt something of my need for

Christ, but I did not know what I needed to do to be saved. Though taught the letter of the Word, I was spiritually ignorant of the plan of salvation; though taught it from my youth up, I knew it not. I felt, but I did not feel what I wished to feel. If ever there was a soul that knew itself to be far off from God, I was that soul; and yet in a moment, in one single moment, no sooner had I heard the words, *Look unto me, and be ye saved, all the ends of the earth,* no sooner had I turned my eyes to Jesus crucified, than I felt my perfect reconciliation with God, and I knew my sins were forgiven.

There was no time for getting out of my heavenly Father's way – it was done, and done in an instant; and in my case, at least, he ran and fell upon my neck to kiss me. I hope that will be the case this morning. Before you can get out of this place, before you can get back to your old doubtings, and fears, and sighings, and cryings, I hope here the Lord of love will run and meet you, and fall upon your neck and kiss you.

After noticing *observation, compassion,* and *swiftness,* do not forget *the nearness:* He *fell on his neck, and kissed him.* This I can understand by experience, but it is too wonderful for me to explain: He *fell on his neck.* If he had stood at a distance and said, "John, I would be very glad to kiss you, but you are too filthy. I do not know what may be under those filthy rags; I do not feel inclined to fall upon your neck just yet; you are too far gone for me. I love you, but there is a limit to the display of love. When I have got you into a proper state, then I may manifest my affection to you, but I cannot just now, while you are so very foul." Oh no; but before he is washed, he falls on his neck – there is the wonder of it.

I can understand how God manifests his love to a soul that is washed in Jesus' blood, and knows it; but how he could fall upon the neck of a foul, filthy sinner *as such?* There it is – not as sanctified, not as having anything good in himself, but as nothing but a filthy, foul, desperate rebel, God falls upon his neck and kisses him. Oh! strange miracle of love! The riddle is unriddled when you recollect that God never had looked upon that sinner, as he was in himself, but had always looked upon him as he was in Christ. And when he fell upon that prodigal's neck, he did in effect only fall upon the neck of his once-suffering Son, Jesus Christ, and he kissed the sinner because he saw him in Christ, and therefore did not see the sinner's loathsomeness, but saw only Christ's comeliness, and therefore kissed him as he would have kissed his Substitute.

Observe how near God comes to the sinner. It was said of that notable saint and martyr Bishop Hooper, that on one occasion a man in deep distress was allowed to go into his prison to tell his tale of conscience; but Bishop Hooper looked so sternly upon him, and addressed him so severely at first, that the poor soul ran away, and could not get comfort until he had sought out another minister of a gentler gaze. Now Hooper really was a gracious and loving soul, but the sternness of his manner kept the repentant one away. There is no such stern manner in our heavenly Father; he loves to receive his prodigals. When he comes, there is no, "Hold off!" no "Keep off!" to the sinner, but he falls upon his neck and he kisses him.

There is yet another thought to be brought out of the metaphor of kissing; we are not to pass that over without dipping our cup in the honey. In kissing his son the father *recognizes relationship.* He said, with emphasis, "You are my son," and the prodigal was

> To his Father's bosom pressed,
> Once for all a child confessed.

Again, that kiss was the seal of *forgiveness.* He would not have kissed him if he had been angry with him; he forgave him, forgave him all. There was, moreover, something more than forgiveness; there was *acceptance* – "I receive you back into my heart as though you were worthy of all that I give to your elder brother, and therefore I kiss you." Surely also this was a kiss of delight – as if he took pleasure in him, delighting in him, feasting his eyes with the sight of him, and feeling more happy to see him than to see all his fields, and the fatted calves, and all the treasures that he possessed. His delight was in seeing this poor restored child. Surely this is all summed up in a kiss.

And if this morning my Father, and your Father, should come out to meet mourning repentant ones, in a moment he will show you that you are his children. You shall say, "Abba, Father," on your road to your own house; you shall feel that your sin is all forgiven, that every particle of it is cast behind Jehovah's back. You shall feel today that you are accepted – as your faith looks to Christ you shall see that God accepts you, because Christ your Substitute is worthy of God's love and God's delight.

No; I trust you shall this very morning delight yourself in God, because God delights himself in you, and you shall hear him whisper in your ear, *Thou shalt be called Hephzibah, . . . for the Lord delighteth in thee* (Isaiah 62:4). I wish I could picture such a text as this as it ought to be. It needs some tender, sympathetic heart, some man who is the very soul of the emotion of pity, to work out the tender touches of such a verse as this.

But, oh! though I cannot describe it, I hope you will feel it, and that is better than description. I come not here to paint the scene, but only to be the brush in God's hand to paint it on your hearts. There are some of you who can say, "I do not want descriptions, for I have felt it; I went to Christ and told him my case, and prayed him to meet me. Now I believe on him, and I have gone my way rejoicing in him."

We will just say these words and be done. In summing up, one may notice that this sinner, though he was a great way off, was *not received to full pardon and to adoption and acceptance by a gradual process, but he was received at once.* He was not allowed to enter into the outhouse first, and to sleep in a barn at night, and then afterwards allowed to come sometimes and have his meals with the servants in the kitchen, and then afterwards allowed to sit at the bottom of the table and by degrees brought near.

No; but the father fell on his neck and kissed him in the first moment; he gets as near to God in the first moment as he ever will. So a saved soul may not enjoy and know so much, but he is as near and dear to God the first moment he believes as he ever will be. He is a true heir of all things in Christ, and as truly so as even when he shall mount to heaven to be glorified and to be like his Lord.

Oh! what a wonder is this! Fresh from his pigpen was he not, yet he was in a father's bosom; fresh from the swine with their gruntings in his ears, and now he hears a father's loving words. A few days ago he was putting husks to his mouth, and now it is a father's lips that are on his cheek. What a change, and all at once. I say there is no gradual process in this, but the thing is done at once, in a moment he comes to his father, his father comes to him, and he is in his father's arms.

Observe again, that there was not a gradual reception, there was *not a partial reception.* He was not forgiven on conditions; he was not received to his father's heart if he would do so-and-so. No; there were no ifs and no buts; he was kissed, and clothed, and feasted without a single condition of any kind whatever. No questions were asked – his father had cast his offenses behind his back in a moment, and he was received without even a reprimand or a rebuke. It was not a partial reception. He was not received to some things and refused others. He was not, for instance, allowed to call himself a child, but to think himself an inferior. No; he wears the best robe, he has the ring on his finger, he has the shoes on his feet, and he joins in eating the fatted calf; and so the sinner is not received to a second-class place, but he is taken to the full position of a child of God. It is not a gradual nor yet a partial reception.

And once more, it is *not a temporary reception.* His father did not kiss him and then turn him out at the back door. He did not receive him for a time, and then afterwards say to him, "Go your way. I have had pity on you; you have now a new start, so go into the far country and mend your ways." No; but the father would say to him what he had already said to the elder brother: *Son, thou art ever with me, and all that I have is thine* (Luke 15:31).

In the parable, the son could not have the goods restored, for he had spent his part. But in the truth itself and as a matter of fact, God does make the man who comes in at the eleventh hour equal with the one who came in at the first hour of the day. He gives every man the penny; and he gives to the child who has been the most wandering the same privileges, and ultimately the same heritage, which he gives to his own who have been these many years with him, and have not transgressed his commandments.

That is a remarkable passage in one of the prophets, where he says, *Ekron as a Jebusite* (Zechariah 9:7), meaning that the Philistine when converted should be treated just the same as the original inhabitants of Jerusalem; that the branches of the olive tree that were grafted in have the same privileges as the original branches. When God takes men from being heirs of wrath and makes them heirs of grace, they have just as much privilege at the first, as though they had been heirs of grace for twenty years, because in God's sight they always were heirs of grace, and from all eternity he viewed his most wandering sons

Not as they stood in Adam's fall,
When sin and ruin covered all;
But as they'll stand another day,
Fairer than sun's meridian ray.

O, I would to God that he would in his infinite mercy bring some of his own dear children home this day, and he shall have the praise, world without end. Amen.

Chapter 3

Prodigal Love for the Prodigal Son

And kissed him. (Luke 15:20)

In the Revised Version (RV), if you will kindly look at the margin, you will find that the text there reads, *And kissed him much.* This is a very good translation of the Greek, which might bear the meaning: "kissed him earnestly," or "kissed him eagerly," or "kissed him often." I prefer to have it in very plain language, and therefore I adopt the marginal reading of the Revised Version, *kissed him much,* as the text of my message, the subject of which will be the overflowing love of God toward the returning sinner.

The first word "and" links us to all that had gone on before. The parable is a very familiar one, yet it is so full of sacred meaning that it always has some fresh lesson for us. Let us, then, consider the preliminaries to this kissing. On the son's side there was something, and on the father's side much more. Before the Prodigal Son received these kisses of love, he had said in the far country, *I will arise and go to my father.* He had, however, done more than that, or else his father's kiss would never have been upon his cheek.

The resolve had become a deed: *He arose, and came to his father.* A bushelful of resolutions is of small value, but a single grain of practice is worth the whole. The determination to return home is good; but it is when the wandering boy begins the business of really carrying out the good resolve that he draws near the blessing. If any of you present here have long been saying, "I will repent; I will turn to God and leave off resolving, and come to practicing," may God in his mercy lead you both to repent and to believe in Christ!

Before the kisses of love were given, this young man was on his way to his father; but he would not have reached him unless his father had come the major part of the way. When you give God an inch, he will give you a yard. If you come a little way to him, when you are *yet a great way off*, he will run to meet you. I do not know that the prodigal saw his father, but his father saw him. The eyes of mercy are quicker than the eyes of repentance. Even the eye of our faith is dim compared with the eye of God's love. He sees a sinner long before a sinner sees him.

I do not suppose that the prodigal traveled very fast. I would imagine that he came very slowly,

> With heavy heart and downcast eye,
> With many a sob and many a sigh.

He was resolved to come, yet he was half afraid. But we read that his father ran. Slow are the steps of repentance, but swift are the feet of forgiveness. God can run where we can scarcely limp, and if we are limping towards him, he will run towards us. These kisses were given in a hurry; the story is narrated in a way that almost makes us realize that such was the case: there is a sense of haste in the very wording of it. His father *ran, and fell on his neck, and kissed him* – kissed him eagerly. He did not delay a moment; for though he was out of breath, he was not out of love. He fell on his neck, *and kissed him much* (RV).

There stood his son ready to confess his sin; therefore did his father kiss him all the more. The more willing you are to acknowledge your sin, the more willing is God to forgive you. When you make a clean breast of it, God will soon make a clear record of it. He will wipe out the sin that you do willingly acknowledge and humbly confess before him. He that was willing to use his lips for confession, found that his father was willing to use his lips for kissing him.

See the contrast. There is the son, scarcely daring to think of embracing his father, yet his father has scarcely seen him before he has fallen on his neck. The condescension of God towards repentant sinners is very great. He seems to stoop from his throne of glory to fall upon the neck of a repentant sinner. God on the neck of a sinner! What a wonderful picture! Can you imagine it? I do not think you can; but if you cannot imagine it, I hope that you will realize it. When God's arm is around our neck, and his lips are on our cheek, kissing us much, then we understand more than preachers or books can ever tell us of his condescending love.

The father *saw* his son. There is a great deal in that word *saw*. He saw who it was; saw where he had come from; saw the clothing of the one who was tending swine; saw the filth upon his hands and feet; saw his rags; saw his repentant look; saw what he had been; saw what he was; and saw what he would soon be. *His father saw him.* God has a way of seeing men and women that you and I cannot understand. He sees right through us at a glance, as if we were made of glass; he sees all our past, present, and future.

When he was yet a great way off, his father saw him. It was not with icy eyes that the father looked on his returning son. Love leaped into them, and as he beheld him, he *had compassion* on him; that is, he felt for him. There was no anger in his heart towards his son; he had nothing but pity for his poor boy who had got into such a pitiful condition. It was true that it was all his own fault, but that did not come into his father's mind. It was the state that he was in, his poverty, his degradation, that pale face of his so pale with hunger, that touched his father to the heart. And God has compassion on the woes and miseries of men. They may have brought their troubles on themselves, and they have indeed done so; but nevertheless, God has compassion upon them. *It is of the Lord's mercies that we are not consumed, because his compassions fail not* (Lamentations 3:22).

We read that the father *ran*. The compassion of God is followed by swift movements. He is slow to anger, but he is quick to bless. He does not take any time to consider how he will show his love to repentant prodigals; that was all done long ago in the eternal covenant. He has no need to prepare for their return to him; that was all done on Calvary. God comes flying in the greatness of his compassion to help every poor repentant soul.

On cherub and on cherubim,
Full royally he rode;
And on the wings of mighty winds
Came flying all abroad.

And when he comes, he comes to kiss. Master Trapp says that if we had read that the father had kicked his Prodigal Son, we would not have been very much astonished. Well, I would have been very greatly astonished, seeing that the father in the parable was to represent God. But still, his son deserved all the rough treatment that some heartless men might have given; and had the story been that of a selfish human father only, it might have been written that "as he was coming near, his father ran at him, and kicked him." There are such fathers in the world, who seem as if they cannot forgive. If he had kicked him, it would have been no more than he deserved. But no, what is written in the Book stands true for all time, and for every sinner – He *fell on his neck, and kissed him*; kissed him eagerly, *kissed him much*.

What does this much kissing mean? It signifies that when sinners come to God, he gives them a loving reception and a hearty welcome. If any one of you, while I am speaking, shall come to God, expecting mercy because of the great sacrifice of Christ, this shall be true of you as it has been true of many of us: He *kissed him much*.

First, this much kissing means much love. It means much love truly *felt*; for God never gives an expression of love without feeling it in his infinite heart. God will never give a Judas kiss and betray those whom he embraces. There is no hypocrisy with God; he never kisses those for whom he has no love. Oh, how God loves sinners! You who repent and come to him will discover how greatly he loves you. There is no measuring the love he bears towards you. He has loved you from before the foundation of the world, and he will love you when time shall be no more. Oh, the immeasurable love of God to sinners who come and cast themselves upon his mercy!

This much kissing also means much love *manifested*. God's people do not always know the greatness of his love to them. Sometimes, however, it *is shed abroad in our hearts by the Holy Ghost which is given unto us* (Romans 5:5). Some of us know at times what it is to be almost too happy to live! The love of God has been so overpoweringly experienced by us on some occasions that we have almost had to ask for a halting of the delight because we could not endure any more. If the glory had not been veiled a little, we would have died of excess of rapture or happiness.

Beloved, God has wondrous ways of opening his people's hearts to the manifestation of his grace. He can pour in, not now and then a drop of his love, but great and mighty streams. Madame Guyon used to speak of the torrents of love that come sweeping through the spirit, bearing all before them. The poor prodigal in the parable had so much love manifested to him, that he might have sung of the torrents of his father's affection. That is the way God receives those whom he saves, giving them not a meager measure of grace, but manifesting an overflowing love.

This much kissing means, further, much love *perceived*. When his father *kissed him much*, the poor prodigal knew, if never before, that his father loved him. He had no doubt about it; he had a clear perception of it. It is very frequently the case that the first moment a sinner believes in Jesus, he gets this "much" love. God reveals it to him, and he perceives it and enjoys it at the very beginning. Think not that God always keeps the best wine to the last; he gives us some of the richest delicacies of his table the first moment we sit there.

I recollect the joy that I had when first I believed in Jesus; and, even now, in looking back upon it, the memory of it is as fresh as if it were but yesterday. Oh, I could not have believed that a mortal could be so happy after having been so long burdened and so terribly cast down! I did but look to Jesus on the cross, and the crushing load was immediately gone; and the heart that could only sigh and cry by reason of its burden began to leap and dance and sing for joy. I had found in Christ all that I wanted, and I rested in the love of God at once. So may it be with you also, if you will but return to God through Christ. It shall be said of you as of this prodigal, *His father saw him, . . . and ran, and fell on his neck, and kissed him [in much love].*

Secondly, this much kissing meant much forgiveness. The prodigal had many sins to confess, but before he came to the details of them, his father had forgiven him. I love confession of sin after forgiveness. Some suppose that after we are forgiven we are never to confess; but oh, beloved, it is then that we confess most truly, because we know the guilt of sin most really! Then do we sorrowfully sing,

My sins, my sins, my Savior,
How sad on thee they fall!
Seen through thy gentle patience,
I tenfold feel them all.

I know they are forgiven,
But still their pain to me
Is all the grief and anguish
They laid, my Lord, on thee.

To think that Christ should have washed me from my sins in his own blood makes me feel my sin the more keenly, and confess it the more humbly before God. The picture of this prodigal is marvelously true to the experience of those who return to God. His father kissed him with the kiss of forgiveness; and yet, after that, the young man went on to say, *Father, I have sinned against heaven, and in thy sight, and am no more worthy to be called thy son.* Do not hesitate, then, to acknowledge your sin to God, even though you know that in Christ it is all put away.

From this point of view, those kisses meant, first, "*Your sin is all gone,* and it will never be mentioned anymore. Come to my heart, my son! You have grieved me sorely, and angered me; but, as a thick cloud, I have blotted out your transgressions, and as a cloud your sins."

As the father looked upon him, *and kissed him much,* there probably came another kiss, which seemed to say, "*There is no soreness left:* I have not only forgiven, but I have forgotten too. It is all gone, clean gone. I will never accuse you of it anymore. I will never love you any the less. I will never treat you as though you were still an unworthy and untrustworthy person." Probably at that there came another kiss; for do not forget that his father forgave him *and kissed him much,* to show that the sin was all forgiven.

There stood the prodigal, overwhelmed by his father's goodness, yet remembering his past life. As he looked on himself and thought, "I have these old rags on still, and I have just come from feeding the swine," I can imagine that his father would give him another kiss, as much to say, "My boy, I do not recollect the past; I am so glad to see you that I do not see any filth on you, or any rags on you either. I am so delighted to have you with me once more that, as I would pick up a diamond out of the mud, and be glad to get the diamond again, so do I pick you up; you are so precious to me." This is the gracious and glorious way in which God treats those who return to him. As for their sin, he has put it away so that he will not remember it. He forgives like a God. Well may we adore and magnify his matchless mercy as we sing,

> In wonder lost, with trembling joy
>   We take the pardon of our God;
> Pardon for crimes of deepest dye;
>   A pardon bought with Jesus' blood;
>
> Who is a pardoning God like thee?
>   Or who has grace so rich and free?

"Well," says one, "can such a wonderful change ever take place with me?" By the grace of God it may be experienced by every man who is willing to return to God. I pray God that it may happen now, and that you may get such assurance of it from the Word of God, by the power of his Holy Spirit, and from a sight of the precious blood of Christ shed for your redemption, that you may be able to say, "I understand it now; I see how he kisses all my sin away; and when it rises, he kisses it away again; and when I think of it with shame, he gives me another kiss; and when I blush all over at the remembrance of my evil deeds, he kisses me again and again, to assure me that I am fully and freely forgiven." Thus, the many kisses from the prodigal's father combined to make his wayward son feel that his sin was indeed all gone. They revealed much love and much forgiveness.

These repeated kisses meant, next, full restoration. The prodigal was going to say to his father, *Make me as one of thy hired servants.* In the far country he had resolved to make that request, but his father, with a kiss, stopped him. By that kiss, his *sonship was acknowledged;* by it the father said to the wretched wanderer, "You are my son." He gave him such a kiss as he would only give to his own son. I wonder how many here have ever given such a kiss to anyone. There sits one who knows something of such kisses as the prodigal received. That father's girl went astray, and, after years of sin, she came back worn-out, to die at home. He received her, found her repentant, and gladly welcomed her to his house.

Ah, my dear friend, you know something about such kisses as those! And you, good woman, whose boy ran away, you can understand something about these kisses, too. He left you, and you did not hear of him for years, and he went on in a very vicious course of life. When you did hear of him, it nearly broke your heart, and when he came back, you hardly knew him.

Do you recollect how you took him in? You felt that you wished that he was the little boy you used to press to your bosom; but now he was grown up to be a big man and a great sinner, yet you gave him such a kiss, and repeated your welcome so often that he will never forget it, nor will you forget it either. You can understand that this overwhelming greeting was like the father saying, "My boy, you are my son. Despite all that you have done, you belong to me; however far you have gone in sin and folly, I own you. You are bone of my bone, and flesh of my flesh." In this parable Christ would have you know, poor sinner, that God will acknowledge you, if you come to him confessing your sin through Jesus Christ. He will gladly receive you; for all things are ready against the day that you return.

> Spread for thee the festal board,
>> See with richest dainties stored,
> To thy Father's bosom pressed,
>> Yet again a child confessed;
> Never from his house to roam,
>> Come and welcome, sinner, come.

The father received his son with many kisses, and so proved that his *prayer was answered.* Indeed, his father heard his prayer before he offered it. He was going to say, *Father, I have sinned,* and to ask for forgiveness; but he got the mercy, and a kiss to seal it, before the prayer was presented. This also shall be true of you, O sinner, who are returning to your God through Jesus Christ! You shall be permitted to pray, and God will answer you. Hear it, poor, despairing sinner, whose prayer has seemed to be shut out from heaven! Come to your Father's bosom now, and he will hear your prayers; and, before many days are over, you shall have the clearest proofs that you are fully restored to the divine favor by answers to your intercessions that shall make you marvel at the Lord's loving-kindness toward you.

Further than this, you shall have all your *privileges restored,* even as this wandering young man was put among the children when he returned. As you see him now in the father's house, where he was received with many kisses, he wears a son's robe, the family ring is on his finger, and the shoes of the home are on his feet. He no longer eats swine's food, but children's bread.

Even thus shall it be with you if you return to God. Though you look so foul and so wretched, and really are even more defiled than you look; and though you smell so strongly of the hogs among which you have been living that some people's nostrils would turn up at you, your Father will not notice these marks of your occupation in the far country with all its horrible defilement. See how this father treats his boy. He kisses him, and kisses him again, because he knows his own child, and, recognizing him as his child, and feeling his fatherly heart yearning for him, he gives him kiss after kiss. He kisses him much, to make him know that he has full restoration.

In this repeated kissing we see, then, these three things: much love, much forgiveness, and full restoration. But these many kisses meant even more than this. They revealed his father's exceeding joy. The father's heart is overflowing with gladness, and he cannot restrain his delight. I think he must have shown his joy by *a repeated look.* I will tell you the way I think the father behaved towards his son who had been dead, but was alive again; who had been lost, but was found.

Let me try to describe the scene. The father has kissed his son, and he bids him to sit down. Then he comes in front of him, and looks at him, and feels so happy that he says, "I must give you another kiss," and then he walks away for a minute. But he is back again before long, saying to himself, "Oh, I must give him another kiss!" He gives him another, for he is so happy. His heart beats fast; he feels very joyful; the old man would like the music to strike up; he wants to be at the dance; but meanwhile he satisfies himself by a repeated look at his long-lost child. Oh, I believe that God looks at the sinner, and looks at him again, and keeps on looking at him, all the while delighting in the very sight of him when he is truly repentant and comes back to his Father's house.

The repeated kiss meant, also, *a repeated blessing,* for every time he put his arms around him, and kissed him, he kept saying, "Bless you; oh, bless you, my boy!" He felt that his son had brought a blessing to him by coming back, and he invoked fresh blessings upon his head. Oh sinner! if you did but know how God would welcome you, and how he would look at you, and how he would bless you, then surely you would at once repent, and come to his arms and heart, and find yourself happy in his love.

The many kisses meant, also, *repeated delight.* It is a very wonderful thing that it should be in the power of a sinner to make God glad. He is the happy God, the source and spring of all happiness; what can we add to his blessedness? And yet, speaking after the manner of men, God's highest joy lies in clasping his willful Ephraims to his breast when he has heard them bemoaning themselves, and has seen them arising and returning to their home. God grant that he may see that sight even now and have delight because of sinners returning to himself!

Yes, we believe it shall be even so, because of his presence with us, and because of the gracious working of the Holy Spirit. Surely that is the teaching of the prophet's words: *The Lord thy God in the midst of thee is mighty; he will save, he will rejoice over thee with joy; he will rest in his love, he will joy over thee with singing* (Zephaniah 3:17). Think of the eternal God singing, and remember that it is because a wandering sinner has returned to him that he sings. He rejoices in the return of the prodigal, and all heaven shares in his joy.

I have not got through my subject yet. As we take a fifth look, we find that these many kisses mean overflowing comfort. This poor young man, in his hungry, faint, and wretched state, having come a very long way, had not much heart left in him. His hunger had taken all energy out of him, and he was so conscious of his guilt that he hardly had the courage to face his father; so his father gives him a kiss, as much as to say, "Come, boy, do not be cast down; I love you."

"Oh, *the past, the past,* my father!" he might moan, as he thought of his wasted years; but he had no sooner said that than he received another kiss, as if his father said, "Never mind the past; I have forgotten all about that." This is the Lord's way with his saved ones. Their past lies hidden under the blood of atonement. The Lord says by his servant Jeremiah, *The iniquity of Israel shall be sought for, and there shall be none; and the sins of Judah, and they shall not be found: for I will pardon them whom I reserve* (Jeremiah 50:20).

But then, perhaps, the young man looked down on his foul garments, and said, "*The present*, my father, *the present* – what a dreadful state I am in!" And with another kiss would come the answer, "Never mind the present, my boy. I am content to have you as you are. I love you." This, too, is God's word to those who are *accepted in the beloved*. In spite of all their vileness, they are pure and spotless in Christ, and God says of each one of them, "*Since thou wast precious in my sight, thou hast been honourable, and I have loved thee* (Isaiah 43:4). Therefore, though in yourself you are unworthy, through my dear Son you are welcome to my home."

"Oh, but," the boy might have said, "*the future*, my father, *the future*! What would you think if I should ever go astray again?" Then would come another holy kiss, and his father would say, "I will see to the future, my boy; I will make home so bright for you that you will never want to go away again." But God does more than that for us when we return to him. He not only surrounds us with tokens of his love, but he also says concerning us, *They shall be my people, and I will be their God: and I will give them one heart, and one way, that they may fear me for ever, for the good of them, and of their children after them: and I will make an everlasting covenant with them, that I will not turn away from them, to do them good; but I will put my fear in their hearts, that they shall not depart from me* (Jeremiah 32:38-40).

Furthermore, he says to each returning one, *A new heart also will I give you, and a new spirit will I put within you: and I will take away the stony heart out of your flesh, and I will give you an heart of flesh. And I will put my spirit within you, and cause you to walk in my statutes, and ye shall keep my judgments, and do them* (Ezekiel 36:26-27).

Whatever there was to trouble the son, the father gave him a kiss to set it all right; and, in like manner, our God has a love token for every time of doubt and dismay that may come to his reconciled sons. Perhaps one whom I am addressing says, "Even though I confess my sin, and seek God's mercy, I shall still be in sore trouble, for through my sin I have brought myself down to poverty."

"There is a kiss for you," says the Lord. *Bread shall be given [thee]; [thy] waters shall be sure* (Isaiah 33:16).

"But I have even brought disease upon myself by sin," says another.

"There is a kiss for you," says the Lord, "for I am Jehovah-Rophi, *the Lord that healeth thee, who forgiveth all thine iniquities; who healeth all thy diseases*" (Exodus 15:26; Psalm 103:3).

"But I am dreadfully down at the heel," says another. The Lord gives you also a kiss, and says, "I will lift you up, and provide for all your needs. *No good thing will [I] withhold from them that walk uprightly*" (Psalm 84:11). All the promises in this Book belong to every repentant sinner who returns to God believing in Jesus Christ, his Son.

The father of the prodigal kissed his son much, and thus made him feel happy there and then. Poor souls, when they come to Christ, are in a dreadful plight, and some of them hardly know where they are. I have known them to talk a lot of nonsense in their despair, and say hard and wicked things of God in their dreadful doubt. The Lord gives no answer to all that, except a kiss, and then another kiss. Nothing puts the repentant one so much at rest as the Lord's repeated assurance of his unchanging love.

Such a one the Lord has often received, *and kissed him much,* that he might fetch him up even from the horrible pit, and set his feet upon a rock, and establish his goings. The Lord grant that many whom I am addressing may understand what I am talking about!

And now for our sixth topic, though you will think I am getting to be like the old Puritans with these many topics. But I cannot help it, for these many kisses had many meanings: love, forgiveness, restoration, joy, and comfort were in them, and also strong assurance.

The father kissed his son much to make him quite certain that it was *all real.* The prodigal, in receiving these many kisses, might say to himself, "All this love must be true, for a little while ago I heard the hogs grunt, and now I hear nothing but the kisses from my dear father's lips." So his father gave him another kiss, for there was no better way of convincing him that the first one was real than repeating it; and if there lingered any doubt about the second, the father gave him yet a third. If, when the dream of old was doubled, then the interpretation was sure, and these repeated kisses left no room for doubt. The father renewed the tokens of his love so that his son might be fully assured of its reality.

He did it so that in the future it might *never be questioned.* Some of us were brought so low before we were converted, that God gave us an excess of joy when he saved us, so that we might never forget it. Sometimes the devil says to me, "You are no child of God." I have long ago given up answering him, for I find that it is a waste of time to argue with such a crafty old liar as he is; he knows too much for me. But if I must answer him, I say, "Why, I remember when I was saved by the Lord! I never can forget even the very spot of ground where first I saw my Savior; there and then my joy rolled in like some great Atlantic billow, and burst in a mighty foam of bliss, covering all things. I cannot forget it."

That is an argument which even the devil cannot answer, for he cannot make me believe that such a thing never happened. The Father kissed me much, and I remember it full well. The Lord gives to some of us such a clear deliverance, such a bright, sunshiny day at our conversion, that from that point on we cannot question our state before him, but must believe that we are eternally saved.

The father put the assurance of this poor returning prodigal beyond all doubt. If the first kisses were given privately, when only the father and son were present, it is quite certain that, afterwards, he kissed him *before men,* where others could see him. He *kissed him much* in the presence of the household, so that they also might not be calling into question that he was his father's child. It was a pity that the elder brother was not there also. You see he was away in the field. He was more interested in the crops than in the reception of his brother.

I have known such a one in modern days. He was a man who did not come out to evening-week services. He was such a man of business that he did not come out on a Thursday night, and the prodigal came home at such a time, and so the elder brother did not see the father receive him. If he lived now, he would probably not come to the church meetings; he would be too busy. So, he would not get to know about the reception of repentant sinners. But the father, when he received that son of his, intended all to know, once and for all, that he was indeed his child. Oh, that you might get these many kisses even now! If they are given to you, you will have, for the rest of your life, strong assurance derived from the happiness of your first days.

I will be done when I have said that I think that here we have a specimen of the intimate communion that the Lord often gives to sinners when first they come to him. *His father saw him, and had compassion, and ran, and fell on his neck, and kissed him [much].*

You see, this was *before the family fellowship.* Before the servants had prepared the meal, before there had been any music or dancing in the family, his father kissed him. He would have cared little for all their songs, and would have valued only slightly his reception by the servants, if, first of all, he had not been welcomed to his father's heart.

So it is with us. We need first to have fellowship with God before we think much of union with his people. Before I go to join a church, I want my Father's kiss. Before the pastor gives me the right hand of fellowship, I want my heavenly Father's right hand to welcome me. Before I become recognized by God's people here below, I want a private recognition from the great Father above; and that he gives to all who come to him as the prodigal came to his father. May he give it to some of you now!

This kissing, also, was *before the Communion table.* You know that the prodigal was afterwards to sit at his father's table, and to eat of the fatted calf; but before that, his father kissed him. He would scarcely have been able to sit easily at the feast without the previous kisses of love. The Communion table, to which we are invited, is very sweet. To eat the flesh and drink the blood of Christ, symbolically, in the ordinance of the Lord's Supper, is, indeed, a blessed thing; but I want to have communion with God by the way of the love kiss before I come there. *Let him kiss me with the kisses of his mouth* (Song of Solomon 1:2). This is something private, ravishing, and sweet. God give it to many of you! May you get the many kisses of your Father's mouth before you come into the church, or to the Communion table!

These many kisses likewise came *before the public rejoicing.* The friends and neighbors were invited to share in the feast. But think how shamefaced the son would have been in their presence if, first of all, he had not found a place in his father's love or had not been quite sure of it. He would almost have been inclined to run away again. But the father had *kissed him much*, and so he could meet the curious gaze of old friends with a smiling face, until any unkind remarks they might have thought of making died away, killed by his evident joy in his father. It is a hard thing for a man to confess Christ if he has not had an overwhelming sense of communion with him.

But when we are lifted to the skies in the rapture God gives to us, it becomes easy, not only to face the world, but also to win the sympathy of even those who might have opposed us. This is why young converts are frequently used to lead others into the light; the Lord's many kisses of forgiveness have so recently been given to them, that their words catch the fragrance of divine love as they pass the lips just touched by the Lord. Alas, that any should ever lose their first love, and forget the many kisses they have received from their heavenly Father!

Lastly, all this was given *before the meeting with the elder brother.* If the Prodigal Son had known what the elder brother thought and said, I would not have wondered at all if he had run off and never come back at all. He might have come near home, and then, hearing what his brother said, have stolen away again. Yes, but before that could happen, his father had given him the many kisses. Poor sinner! you have come in here, and perhaps you have found the Savior. It may be that you will go and speak to some Christian man, and he will be afraid to say much to you. I do not wonder that he should doubt you, for you are not, in yourself, as yet a particularly nice sort of person to talk to. But, if you get your Father's many kisses, you will not mind your elder brother being a little hard upon you.

Occasionally I hear of one who wished to join the church, saying, "I came to see the elders, and one of them was rather rough with me. I shall never come again." What a stupid man you must be! Is it not their duty to be a little rough with some of you, lest you should deceive yourselves, and be mistaken about your true state? We desire lovingly to bring you to Christ, and if we are afraid that you really have not yet come back to God, with repentance and faith, should we not tell you so, like honest men?

But suppose that you have really come, and your brother is mistaken; go and get a kiss from your Father, and never mind your brother. He may remind you of how you have squandered your living, painting the picture even blacker than it ought to be; but your Father's kisses will make you forget your brother's frowns.

If you think that in the household of faith you will find everybody amiable, and everyone willing to help you, you will be greatly mistaken. Young Christians are often frightened when they come across some who, from frequent disappointment of their hopes, or from a natural spirit of caution, or perhaps from a lack of spiritual life, receive only coldly those upon whom the Father has lavished much love. If that is your case, never mind these cross-grained elder brethren; get another kiss from your Father. Perhaps the reason it is written, "He kissed him *much*" was because the elder brother, when he came near him, treated him so coldly, and so angrily refused to join in the feast.

Lord, give to many poor trembling souls the will to come to you! Bring many sinners to your blessed feet, and while they are yet a great way off, run and meet them; fall on their neck, give them many kisses of love, and fill them to the full with heavenly delight, in the name of the Lord Jesus Christ. Amen.

Chapter 4

The Reception of Sinners

*But the father said to his servants, Bring forth the best robe,
and put it on him; and put a ring on his hand, and shoes
on his feet: And bring hither the fatted calf, and kill it; and
let us eat, and be merry.* (Luke 15:22-23)

Previously we spoke on the consecration of priests. That theme might
seem too high for troubled hearts and trembling consciences who
fear that they shall never be made priests and kings unto God. So glorious a privilege appears to them to hang in the dim and distant future,
if, indeed, they reach it at all. Therefore, at this time, we will go down
from the elevated regions to comfort those who are seeking the Lord,
with the view of helping them in their turn to climb also.

We speak this morning not of the consecration of priests, but of
the reception of sinners, and this, according to our text, is a very joyful business; it is even described as a merrymaking, accompanied with
music and with dancing. We very frequently speak of the sorrow for
sin that accompanies conversion, and I do not think we can speak of
it too often; but yet there is a possibility of our overlooking the equally
holy and remarkable joy that accompanies the return of a soul to God.

It has been a very common error to suppose that a man must pass
through a very considerable time of despondency, if not of horror of mind,
before he can find peace with God. Now in this parable the father seems

determined to cut short that period; he stops his son in the very middle of his confession, and before he can ask to be made as one of the hired servants, his mournful style is changed to rejoicing, for the father has already fallen on his neck and kissed his trembling lips into a sweet silence.

It is not the Lord's desire that sinners should delay long in the state of unbelieving conviction of sin. It is something wrong in themselves that keeps them there; either they are ignorant of the freeness and fullness of Christ, or they harbor self-righteous hopes, or they cling to their sins. Sin lies at the door; it is no work of God that blocks the way. He delights in their delight, and enjoys their joy.

It is the Father's will that the repentant sinner should at once believe in Jesus, at once find complete forgiveness, and immediately enter into rest. If any of you came to Jesus without the dreary interval of terror that is so frequent, I pray you do not judge yourselves as though your conversions were doubtful – they are all the more genuine instead of all the less genuine because they bear the marks of the gospel rather than of the law. The weeping of Peter, which in a few days turns to joy, is far better than the horror of Judas, which ends in suicide.

Conversions, as recorded in Scripture, are for the most part exceedingly rapid. People were pricked in the heart at Pentecost, and the same day they were baptized and added to the church because they had found peace with God through Jesus Christ. Paul was struck down with conviction, and in three days he was a baptized believer. Perhaps the figure is inept, but I was about to say that sometimes God's power is so very near us that the lightning flash of conviction is often accompanied at the very same moment with the deep thunder of the Lord's voice, which drives away our fears and proclaims peace and pardon to the soul.

In many cases the sharp needle of the law is immediately followed by the silken thread of the gospel; the showers of repentance are succeeded at once by the sunshine of faith; peace overtakes repentance and walks arm in arm with her into yet fuller rest.

Having thus reminded you that God would have repentant ones very soon rejoice, I want to spend this morning in setting forth the joy that is caused by pardoned sin. That joy is threefold. We will talk about it, first, as *the joy of God over sinners;* secondly, as *the joy of sinners in God;* and thirdly, what is so often forgotten, as *the joy of the servants,* for they too rejoiced, for the father said, *Let us eat, and be merry.* And one of the points of the parable is just this, that as in the case of the lost sheep, the shepherd calls together his friends and neighbors; and as in the case of the piece of money, the woman calls her neighbors together; so in this case, also, others share in the joy that chiefly belongs to the loving father and the returning wanderer.

First is the joy of God over sinners. It is always difficult to speak of the ever-blessed God appropriately when we have to describe him as touched by emotions. I pray, therefore, to be guided in my speech by the Holy Spirit. We have been educated into the idea that the Lord is above emotions, either of sorrow or pleasure. That he cannot suffer, for instance, is always laid down as a self-evident presumption. Is that quite so clear? Cannot he do or bear anything he chooses to? What does the Scripture mean that says that man's sin before the flood made the Lord repent that he had made man on the earth, *and it grieved him at his heart* (Genesis 6:6)? Is there no meaning in the Lord's own language, *Forty years long was I grieved with this generation* (Psalm 95:10)? Are we not forbidden to grieve the Holy Spirit? Is he not described as having been vexed by ungodly men? Surely, then, he can be grieved: it cannot be an altogether meaningless expression.

For my part, I rejoice to worship the living God, who, because he is living, does grieve and rejoice. It makes one feel more love for him than if he dwelt on some serene Mount Olympus, careless of all our woes because he is incapable of any concern for us, or interest in us, one way or the other. To look upon him as utterly impassive and incapable of anything like emotion does not, to my mind, exalt the Lord, but rather brings him down to be comparable to the gods of stone or wood, which cannot sympathize with their worshippers.

No, Jehovah is not indifferent. He is the living God, and everything that goes with life – pure, perfect, holy life – is to be found in him. Still, such a subject must always be spoken of very tenderly, with solemn awe, because, even though we know something of what God is, for we are made in the image of God, and the best likeness of God undoubtedly was man as he came from his Maker's hand, yet man is not God, and even in his perfectness he must have been a very tiny miniature of God; while now that he has sinned he has blotted and blurred that image.

The finite cannot fully mirror the Infinite, nor can the grand, glorious, and essential properties of the Deity be communicated to creatures; they must remain peculiar to God alone. The Lord is, however, continually represented as displaying joy. Moses declared to sinful Israel that if they returned and obeyed the voice of the Lord, the Lord would again rejoice over them for good, as he rejoiced over their fathers (see Deuteronomy 30:9). The Lord is said to rejoice in his works and to delight in mercy, and surely we must believe it. Why should we doubt it? Many passages of Scripture speak very impressively of God's joy in his people.

Zephaniah puts it in the strongest manner: *He will save, he will rejoice over thee with joy; he will rest in his love, he will joy over thee with singing* (Zephaniah 3:17). Our God is forever the happy or blessed God; we cannot think of him as other than supremely blessed. Still, from the Scriptures we gather that he displays on certain occasions a special joy that he would have us recognize. I do not think that it can be a mere parable, but it is a real fact, that the Lord does rejoice over returning and repenting sinners.

Every being manifests its joy according to its nature, and seeks means for its display suitable to itself. It is so with men. When the old Romans celebrated a triumph because some great general returned as a victor from Africa, Greece, or Asia with the spoils of a long campaign, how did the fierce Roman nature express its joy? Why, in the Colosseum, or in some yet more grand amphitheater, where buzzing nations choked the ways, and where they gathered in their myriads to behold not only beasts, but also their fellow man, "butchered to make a Roman holiday." Cruelty upon an extraordinary scale was their way of expressing the joy of their iron hearts.

Look at the self-indulgent man! He has had a prosperous season, and has made a lucky hit, as he calls it, or some event has occurred in his family that makes him very jubilant; what will he do to show forth his joy? Will he bow the knee in gratitude, or lift a hymn of praise? Not he. He will hold a drinking bout, and when he and his fellows are mad with wine, his joy will find expression! The sensual show their joy by sensuality.

Now God, whose name is good and whose nature is love, when he has joy, expresses it in mercy, in loving-kindness, and in grace. The father's joy in the parable before us showed itself in the full forgiveness accorded, in the kiss of perfect love bestowed, in the gift of the best robe, the ring, and the sandals, and in the gladsome festival that filled the whole house with holy mirth. Everything expresses its joy according to its nature; infinite love, therefore, reveals its joy in acts of love.

The nature of God being as much above ours as the heavens are above the earth, the expression of his joy is therefore all the loftier, and his gifts the greater. Still, there is a likeness between God's way of expressing joy and ours, which it will be profitable to note. How do we express ourselves, ordinarily, when we are glad? We do so very commonly by a display of *generosity*.

When in the olden time our kings came into the city of London, or a great victory was celebrated, the conduit in Cheapside ran with red wine, and even the gutters flowed with it. Then there were tables set in the street, and my lords, and the aldermen, and the mayor kept open house, and everybody was fed to the full. Joy was expressed by hospitality. You have seen the picture of the young heir coming of age, and have noticed how the artist depicts the great yard of the manor house as full of men and women who are eating and drinking to their hearts' content.

At Christmas seasons, and upon marriage days and harvest homes, men ordinarily express their joy by bountiful provision; so also does the father in this wondrous parable exhibit the utmost generosity, representing thereby the boundless liberality of the great Father of spirits, who shows his joy over repentant ones by the manner in which he entertains them. The best robe, the ring, the shoes, the fatted calf, and the *Let us eat, and be merry* all show by their bountifulness that God is glad. His oxen and his fatlings are killed, for the feast of mercy is the banquet of the Lord. So unrivaled are the gifts of his gracious hand that the receivers of his favors have cried out in amazement, *Who is a God like unto thee?* (Micah 7:18).

Beloved, consider a while the Lord's bounty to returning sinners, blotting out their sins like a cloud, and like a thick cloud their iniquities, justifying them in the righteousness of Christ, endowing them with his Holy Spirit, regenerating them, comforting them, illuminating them, purifying them, strengthening them, guiding them, protecting them, filling them with all his own fullness, satisfying their *mouth with good things* (Psalm 103:5), and crowning them with tender mercies. I see in the bounty of God with which he so liberally endows returning sinners a mighty proof that his inmost soul rejoices over the salvation of men.

At glad times men generally manifest some *specialty* in their generosity. On the day of the young heir's coming of age, the long-stored cask of wine is opened, and the best bullock is roasted whole. So here in the parable we read: **Bring forth** *the best robe* (emphasis added), indicating that it had been laid by and kept in store until then. Nobody had used that robe; it was locked up in the wardrobe, only to be brought out on some very special occasion. This was the happiest day that ever had made glad the house, and therefore, *Bring forth the best robe,* for no other will suffice.

Meat is needed for the banquet. Let a calf be killed. Which shall it be? A calf taken at random from the herd? No, but *the fatted* calf that has been standing in the stalls, and is well fed, and has been reserved for a festival. Oh, beloved, when God blesses a sinner, he shows his joy by giving him the reserved mercies, the special treasures of everlasting love, the precious things of grace, the secret of the covenant: yes, he has given to sinners the best of the best in giving them Christ Jesus and the indwelling of the Holy Spirit.

The best that heaven gives, God bestows on sinners when they come to him. No scraps and odds and ends are dealt out to hungry and thirsty seekers, but in princely lavishness of unlimited love the heavenly Father deals out abundant grace. I would that sinners would come and try my Lord's hospitality; they would find his table to be more richly loaded than even that of Solomon, though thirty oxen and a hundred sheep did not suffice for one day's provision for the household of that magnificent king. If they would but come, even the largest-hearted among them would be awestruck as they saw how richly God supplied all their need, *according to his riches in glory by Christ Jesus* (Philippians 4:19).

> Rags exchanged for costly treasure.
> Shoes and ring and heaven's best robe!
> Gifts of love which knows no measure;
> Who can tell the heart of God?
> All his loved ones – his redeemed ones,
> Perfect are in his abode.

We also show our joy by a *concentration of thought* upon the object of it. When a man is carried away with joy, he forgets everything else, and gives himself up to the one delight. David was so glad to bring back the ark of the Lord that he danced before the Lord with all his might, being clad only with a linen ephod. He laid aside his stately garments and thought so little of his dignity that Michal sneered at him; he was so much absorbed in adoring his Lord that all regard for appearances was quite gone.

Observe well the parable, and hear the father say, *Bring forth the best robe, and put it on **him**; and put a ring on **his** hand, and shoes on **his** feet: . . . and let us eat, and be merry: for **this my son** was dead, and is alive again* (emphasis added). The son alone is in the father's eye, and the whole house must be ordered in reference to him. Nothing is to be thought of today except the long-lost son; he is paramount in the wardrobe, the jewel room, the farmyard, the kitchen, and the banqueting chamber. He that was lost, he that was dead, he being found and alive engrosses the whole of the father's mind. Sinner, it is wonderful how God sets all his thoughts on you according to his promise: *I will set mine eyes upon them for good* (Jeremiah 24:6); and again, *So will I watch over them, to build, and to plant, saith the Lord* (Jeremiah 31:28).

The Lord thinks upon the poor and needy, his eyes are upon them, and his ears are open to their cry. He thinks as much of each repentant sinner as if he were the only being in the universe. O repentant one, for you is the working of the Lord's providence to bring you home, for you is the training of his ministers that they might know how to reach your heart, for you are the gifts of the Spirit upon them that they might be powerful with your conscience; yes, for you his Son, his eternal Son once bleeding on the cross, is now sitting in the highest heavens making intercession for you.

I saw in Amsterdam the diamond-cutting, and I noticed great wheels, a large factory, and powerful engines, and all the power was made to bear upon a small stone no larger than the nail of my little finger. All that huge machinery for that little stone, because it was so precious! It seems to me that I see you poor insignificant sinners, who have rebelled against your God, brought back to your Father's house, and now the whole universe is full of wheels and all those wheels are working together for your good, to make out of you a jewel fit to glisten in the Redeemer's crown. God is not represented as saying more of creation than that *it was very good* (Genesis 1:31), but in the work of grace he is described as singing for joy. He breaks the eternal silence and cries, "My son is found."

As the philosopher when he had compelled nature to yield her secret ran through the street crying, "Eureka! Eureka! I have found it! I have found it!" so does the Father dwell on the words, *My son was dead, and is alive again; he was lost, and is found.* The whole of Scripture aims at the bringing back again of the Lord's banished, for this the Redeemer leaves his glory, for this the church sweeps her house and lights her candle, and when the work is done, all other bliss is secondary to the surpassing joy of the Lord, of which he bids his ransomed ones to partake, saying, *Enter thou into the joy of thy Lord* (Matthew 25:23).

We also show our joy by *a willingness of motion.* I mentioned David just now. It was so with him when he danced before the ark. I cannot imagine David walking slowly before the ark or creeping after it like a mourner at a funeral. I often notice the difference between your coming to this place and people going to other places of worship. I observe a very solemn, stately, and somber motion in almost everybody else, but you come tripping along as if you were glad to go up to the house of the Lord; you do not regard the place of our joyous assemblies as a sort of religious prison, but as the palace and banqueting house of the great King.

When anyone is joyous, he is sure to show it by the quickness of his motions. Listen to the father; he says, *Bring forth the best robe, and put it on him; and put a ring on his hand, and shoes on his feet: and bring hither the fatted calf, and kill it; and let us eat, and be merry.* As quickly as possible he pours out sentence after sentence. There is no delay, no interval between the commands. Might he not have said, "Bring forth the best robe and put it on him, and let us look at him a while, and sit down and prepare him for the next step; and in an hour's time, or tomorrow, we will put a ring on his hand; and then soon we will put shoes on his feet. He is best without shoes for the present, for perhaps if he has shoes on, he will run away. As to the festival, perhaps we had better rejoice over him when we see whether his repentance is genuine." No, no, no, the father's heart is too glad; he must bless his boy at once, heap on his favors, and multiply his tokens of love. When the Lord receives a sinner, he runs to meet him, he falls on his neck, he kisses him, he speaks to him, he forgives him, he justifies him, he sanctifies him, he puts him among the children, he opens the treasures of his grace to him, and all in quick succession.

Within a few minutes after he has been cleansed from sin, the prodigal is robed, and adorned, and equipped with shoes for service. The love of our Redeemer's heart made him say to the poor thief, *Today shalt thou be with me in paradise* (Luke 23:43); he would not let him linger in pain on the cross, but carried him away to paradise in an hour or two. Love and joy are ever quick of foot. God is slow to anger, but he is so plentiful in his mercy that his grace overflows and rushes on like a torrent when it leaps along the ravine.

Once more, the joy of the father was shown as ours often is by *open utterance*. It is hard for a glad man to hold his tongue. What can mute people do when they are very happy? I cannot imagine how they endure silence at such times; it must then be a terrible misfortune. When you are very happy, you must tell somebody. So does this father. He pours out his joy, and the utterance is very simple. *My son was dead, and is alive again; he was lost, and is found.* Yet, simple as it is, it is poetry.

The poetry of the Hebrews consisted of parallelism, or a repetition of the sense or a part of the words. So here are two lines that pair with each other, and make a verse of Hebrew poetry. Glad men when they speak naturally and simply always say the right thing in the very best manner, using nature's poetry, as does the father here.

Note, also, that there is reiteration in his utterance. He might have been satisfied to say, *This my son was dead, and is alive again.* No; the fact is so sweet that he must repeat it: *He was lost, and is found.* Even thus we speak when we are very full of sweet content; the heart bubbles up with a good matter, and over again and over again we rehearse our joy. When the morsel is sweet, we roll it under the tongue. We cannot help it.

So, the Lord rejoices over sinners, and tells his joy in Holy Scripture in varied phrases and metaphors, and though those Scriptures are simple in their style, yet they contain the very essence of poetry. The poets of the Bible stand in the first rank among the sons of song, God himself condescending to use poetry to utter his joy because a more prosaic manner would be all too cold and tame.

Hear how he puts it: *As the bridegroom rejoiceth over the bride, so shall thy God rejoice over thee* (Isaiah 62:5). *I will rejoice in Jerusalem, and joy in my people* (Isaiah 65:19). We might have been left in the dark about this joy of God; we might have been coldly informed that God would save sinners, and we might never have known that he found such joy in it. But the divine joy was too great to be concealed; the great heart of God could not restrain itself, he must tell out to all the universe the delight that the exercise of mercy brought to him. It was suitable that he should make merry and be glad, and therefore he did it, for nothing that is suitable to be done will ever be neglected by the Lord our God.

Thus, dear friends, have I feebly spoken of the joy of God, and I want you to notice that it is a delight in which every attribute of God takes a share. Condescension ran to meet the son, love fell on his neck, grace kissed him, wisdom clothed him, truth gave him the ring, peace put shoes on his feet, wisdom provided the feast, and power prepared it.

No one attribute of the divine nature quarrels with the forgiveness and salvation of a sinner; not one attribute holds back from the beloved purpose. Power strengthens the weak, and mercy binds up the wounded; justice smiles upon the justified sinner, for it is satisfied through the atoning blood, and truth puts forth her hand to guarantee that the promise of grace is fulfilled; unchangeableness confirms what has been done, and omniscience looks around to see that nothing is left undone. The whole of the Deity is brought to bear upon a poor worm of the dust, to lift it up and transform it into an heir of God, a joint heir with the Only Begotten. The joy of God occupies the whole of his being, so that when we think of it, we may well say, *Bless the Lord, O my soul: and all that is within me, bless his holy name* (Psalm 103:1), since all that is within him is engaged to bless his saints.

This joy of the Lord should give every sinner great confidence in coming to God by Jesus Christ, for if you would be glad to be saved, he will be glad to save you; if you long to lay your head in your Father's bosom, your Father's bosom longs to have it there; if you yearn to say, "I have sinned," he equally longs to say to you, by acts of love, "I forgive you freely." If you long to be his child in his own house once more, the door is open, and he himself is on the watch. Come and welcome, come and welcome, and delay no more.

I will now speak of the joy of the sinner. The son was glad. He did not express it in words, as far as I can see in the parable, but he felt it nonetheless – but all the more. Sometimes silence is discreet, and it was so in this case; at other times it is absolutely forced upon you by an inability to utter the emotion, and this also was true of the prodigal. The son's heart was too full for utterance in words, but he had speaking eyes and a speaking countenance as he looked on that dear father.

As he put on the robe, the ring, and the shoes, he must have been too astonished to speak. He wept in showers that day, but the tears were not salty with grief, they were sweet tears, glittering like the dew of the morning. What do you think would make the son glad? Why, the father's love, the father's forgiveness, and restoration to his old place in the father's heart. That was the point. But then each gift would serve as a token of that love and make the joy overflow. There was *the robe* put on – the clothing of a son, and of a son well beloved and accepted. Have you noticed how the robe answered to his confession? The sentences match each other thus: *Father, I have sinned. Bring forth the best robe, and put it on him.* Cover all his sins with Christ's righteousness; put away his sin by imputing to him the righteousness of the Lord Jesus.

The robe also met his condition. He was in rags; therefore, *bring forth the best robe, and put it on him,* and you shall see no more of his rags. It was proper that he should be thus arrayed, in token of his restoration. He who is re-endowed with the privileges of a son should not be dressed in sordid clothes, but should wear garments suitable to his position. Moreover, as a festival was about to begin, he ought to wear a festive garment. It would not be respectable for him to feast and be merry in his rags. Put the best robe on him so that he may be ready to take his place at the banquet. So when the repentant one comes to God, he is not only covered as to the past by the righteousness of Christ, but he is also prepared for the future blessedness that is reserved for the pardoned ones; yes, he is fitted to begin the rejoicing at once.

Then came *the ring,* a luxury rather than a necessity, except that now that he was a son, it was well that he should be restored to all the honors of his relationship. The signet ring in the East in former times conferred great privileges. In those days men did not sign their names, but stamped with their signet upon wax, so that the ring gave a man power over property, and made him a sort of other self to the man whose ring he wore. The father gives the son a ring, and how complete an answer was that gift to another clause of his confession. Let me read the two sentences together: *[I] am no more worthy to be called thy son. Put a ring on his hand.* The gift precisely meets the confession.

It also corresponded with his changed condition. How unusual that the very hand that had been feeding swine should now wear a ring. There were no rings on his hands when they were soiled at the trough, I warrant you; but now he is a swine feeder no longer, but an honored son of a rich father. Slaves wear no rings. Juvenal laughs at certain freedmen because they were seen walking up and down the Via Sacra with conspicuous rings on their fingers, the emblems of their newfound liberty. The ring indicated the repentant one's liberty from sin, and his enjoyment of the full privileges of his Father's house.

O beloved, the Lord will make you glad if you come to him, by putting the seal of the Holy Spirit's indwelling upon you, which is both the pledge of the inheritance and the best adornment of the hand of your practical character. You shall have a sure and honorable token, and shall know that all things are yours, whether things present, or things to come. This ring upon your finger will declare your marriage union to Christ, will set forth the eternal love that the Father has fixed upon you, and will be the abiding pledge of the perfect work of the Holy Spirit.

Then they put *shoes* on his feet. I suppose he had worn out his own. In the East, servants do not usually wear shoes at home, and especially in the best rooms of the house. The master and the son wear the sandals, but not the servants, so that this order was an answer to the last part of the repentant son's prayer, *Make me as one of thy hired servants.* "No," says the father, "put shoes on his feet." In the forgiven sinner the awe that puts off its shoes is to be defeated by the familiarity that wears the shoes that infinite love provides.

The forgiven one is no longer to tremble at Sinai, but he is to come unto Mount Zion, and to have familiar interaction with God. Thus, also the restored one had shoes put on his feet for filial service – he could run upon his father's errands or work in his father's fields. He had now in every way all that he could want – the robe that covered him, the ring that adorned him, and the shoes that prepared him for travel or labor.

Now you awakened and anxious ones who are longing to draw near to God, I would that this description of the joy of the prodigal would induce you to come at once. Come, you naked, and he will say, *Bring forth the best robe.* Come, you that see your natural deformity through sin, and he will adorn you with a ring of beauty. Come, you who feel as if you could not come, for you have bleeding, weary feet, and he will shoe you with the silver sandals of his grace. Only do but come, and you shall have such joy in your hearts as you have never dreamed of. There shall be a young heaven born within your spirit, which shall grow and increase until it comes to the fullness of bliss.

The time has now come for us to dwell upon the joy of the servants. They were to be merry, and they were merry, for the music and the dancing that were heard outside could not have proceeded from one person only; there must have been many to join in it, and who should these be but the servants to whom the father gave his commands? They ate, they drank, they danced, they joined in the music. There are many of us here who are the servants of our own heavenly Father; though we are his children, we delight to be his servants. Now, whenever a sinner is saved, we have our share of joy. We have joy, first, *in the Father's joy.* They were so glad, because their lord was glad – good servants are always pleased when they see that their master is greatly gratified, and I am sure the Lord's servants are always joyous when they feel that their Lord is well pleased.

That servant who went out to the elder brother showed by his language that he was in sympathy with the father, for he pleaded with the son upon the matter; and when you are in sympathy with God, my dear brother or sister, if the Lord lets you see poor sinners saved, you must and will rejoice with him. It will be to you better than finding a purse full of money, or making a great gain in business; yes, nothing in the world can give you more delight than to see some brother of yours or some child of yours made to rejoice in Christ.

A mother once beautifully said, "I remember the new and strange emotions that trembled in my breast when as an infant he was first folded to my heart – my firstborn child. The thrill of that moment still lingers; but when he was 'born again,' clasped in my arms as a new creature in Christ Jesus, my spiritual child, my son in the gospel, pardoned, justified, adopted, saved, forever saved – oh! it was the very depth of joy, joy unspeakable! My child was a child of God! The prayers that preceded his birth, that cradled his infancy, that circled his youth were answered. My son was Christ's. The weary watchings, the yearning desires, the trembling hopes of years were at rest. Our firstborn son was avowedly the Lord's." May every father and mother here know just such joy by having sympathy with God.

But they had sympathy with *the son*. I am sure they rejoiced to see him back again, for somehow usually even bad sons have the goodwill of good servants. When young men go away, and are a great grief to their fathers, the servants often stick to them. They will say, "Well, Master John was very inconsiderate and licentious, and he vexed his father a great deal, but I would like to see the poor boy back again."

Especially is this true of the old servants who have been in the house since the boy was born: they never forget him. And you will find that God's old servants are always glad when they see prodigal children return; they are delighted beyond measure, because they love them after all, notwithstanding their wanderings. Sinner, with all your faults and hardness of heart we do love you, and we would be glad for your sake to see you delivered from eternal ruin and from the wrath of God that now abides on you, and brought to rejoice in pardoned sin, and acceptance in the beloved.

We should rejoice for the sinner's sake, but I think the servants rejoiced most of all when *they were the instruments* in the father's hand of blessing the son. Just look at this. The father said to the servants, *Bring forth the best robe.* He might have gone to the closet himself with a key and opened it, and brought out the robe himself; but he gave them the pleasure of doing it.

When I get my orders from my Lord and Master on the Lord's Day morning to bring forth the best robe, I am delighted indeed. Nothing delights me more than to preach the imputed righteousness of Jesus Christ, and the substitutionary sacrifice of our exalted Redeemer. *Bring forth the best robe.* Why, my Master, I might be content to stay out of heaven if you would always give me this work to do – to bring forth the best robe and extol and exalt Jesus Christ in the eyes of the people.

Then he said, *Put it on him.* When our Lord gives us grace to do that, there is more joy still. How many times I have brought forth the best robe, but could not put it on you. I have held it up, and lectured on its excellencies, and pointed to your rags, and said what a delightful thing it would be if I could put it on you, but I could not. But when the heavenly Father, by his divine grace and the power of the Spirit, makes us the means of bringing these treasures into the possession of poor sinners, oh, what joy!

I would rejoice to bring forth the ring of the Spirit's sealing work, and the shoes of the preparation of the gospel of peace, for it is a joy to exhibit these blessings, and a greater joy still to put them upon the poor, returning wanderer. God be thanked for giving his servants so great a pleasure! I would not have dared to describe the Lord's servants as putting on the robe, the ring, and the shoes, but as he has himself done so I am delighted to use the Holy Spirit's own language.

How sweet was the command, *Put it on **him*** (emphasis added). Yes, put it on the poor trembling, ragged, shivering sinner. *Put it on **him***, even on him, though he can hardly believe such mercy to be possible. *Put it on **him**?* Yes, on *him*. He who was a drunkard, a swearer, an adulterer? Yes, put it on *him*, for he repents. What joy it is when we are enabled by God's commission to throw that glorious mantle over a great sinner. As for the ring, put it on *him*; that is the beauty of it. And as for the shoes, put them on *him*; that they are for him is the essence of our joy – that such a sinner, and especially when he is one of our own household, should receive these gifts of grace is wonderful! It was most kind of the father to divide the labor of love. One would put on the robe, another the ring, and a third the shoes.

Some of my brethren can preach Jesus Christ in his righteousness gloriously, and they put on the best robe; others seem most gifted in dwelling upon the work of the Spirit of God, and they put on the ring; while yet another class are practical preachers, and they put on the shoes. I do not mind which I have to do, if I may but have a part in helping to bring to poor sinners those matchless gifts of grace, which at infinite expense the Lord has prepared for those who come back to him.

How glad those were who helped to dress him I cannot tell. Meanwhile, another servant was gone off out of doors to bring in the fatted calf, and perhaps two or three were engaged in killing and dressing it, while another was lighting a fire in the kitchen, and preparing the spits for the roast.

One laid the table, and another ran to the garden to bring flowers to make wreaths for the room – I know I would have done that if I had been there. All were happy. All were ready to join in the music and dancing.

Those who work for the good of sinners are always the gladdest when they are saved. You who pray for them, you who teach them, you who preach to them, you who win them for Christ – you shall share their merriment.

Now, dear brethren, we are told that *they began to be merry,* and according to the description, it would seem that they were merry indeed, but still they only *began.* I see no indication that they ever left off. *They began to be merry,* and as merriment is apt to grow beyond all bounds when it once starts, who knows what they have come to by this time. The saints begin to be merry now, and they will never cease, but will rejoice evermore. On earth all the joy we have is only beginning to be merry; it is up in heaven that they get into full swing. Here our best delight is hardly better than a neap tide at its ebb; there the joy rolls along in the majesty of a full spring tide.

> Oh what rapturous hallelujahs
> In our Father's home above!
> Hallelujah! Hallelujah!
> O'er the embraces of his love!
>
> Wondrous welcome – God's own welcome,
> May the chief of sinners prove.
> Sweet melodious strains ascending,
> All around a mighty flood.
>
> Servants, friends, with joy attending –
> Oh! the happiness of God!
> Grace abounding, all transcending,
> Through a Savior's precious blood.

Let us begin to be merry this morning. But we cannot unless we are laboring for the salvation of others in all ways possible to us. If we have done and are doing that, let us praise and bless the Lord, and rejoice with the reclaimed ones, and let us keep the feast as Jesus would have it kept; for I hope there is no one here of the elder brethren who will be angry and refuse to go in. Let us continue to be merry as long as we live, because the lost are found and the dead are made alive. God grant you to be merry on this account, world without end. Amen.

Chapter 5

You Are a Steward

Give an account of thy stewardship. (Luke 16:2)

W e have heard many times in our lives that we are all stewards to almighty God. We told it as a solemn truth of our religion, that the rich man is responsible for the use that he makes of his wealth; that the talented man must give an account to God of the interest that he gets upon his talents; that every one of us, in proportion to our time and opportunities, must give an account for himself before almighty God.

But, my dear brothers and sisters, our responsibility is even deeper and greater than that of other men. We have the ordinary responsibility that falls upon all who profess religion, to give an account of all we have to God; but besides this, you and I have the extraordinary responsibilities of our official standing – you, as teachers for Christ in your classes; and others of us as preachers for him before the great congregation.

The first responsibility is too heavy for any man to fulfill. Apart from divine grace, it is not possible that any man would so use all that God has given him as to be accepted at last with a *Well done, thou good and faithful servant* (Matthew 25:21); yet even if that were possible, it would still remain an utter impossibility for us fully to sustain the fearful weight of responsibility that rests upon us as teachers of the Word of God to our fellow immortals. Upon *our* necks there are two yokes; sovereign grace can make them light and easy, but apart from that they will irritate our shoulders, for they are, of themselves, too heavy for us to bear.

Common responsibility is as Solomon's whip; but extraordinary responsibility derived from official standing, when not regarded, will be as the scorpion of Rehoboam, and its little finger shall be thicker than its father's loins. Woe unto the watchman who warns them not; woe unto the minister who fails to teach the truth; woe unto the Sunday school teacher who is unfaithful to his trust.

Now, let us try to stir one another up, upon this seriously important matter. You will pray for me while I preach, that I may utter some things that may do good to all now present, and I will labor that God may, in answer to your prayers, give me words and thoughts that shall be blessed to you.

Now, first, let me show *the meaning of our being stewards;* then let us consider *that kind of account we shall have to give;* and lastly, let us notice *the days of reckoning when we ought to cast up our account,* and *the days of reckoning when we must give in our account.*

First, then, the steward – What is he?

In the first place, the steward is a servant. He is one of the greatest of servants, but he is only a servant. Perhaps he is the bailiff of a farm, and looks, to all intents and purposes, like a country farmer: he rides over his master's estate, and has many men under him; still he is only a servant, he is under authority, he is only a steward. Perhaps he is a steward in the house of some gentleman who employs him to see after the whole of his establishment in order that he may be free from cares. In that capacity he is himself a master, but still he is a servant, for he has one over him. Let him be as proud as he pleases, but he has little to be proud of, for the only rank he holds in life is the rank of a servant.

Now, the minister and the Sunday school teacher specially stand in the rank of servants. Why, we are none of us our own masters; we are not independent gentlemen who may do as we please; our classes are not our own farms, which we may until in our own manner, and neglect if we please, out of which we may produce any harvest or none at all, at our own discretion. No, we are nothing better than stewards, and we are to labor for our Master in heaven.

What a strange thing it is to see a minister or a teacher giving himself fine airs, as if he were everybody in the world, and might do as he pleased. Is it not an anomaly? How is he to talk about the sacrifices that he makes when he is spending only his master's property? How is he to boast about the time that he expends when his time is not his own? It is all his master's.

He is a servant, and therefore, do he what he may, he only discharges the duty for which he is well rewarded. He has no reason to be proud, or to lord it over others, for whatever his power among them may be, he is himself neither more nor less than a servant. Let each of us try to recollect that from this time on "I am only a servant."

If a superintendent puts a teacher in a class that she does not like, she will recollect that she is a *servant*. She does not allow her servants at home to stand up and say they are not going to do kitchen work but will only wait on tables; they are servants, and they must do as they are bidden; and if we felt that we were servants, we should not object to do what we are told for Christ's sake. Though we would not do it at the dictation of men, yet for Christ's sake we do it as unto the Lord.

We do not suppose that our servants will come to us at night and expect us to say to them, "You have done your work very well today"; we do not imagine that they will look for constant commendation. They are servants, and when they get their wages, that is their commendation on their work. They may judge that they are worth their money, or else we should not keep them.

When you do your work for Jesus, remember that you are only a servant. Do not expect always to have that encouragement that some people are constantly crying for. If you get encouragement from your pastor, from other teachers, or from your friends, be thankful; but if you do not get it, go on with your work nevertheless. You are a servant, and when you receive your reward that is of grace and not of debt, then you will have the highest commendation that can be passed upon you, the applauses of your Lord, and eternal glory with him whose you are, and whom you desire to serve.

But still while the steward is a servant, he is an *honorable one*. It does not do for the other servants in the house to tell him that he is a servant. He will not endure that. He knows it and feels it; he desires to act and work as such, but at the same time, he is an honored servant. Now, those who serve Christ in the office of teaching are honorable men. I remember hearing a very unsuitable discussion between two persons as to whether the minister was not superior to the Sunday school teacher. It reminded me of that talk of the disciples as to who among them was the greatest. Why, we are all of us "the least," if we feel according to the truth, and though we must each of us exalt our office as God has given it to us, yet I see not anywhere in the Bible anything that should lead me to believe that the office of the preacher is more honorable than that of the teacher.

It seems to me that every Sunday school teacher has a right to put a title before his name as much as I have, or if not, if he carries out his responsibility, then he certainly is a "Right Honorable." He teaches his congregation and preaches to his class. I may preach to more, and he to less, but still he is doing the same work, though in a smaller sphere. I am sure I can sympathize with Mr. Carey, when he said of his son Felix, who left the missionary work to become an ambassador, "Felix has dribbled into an ambassador;" meaning to say, that he was once a great person as a missionary, but that he had afterwards accepted a comparatively insignificant office.

So, I think we may say of the Sunday school teacher, if he gives up his work because he cannot attend to it on account of his enlarged business, he dribbles into a rich merchant. If he forsakes his teaching because he finds there is so much else to do, he dribbles into something less than he was before, with one exception – if he is obliged to give up to attend to his own family, and makes that family his Sunday school class, there is no dribbling there; he stands in the same position as he did before.

I say they who teach, they who seek to pluck souls as brands from the burning, are to be considered as honored persons, second by far to him from whom they received their commission; but still in some sweet sense lifted up to become fellows with him, for he calls them his brethren and his friends. *The servant knoweth not what his lord doeth: but I have called you friends; for all things that I have heard of my Father I have made known unto you* (John 15:15).

Only one more thought here. The steward is also a servant *who has very a great responsibility attached to his position.* A sense of responsibility seems to a right man always a weighty thing. To do a thing where there is no responsibility involved at all is a very slight matter, and therefore we find in ordinary affairs that the labor that involves no trust is but poorly paid. But where there is a large amount of trust placed, the labor is paid in proportion. Now the work of the Sunday school teacher is one of the most responsible in the world. It has sometimes staggered me to think how greatly God trusts you and me.

You remember the story of the Prodigal Son. It finds a counterpart in each of us, who after wandering long in sin have come home to Jesus. I sometimes think that a prudent father, when the prodigal was restored to his house, would receive him to his heart, would press him to his bosom, and give him a share of all his wealth, but would be very slow to trust him in any matter of responsibility. The next market day the old gentlemen would say, "Now John, I love you with all my heart, but you know you ran away once, and spent your living riotously. I must send your elder brother to the market; I cannot trust you with my purse. I love you; I have totally forgiven you, but at the same time I cannot yet rely upon you." Why does God not say so to us?

Instead of that, when he takes poor prodigals to his heart, he trusts us with his most precious jewels – he trusts us with immortal souls. He permits us to be the means of seeking his lost sheep, and then allows us to feed the lambs after they are gathered. He puts the prodigal into the most important station, and has confidence in him. Then my brethren and sisters, seeing he has been gracious enough to place confidence in such unworthy persons, shall we deceive him? Oh no; let us earnestly labor as stewards so that every part of the estate committed to us shall be found in good order when our Master comes, and so that every jot and tittle of our account shall be found correct when he sums it up in the great day of the audit before his throne.

Our office is a very, very solemn one. Some think little of it. Some take it upon themselves very lightly. Giddy youths are enticed into the school and not rendered more sober by their connection with it. Let such depart from us. We want none but those who are sober, none but those who solemnly weigh what they are doing and who enter upon the work as a matter involving life or death; not as a trivial affair that concerns the interests of time, but an awfully solemn thing that even an angel would be incapable of performing unless he had the abundant assistance of God the Holy Spirit. I have thus endeavored very simply to set forth the idea couched in the word *stewardship*. We are servants highly honored, very responsible, and much trusted.

And now, the account – *Give an account of thy stewardship.* Let us briefly think of this giving an account of our stewardship.

Let us first notice that when we shall come to give an account of our stewardship before God, that account must be given *personally* by every one of us. While we are here, we talk in the mass; but when we come before God, we shall have to speak as individuals. You hear persons boasting about "*our* Sunday school." Many persons are wicked enough to call the Sunday school "their school," when they never see it by the year together. They say, "I hope *our* school is flourishing," when they never subscribe a half-penny, when they never give the teachers a word of encouragement, or even a smile, and do not know how many children the school contains. Yet they call it theirs.

Thieves that they are, taking to themselves that which does not belong to them! Well, but we, in our measure, make the same mistake. As a ministry, we often talk of the doings of the "body," and what wonders have been done by the "denomination." Now, let us recollect, when we come before God, there will be no judging us in denominations, no dealing with us in schools and in churches, but the account must be given for each one by himself. So then, you who have the infant class, you will have to give your own account. It was but the other day that you were finding fault with the conduct of the senior class, and you were told then to look at home. Conscience told you so.

But at last, when you shall have to stand before God, you will have no account to give of the senior class, but of that infant class committed to you. And you, my sister, you have been seven or eight years a teacher – you must give an account for yourself, not for that other teacher of another class, of whom you have often boasted, because she has been the means of bringing six or seven children to Christ lately. Remember, her six won't be put with your none at all, in order to make the total at the year's end look respectable; but there will stand your great blank at the end of your labors, and there will remain the dark mark for your negligence, for your unpunctuality, for your carelessness in your class, without the relief of the bright side of the diligent teacher's success.

You must be judged each of you for yourself, not in parties, but one by one. This makes it terrible work for a man to be looked at all alone. I have known people who could not bear to stand up in a pulpit; the very fact of so many eyes looking upon them seemed so horrible. But how will it be when we must stand up and hear our hearts read by the all-searching eye of God, and when the whole of our career in the offices that we now hold will be published before the sun, and that, I repeat it, without the blitz of the success of others, without any addition to our labors derived from the diligence of other teachers?

Come, Mr. Steward, what is your account? Not that one, sir, not that one; *your* account. "Lord, I have brought in the account of the Sunday school books."

"No, not that; the account of *your own* class."

"Well, my Master, I have brought in the account of the class for the last twenty-five years, showing how many were converted."

"No, not that; the account of *your own class while you were its teacher.*"

"Well, I have brought in the account of the class during the time I was a teacher with So-and-so."

"No, not that; the account of the class while you were the teacher of it *alone;* the account of how you taught, what you taught, how you prayed, how earnestly you labored, how diligently you studied, and what you sought to do for Christ." Not the addendums of the other teacher who helped you in another part of the duty, but your own personal account alone must be brought in before God. *Give an account of **thy** stewardship* (emphasis added).

Putting it in this light, what account will some of you give at the last and great day? Just let me stop a minute to charge your memories. What kind of account will it be? I trust a very large number here can humbly in their hearts say, "I have done but little, but I did *that* sincerely and prayerfully; may God accept it through Jesus Christ!" But I fear there are some others, who, if they are true to their consciences, will say, "I have done but little; I did that little carelessly; I did it without prayer; I did it without the help of the Holy Spirit."

Then, my brother and sister, I hope you will add after that, "Oh, my God, forgive me, and help me from this good hour to be diligent in this divine business, fervent in my spirit, serving the Lord." And may God bless you in that prayer! Make no resolve but offer a prayer that is better far; and may you be heard in heaven, the dwelling place of God.

And note again, that while this account must be personal, it must be *exact.* You will not, when you present your account before God, present the gross total, but every separate item. When you give your account of your stewardship, it will be thus. You had so many children. What did you say to this child, and to this, and to this, and to the other? How often did you pray for that child with his bitter temper; for that child with his unbending obstinacy; for that child with his glowingness and his sweet affection; for that child, that sulky one; for that child, the headstrong, vicious one, that had learned all the evils of the street, and seemed to taint others? What did you do for each one of these? How did you labor for the conversion of every one?

And to make the account still more particular, it will run thus – What did you do for each child on each Sabbath? You heard one child utter an ill word; did you scold him? You saw another child oppress a little one; did you deliver the little one out of his hand and rebuke him, and teach both children to love each other? Did you notice the follies of each, and strive to understand the temperament of each, so that you could fit your discourse or your prayer to each? Did you labor in birth for the conversion of each one? Did you agonize in prayer with God, and then did you agonize in exhortation with them, pleading with them to be reconciled to Christ?

I believe the account will be far more minute than this, when God shall come to try our hearts and minds as well as our works and ways. My poor way of putting it does but cloud the truth that I seek to bring forth, but nevertheless so shall it be; a special and exact account shall be given. And then there shall be an account given for every opportunity, not only for every child, but also for every opportunity of doing good to the child. Did you benefit yourself that afternoon, when the child was in a peculiarly solemn state because his little brother lay at home dead? Did you seek to send the arrows home when Providence had made a wound in his little heart because he had lost his dear mother? Did you seek to turn every event that occurred in the school to account, whether it was joyous or the reverse?

God gave you the opportunity, and he will at last ask you what you did with it. We shall many of us make but a sorry account, for we have neglected much that we ought to have done; and the general confession must be ours as teachers: "We have done those things that we ought not to have done, and we have left undone those things that we ought to have done."

And then remember, again, the account will be exact as to everything that we did. We shall not only be examined as to how we addressed the school; we may have had peculiar gifts for that, and we may have done well; but it will also be: "How did you address your own class?" and not that alone, but also "How did you study the lessons?" If you had no time it will not be required of you to do what you could not do; but if you had much leisure, how did you spend it? Was it for your children, for your Master's good, that you might find polished shafts to shoot forth from your bow, that God might bless you by giving you strength to send them home into the heart?

And then, what did you do in your closet? Were you cold and careless there? Were your children forgotten, or did you bring them on your heart, and in your arms, and with tears and cries commend them to Christ? Ah, Sunday school teachers, your closet shall be turned into the open air one day, and the contents of your secret chambers be published before the sun. Oh, you whose cobwebbed closets witness against you; oh, you against whom the beam out of the wall exclaims because your voice has not been heard there, against whom the very floor might bear witness because it has never felt the weight of your knees, how will you stand this searching test? How will you endure this day of burning, when God shall try you for everything you did, and everything you did not do that you ought to have done, in connection with the work of teaching your children? The account must be exact and precise, as well as personal. I shall not stop to enlarge upon that; your own conscience and judgment can enlarge upon it at home.

Now remember, once again, that the account must be *complete.* You will not be allowed to leave out something, and you will not be allowed to add anything. Perhaps some of you would like to begin with tomorrow, or next Sabbath day, and strike out the past. No, Sunday school teacher, when God says, *Give an account of thy stewardship,* you will have to begin with the day when you first were a teacher. Ah, my God, how many there are who profess to preach the Word, who might well beg that you would let many a year of their ministry be buried in forgetfulness!

Ah, might not some of us fall upon our knees and say, "Lord, let me give account of my diligent years, not of my idle years"? But we must begin with our ordination, and we must end with our death; and you must begin with the first hour when you sat down in your class, and you must end when life ends, and not until then. Does not this put a very solemn aspect upon your account, some of you? You are always saying, "I will be better tomorrow." Will that blot out yesterday? "I must be more diligent in the future." Will that redeem the lost opportunities that have departed in the years gone by? No; if you have loitered long, and lingered much, you will find the hardest running of today will not make up for the loitering of yesterday.

There have been some men who, after spending many years in sin, have been doubly diligent for Christ afterwards, but they have always felt that they have only done the day's work in the day, and they mourned over those years that the locusts had eaten, as gone beyond recall. Oh! catch the moments as they fly, Sunday school teachers; use the days as they come. Do not be talking about making up for the badness of the first part of the account by the brilliant character of the conclusion; you cannot do it. You must give an account for each day separately, for each year by itself; and do what you may to retrieve your losses, the losses that still stand upon the book, and the Master will say, at last, "How did these get here?"

And, though they are all covered up in sovereign grace, if you believe in Christ Jesus, still you would not wish to have any the more stains for that. Because Christ has washed you, you do not desire to make yourself filthy; because he has redeemed you, you do not desire to commit sin.

No, live, my brothers and sisters, as Sunday school teachers should live. Live as if your own salvation depended upon the strictness of your fulfilling your duty; and yet remember that your salvation does not depend upon that, but on your personal interest in the everlasting covenant, and in the all-prevailing blood of the Lord Jesus Christ, who is Israel's strength and Redeemer.

And now, though there are many other things I might say, I fear lest I might weary you; therefore, let me notice some occasions when it will be well for you all to give an account of your stewardship, and then notice when you must give an account of it.

You know there is a proverb that "short reckonings make long friends," and a very true proverb it is. A man will always be at friendship with his conscience as long as he makes short reckonings with it. It was a good rule of the old Puritans, that of making honest and full confession of sin every night; not to leave a week's sin to be confessed on Saturday night, or Sabbath morning, but to recall the failures, imperfections, and mistakes of the day, in order that we might learn from one day of failure how to achieve the victory on the next day, and that by washing ourselves daily from our sins, we might preserve the purity and whiteness of our garments.

Brothers and sisters, do the same; make short reckonings. And it will be well for you every Sabbath evening, or at any other time, if so it pleases you, to make a reckoning of what you do on the Sabbath. I do not say this in order that you may be encouraged in any self-righteous congratulation that you have done well, because, if you make your reckoning correct, you will never have much cause to congratulate yourself, but will always have cause to mourn that you did your duty so ill compared with what you ought to have done.

When the Sabbath is over, and you have been twice to the house of God to teach your class, just sit down and try to recollect what were the points in which you failed. Perhaps you exhibited a hasty temper; you spoke to a boy too sharply when he was a little rebellious. Perhaps you were too complacent; you saw sin committed, and ought to have rebuked it, and you did not do so. If you find out your own failing, that is half the way to a cure. Next Sabbath you can try and set it right.

Then, there are times that Providence puts in your way that will be excellent seasons for reckoning. For instance, every time a boy or girl leaves the school, there is an opportunity afforded you of thinking to yourselves, "Well, how did I deal with Betsy? How did I treat John? Did I give William such teaching as will help him in his future life, to maintain integrity in the midst of temptation, and preserve righteousness when he shall be subjected to imminent perils? How did I teach the girl? Did I so teach her that she will know her duty when she goes into the world? Did I strive with all my might to lead her to the foot of the cross?"

There are many solemn questions that you may put concerning the child. And when you meet with any of them grown up in later years, you will find that to be a very proper season for giving an account of your stewardship to your conscience, by seeing whether you really did with that person, when a child, as you could have desired.

Then, there is a peculiar time for casting up accounts when a child dies. Ah! what a host of thoughts cluster around the deathbed of a child whom we have taught. Next to the father and the mother, I would think the Sunday school teacher will take the most interest in the dying one. You will recollect, "There lies withering the flower that my hand has watered; there is an immortal soul about to pass the gates of eternity, whom I have taught.

"O God, have I taught this dying child the truth, or have I deceived him? Have I dealt faithfully with him? Have I told him of his ruin? Have I set before him how he was fallen in Adam and depraved in himself? Have I told him about the great redemption of Christ? Have I shown him the necessity of regeneration and the work of the Holy Spirit? or have I amused him with tales about the historical parts of the Bible, and pieces of morality, and kept back the weightier matters of the law? Can I put my hand into his dying hand, and silently lifting my heart to heaven, can I say, "O God, you know I am clear of his blood"?

Ah! that is a thing that stings the minister often – when he recollects that any of his congregation are dying. When I stand sometimes by the deathbed of any of the ungodly in my congregation, it brings many a fearful thought to me. Have I been as earnest as I ought to have been? Did I cry to this man, *Escape for thy life; look not behind thee, neither stay thou in all the plain; escape to the mountain* (Genesis 19:17)? Did I pray for him, weep over him, tell him of his sin, preach Christ simply, plainly, and boldly to him? Was there not an occasion when I used lightness when I ought to have been solemn? Might there not have been a season when I uttered something by mistake, which may have been a pillow for the armhole of his conscience on which he might rest? Have I not helped to smooth his path to hell, instead of putting blocks in his way, and chains across his path, that he might be turned out of it and led to seek the Savior?

Ah! while we know that salvation is all of grace, let none of us imagine we are free from the blood of souls, unless we warn them with diligence, unless we preach with faithfulness; for this same Bible which tells me that Christ shall see the labor of his soul and be satisfied, also tells me that if I warn them not, their blood, if they perish, shall be required at my hand.

But now, teacher, let me tell you an occasion when you *must* give your account. You may put off all these seasons if you like; you may live as carelessly as you please, but if you have a particle of heart in you, you will have to give an account when you are sick and cannot go to your class. If your conscience is worth having – which some people's consciences are not, for they are dead and seared – if your conscience is an awakened one, when you are put out of your work, you will begin to think about how you did it.

You should read the letters of that holy man Rutherford. If ever there was a man who preached the gospel sweetly and with divine unction, I should think it must have been him; and yet when he was shut up in Aberdeen, and could not get out to his much-loved flock, he began to say, "Ah, if the Lord will let me go out to preach again, I will never be such a dull drone as I was accustomed to being. I will preach with tears in my eyes, so that the people may be comforted, and the sinners converted."

Perhaps when you are lying ill in your bedroom, little Jane comes to see you, and says, "I hope you will soon get well, teacher"; or William or Thomas calls and inquires about you every Sunday afternoon, and asks the servant to give his love to you, and hopes that the teacher will soon come back again. Then is the time when I know you will be sure to cast up your account. You will say, "Ah, when I get back to my class, I won't teach them as I used to do; I will study my lesson more, I will pray more. I won't be so hot or so fast with them as I was accustomed to being. I will bear with their ill manners. Ah, if my Master will give me, like Hezekiah, another fifteen years of labor, and will give me more grace, I will strive to be better." You will be sure to cast up your accounts when you get sick.

But if you do not do it then, I will tell you when you must; that is when you come *to die*. What a dreadful thing it must be, to be an unfaithful preacher on a deathbed. (Oh, that I may be saved from that!) To be upon one's bed when life is over; to have had great opportunities, mighty congregations, and to have been so diligent about something else as to have neglected to preach the full and free gospel of our Lord Jesus Christ! It seems to me, as I lie in my bed dying, that I should see apparitions and grim things in the room. One would come and stare upon me and say, "Ah! you are dying. Remember how many times I sat in the front of the gallery, and listened to you, but you never once told me to escape from the wrath to come; you were talking to me about something I did not understand; but the simple matter of the gospel you never preached to me, and I died in doubt and trembling. And now you are coming to me to the hell which I have inherited because you were unfaithful." And when in our gray and dying age we see the generations that have grown up around our pulpits, we shall think of them all. We shall think of the time when as youths we first began to preach; we shall recollect the youths that then crowded in, then the men, and then the gray heads that passed away. And it seems to me that as they come on in grim procession, they will every one of them leave a fresh curse upon our conscience because we were unfaithful. The deathbed of a man who has murdered his fellows, of some grim tyrant who has let the bloodhounds of war loose upon mankind, must be an awful thing.

When the soldier, and the soldier's widow, and the murdered man of peace rise up before him; when the smoke of devastated countries seems to blow into his eyes and make them sore and red; when the blood of men hangs on his conscience like a great red sense of gloom; when bloody murder, the grim chief officer, draws red curtains around his bed, and when he begins to approach the last end where the murderer must inherit his dreary doom, it must be a fearful time indeed.

But it seems to me that to have murdered souls must be more awful still – to have distributed poison to children instead of bread, to have given them stones when they asked us for good food, to have taught them error when we ought to have taught them the truth as it is in Jesus, or to have spoken to them with cold listlessness when earnestness was needed. Oh, how your children seem to curse you when you lie there and have been unfaithful to your charge.

Yes, you will have to cast up your account then; and let me tell you, though your hope must all be fixed on Jesus, and that must be the consolation of your life and death, yet it will be very sweet to remember when you come to die that you have been successful in winning souls to Christ.

Ah! that will bring a little life into the cheek of the teacher who has tuberculosis, who was sickened young, when you remind her that there was a little girl who, a year before she was taken ill, kissed her hand and said, "Good-bye, teacher; we shall meet in heaven. Do you not recollect, teacher, telling me the story of Jesus on the cross, and taking me home one Sunday afternoon, and putting your arms around my neck, and kneeling down and praying that God would bless me? Oh, my teacher, that brought me to Jesus."

Yes, teacher, when you are lying on your bed, pale with tuberculosis, you will recollect that there is one up there beside your Savior who will receive you into eternal habitations – that young spirit who has gone before you, who by your means was emancipated from the wickedness and bondage of a sinful world.

Happy is the teacher who has the hope of meeting a whole band of such in heaven. Such a thought often cheers me. Let the world say what it will; I know when I die there is many a spirit that will think of me in after years as the man who preached the gospel to him; many a drunkard brought to Jesus, and many a harlot reclaimed. And to the teacher it must be the same to think that when he claps his wings and mounts from this lower valley of earth to heaven, he will see a bright spirit coming down to meet him, and he will hear the spirit saying, "Sister spirit, come away."

And when he opens his eyes, he will see that the song came from the lips of one to whom he had been blessed as the means of conversion. Happy are you who shall be welcomed at the gates of paradise by your spiritual sons and daughters, and who shall have beside your Master's welcome, the welcome of those whom he has given you to be jewels in your crown of glory forever and ever.

Now to conclude. We must all give an account to God in the day of judgment. That is the thing that makes death so terrible. Oh Death, if you were all, what are you but a pinch, and all is over! But after Death the judgment. This is the sting of the dragon to the ungodly. The last great day has come. The books are opened – men, women, and children are assembled. Many have come, and some on the right, and some on the left have already heard the sentence. It is now your turn. Teacher! What account will you render? In the first place, are you in Christ yourself? Or have you taught to others what you did not know yourself? Have I any such here? Doubtless, I have; for alas! there are many such in our schools.

Oh, my friend, what will you say when the Master, opening the book, shall ask you, "What did you do to declare my statutes?" Will you look at him and say, "Lord, I taught in your schools, and you have eaten and drunk in our streets." If you should say so, he will say, *I never knew you: depart from me, ye that work iniquity* (Matthew 7:23). Then, what have you to say with regard to your schools? For although our state at last will really be settled according to our interest in Christ, you will be judged by your works, as evidences.

The Scripture always says that we are to be judged according to our works. Well then, the book is opened. You hear your own name read, and you hear that one brief sentence – "Inasmuch as *thou hast been faithful over a few things, I will make thee ruler over many things: enter thou into the joy of thy lord*" (Matthew 25:21).

Oh, heaven of heavens! and is this the reward of the little trouble of teaching a few children? Oh Master, you give ingots of gold for our grains of dust; our fragments of service you reward with crowns and kingdoms! But he turns to others, and to you he says, "*Inasmuch as ye did it not to one of the least of these, ye did it not to me. Depart from me, ye cursed, into everlasting fire, prepared for the devil and his angels*" (Matthew 25:45, 41). Which of these two shall be said to *me*? Which of these two shall be said to *you*?

Oh! as in God's sight I charge you by him who is the judge of the quick and the dead, by the swiftness of his chariot-wheels that now are bringing him here, by the solemnity of his awful tribunal, by that sentence that shall never be reversed, judge yourselves, for then you shall not be judged. Give an account of your stewardship to your conscience and to your God. Confess your sins, seek his help, and begin from this hour, by his Holy Spirit, to undertake his work afresh; so shall you stand before his face, clothed in the righteousness of your Redeemer and washed in his blood. Though not boasting in your works, you shall be able to stand accepted in him, and your works shall follow when you rise from your labors, and you shall be among the blessed that die in the Lord.

Chapter 6

The Bridgeless Gulf

Beside all this, between us and you there is a great gulf fixed: so that they which would pass from hence to you cannot; neither can they pass to us, that would come from thence. (Luke 16:26)

For the last few months, I have been led to blow the silver trumpet, sounding forth the love and mercy of our God in Christ. Many times in your hearing I have preached a full Christ for empty sinners and have set forth the freeness and graciousness of the divine proclamation that in the gospel is made to the chief of sinners. I have not, concerning that point, shunned to declare unto you the whole counsel of God. But I feel that I must now blow a blast upon the rough ram's horn, for sometimes our congregations need to be reminded of the law and terrors of God and of the judgment to come. Our experience is, that the preaching of judgment is greatly blessed of God; we have remarked that a very large number of conversions have occurred under those sermons in which the declaration of God's wrath against all iniquity has been the most plain and solemn.

A thunderstorm clears the air; there are pestilences that would gather beneath the wings of calm that can only be purged away by the lightning flash. When God sends his servant with heavy tidings, his message of alarm cleanses the spiritual atmosphere, and kills the sloth, pride, indifference, and lethargy that otherwise might fall upon the people.

As the sharp needle prepares the way for the thread, so the piercing law makes a way for the bright silver thread of divine grace. The lancet is quite as needful as the healing balm. The law is our teacher to bring us to Christ; like the old Greek teacher who led the boy to school, so the law leads us to Christ, who teaches and instructs us, and makes us wise unto salvation.

Those who preached the law, as well as the gospel, in the puritanical times, were the most fruitful soul winners. We find our blessed Lord and Master, whose heart was overflowing with compassion, and whose very nature was love, often dwelling upon the wrath to come; and indeed his utterances are more forceful and terrible than the most burning threatening from the lips of thundering prophets of old.

God grant that this morning, the effect that so anxiously I desire may follow from that burden of the Lord that now weighs so heavily upon me. May the Master gather out this day a seed unto himself, who shall be saved from the wrath to come, and be to all eternity the reward of the Redeemer's labors. Lift up your hearts to God, you who know him and have power with him, and ask that now the divine Spirit may work mightily, that hearts may be broken and sinners led to Jesus.

Beside all this, between us and you there is a great gulf fixed. Human ingenuity has done very much to bridge great gulfs. Scarcely has the world afforded a river so wide that its floods could not be overleaped; or a torrent so furious that it could not be made to pass under the yoke. High above the foam of Columbia's glorious waterfall, man has hung aloft his slender but substantial road of iron, and the shriek of the locomotive is heard above the roar of Niagara. This very week I saw the first chains that span the deep rift through which the Bristol Avon River finds its way at Clifton; man has thrown his suspension bridge across the chasm, and men will soon travel where only that which has wings could a little while ago have found a way.

There is, however, one gulf that no human skill or engineering ever shall be able to bridge; there is one chasm that no wing shall ever be able to cross; it is the gulf that divides the world of joy in which the righteous triumph, from that land of sorrow in which the wicked feel the hurt of the Lord's sword. Whatever other arguments there may be as to why the righteous should have no communion with the wicked in a future state, beside all these other things, any one of which is enough and sufficient of itself, there is a great gulf fixed, so that there can be no passage from the one world to the other.

In trying solemnly to speak upon this matter, I shall commence with this – there is no passage from heaven to hell; *they which would pass from hence to you, cannot.* Glorified saints cannot visit the prison house of lost sinners. Long enough were the righteous mingled with the wicked; sufficient was the evil time in which the wheat was choked with the tares; quite long enough was the period in which the chaff lay upon the same floor, side by side with the wheat. Patience had its perfect work. They did both grow together until the time of the harvest; it is not necessary, now that the harvest has come, that they should lie together any longer.

It would be inconsistent with the perfect joy and the state of blissful appearance of the righteous, with its perfect calm and purity, that sin should be admitted into their midst, or that they should be permitted to find companionships in the abodes of evil. It would not be glorious to the Lord Jesus Christ that they should cease from beholding his beauties and adoring his person, in order to aid his enemies and comfort his desperate foes.

Shall the courtiers of heaven become traitors to their King, that they may relieve his unyielding adversaries? Shall the princes of the blood imperial, who wear eternal coronets, lay aside their robes of honor to become menial servants to the damned in hell who would not, when Christ was preached to them, bow the knee and kiss the Son? This must not and cannot be. Besides, the decree of God, like a great mountain of brass, has forever shut the righteous in with holiness, with happiness, and with God, and they cannot, if they would, must not cross the great gulf that divides them from the world of the wicked.

It follows that *the most earnest and diligent preacher* must then renounce all hope of converting sinners. God has raised up some apostolic spirits whose presence in a nation is like the rising of the sun; darkness flies before them, and the light of salvation streams from them to tens of thousands. When they lift up their hands to preach, God gives them power to shake the gates of hell; and when they bend the knee to pray, they unlock the gates of heaven.

Men like Baxter with bursting hearts of love, or Joseph Alleine with glowing tongue, or Whitfield with seraph's fire, or Wesley with cherub's zeal – these are the men who bless their age and are most truly great. These men can go to the borders of the earth if they will; their commission is co-extensive with the human race – *Go ye into all the world, and preach the gospel to every creature* (Mark 16:15); *Lo, I am with you always, even unto the end of the world* (Matthew 28:20).

These men are never so happy as when they are preaching. Woe is unto them if they preach not the gospel, and when they preach it and God helps them, they are like Elihu, refreshed by the effort. They were born to preach the gospel and to win sinners to Christ, and they are never content unless they are fulfilling their high commission. But they must cease from their labors soon, for in heaven they are not needed, and from hell they are excluded.

O sinner, even our voice, feeble though it be, may win you to Jesus now; but if you die unrepentant, it can never woo you again to a Savior. *Now* is my time to preach to you, and set open mercy's door before you, but *then* I can never warn you, nor invite you; never again I can depict the agonies of my Lord and Master and endeavor to attract you by the story of his love, his dying and bleeding love. No, it will be all over then. *They may rest from their labours; and their works do follow them* (Revelation 14:13). They must bring their sheaves with them, for they cannot return to another field to sow, nor journey to other broad acres to reap. Burning as their hearts will still be with divine love, they will have to exercise it in another way.

Their passionate longings for God's glory will find other channels in which to flow. They will bow their heads and adore him day and night, but they can no longer serve him in gospel ministry. The ambassador who rolls up his commission for God has run up the black flag of damnation and hangs out no more signals of peace. Poor sinner, rather would I win you now, for it is now or never with you and me.

The efforts of the most urgent visitor, the most earnest friend, must cease with death. Some of you have friends who can get nearer to your heart than I can. You can afford sometimes to forget my poor words and go your way to sin again; but you have a sister, and when she pleads with you, you do feel it; you have one loving friend, and when he speaks to you, you cannot be deaf; your conscience has often been impressed by him, and sometimes through him the strivings of the Spirit have been very mighty with your soul.

I love, my brethren and sisters, to see you earnest for the souls of others. God may give *you* some souls whom he will never give to me, and so long as they be but saved, though I have a holy covetousness and earnestly desire to bring many to Christ, yet I will as genuinely rejoice in their salvation by your instrumentality as if it had been accomplished by my own. Go and labor with all your might. Tell what Christ has done for you. With pleading, loving utterances, beg them to be reconciled to God.

But oh! remember you can only do that in *this* life, for when the gates are shut, you are shut in for your reward, and all the world is shut out from your efforts. O my friend, do you hear this? Not only will there be no public congregations, no Sabbaths, and no houses of prayer, but there shall also be no private messengers, and no earnest Christians who shall privately seek your soul's good. What do you say to this? Does not this give an awful value to those tender words of compelling love? Turn you at the gentle rebuke, for otherwise you shall be suddenly destroyed, and that without remedy.

Those who are nearest and dearest must be divided from you, if you perish in your sins. A mother can put her arms around her child's neck and pray for him here; she may affectionately exhort her son to seek peace with God now; she may earnestly and incessantly follow him with her holy pleadings, but she can never come to him from the realms of glory if once he is lost. *They which would pass from [us] to you cannot.* Do you hear it, young man? Those glistening eyes of a mother's love shall never weep again for you. That touching voice that sometimes awoke the echoes of your heart shall never plead again. O ungodly woman, you shall never see your godly child.

Father, is it that daughter you are thinking of who loved and feared God in childhood and was taken from you? Did she say to you when she was dying, "Follow me to heaven, my father"? You have heard her voice for the last time; that child will never see her father again unless he turns from his evil ways. It seems to me that if she could be in heaven what she was on earth, she would fling her arms around your neck and seek to draw you to the glorious throne of the Most High; but oh! it cannot be.

A just God condemns the unrepentant sinner, and just men acquiesce to the divine sentence. See then, O you ungodly ones who are present today, you often think our company a great nuisance, and perhaps while I am preaching, my alarming words annoy you. Ah, we shall not annoy you long. Does your mother tease you when she bids you to seek the Lord? She will not tease you long.

When I bring home the judgment to come, is the subject obnoxious to you? I shall not ask your patience for long. We shall be separated; if you go your way and follow after sin and wrath, there will come a dividing time, and O let me say to you, you would give worlds if you had them; you would give them if they were solid diamonds, to hear again the voice that now fatigues you, and to listen once more to those plaintive invitations that vex you and spoil your cheeriness. Ah, how you would bless God if he would let you come back again and have once more those Sabbaths that were so dull and dreary, and permit you to go up once more to the house of God that now perhaps is like a prison house to your vain and frivolous spirits.

O sirs, I say you may well have patience with us for a little time and bear with our compulsions, for we shall not plague you much longer. We implore you to come to Jesus; we would pluck you by your garments and beg you to flee from the wrath to come; forgive us for being thus in earnest, for even if we should fail with you, you will soon escape the compulsions of our love. A few short months of mortal life, and then you will be far away from all religious discourses and all spiritual talk of things to come; you will be in your own company, but I warn you, this will yield you little enough content.

Dear friends, how earnest this ought to make the people of God to work while it is called today. If this is our only time for doing good, let us do good while we can. I hear people sometimes say, "Mr. So-and-so does too much; he works too hard." Oh! none of us do half enough. Do not talk about working too hard for Jesus Christ; the thing is impossible. Are souls perishing, and shall I sleep? My idle, lazy flesh, shall you keep me still while men are dying and hell is filling? Brethren and sisters, let us be lukewarm no longer.

If God makes us lights in the world, let us spend ourselves as a candle does, which consumes itself by shining. As the poor workgirl, who has but one light, works with desperate pace because that will soon be burned out, so let us be urgent in season and out of season, watching, praying, and laboring for the souls of men. We are not earnest enough about immortal souls. If we had but a view of the shortness of life, the fleeting character of time, and the terrors of eternal wrath; if we could but see lost souls, and understand their unutterable woe, we would shake ourselves from the dust, and go forth to work while it is called today.

As we cannot go from heaven to hell, so the text assures us, *neither can they pass to us, that would come from thence.* The lost spirits in hell are shut in forever. I see the angel standing at that iron door; I hear the awful key as it grates among the tremendous cells, and when that gate is closed, he hurls the key into the abyss of oblivion, and the captives are firmly imprisoned, bound in fetters that will never break, in chains that never rust. The sinner cannot come to heaven for a multitude of reasons, and among them is this: *His own character* forbids it. As a man lives and dies, so will he be throughout eternity. The drunkard here will have all a drunkard's thirst there without the means of gratifying it. The swearer here will become a yet more ripe and proficient blasphemer.

Death does not change, but fixes character; it petrifies it. *He which is filthy, let him be filthy still: . . . and he that is holy, let him be holy still* (Revelation 22:11). The lost man remains a sinner and a growing sinner and continues to rebel against God. Would you have such a man in heaven? Shall the thief prowl through the streets of the New Jerusalem? Shall the atmosphere of paradise be polluted by an oath? Shall the songs of angels be disturbed by the foulness of lewd conversation? It cannot be.

Heaven would be no heaven if the sinner could be permitted to enter it. *Except a man be born again, he cannot see the kingdom of God* (John 3:3), and as there is no hope of the finally lost ever being born again, that kingdom of God they cannot see. Sinner, if you are not fit for heaven now, have you any right to hope you ever will be? If you die without God and without hope, where must your destiny be? Without a God, can you dwell in heaven – God's own dominions? Without hope, can you enter where hope is consummated in full fruition? Never. The enemies of God shall never be permitted to defy him to his face and vent their blasphemies in his own palace; they must be driven from his presence, and driven from that presence forever.

Moreover, not only does the man's character shut him out, but also *the sinner's doom*. What was it? *These shall go away into **everlasting** punishment* (emphasis added). If it is everlasting, how can they enter heaven? What does the Savior say? *Where their worm dieth not, and the fire is not quenched* (Mark 9:48). If there be any truth in that metaphor, then the lost are lost forever; the worm would die if they entered heaven; and the fire would be quenched if they obtained celestial seats.

How does the Holy Spirit put it? Does he not describe the wrath to come as a bottomless pit? It would not be such if they could get a handhold, and afterwards climb upward to the starry thrones of angels. Brethren, he that dooms men, he that has put it in the strong expression, *He that believeth not shall be damned,* will certainly and literally carry out his own words; and if it be so, it shall never be possible for them to break their prison of fire, and enter the land of joy and peace.

Moreover, sinner, you cannot go out of the prison house because *God's character* and God's Word are against you. Shall God ever cease to be just? But if he is just, he must never cease from punishing you when you are finally condemned. *Holy, holy, holy, Lord God Almighty* (Revelation 4:8) is the never-ceasing cry of cherubim, but as long as he is *holy, holy, holy,* you can never be acceptable to him. Shall God ever cease to be true? But remember, as long as he is true to his own threatenings, he must and will send his arrows through you, and make his fierce wrath consume you.

Then there stands his decree: *He that believeth not shall be damned;* this is the great gulf, that fixed chasm by which the unrepentant sinner is as firmly as firmest destiny bound like Prometheus to the rock forever, never to be loosed in time or in eternity. It must not be – it shall not be – if God be God, and if his decree be not a falsehood and a vanity, you must not come out of the place of your torment.

No, yet more; for remember, sinner, there never was but one bridge between fallen man and a holy God. That bridge you reject. The person of the Mediator, his substitution, his righteousness, his painful death – these make the only road from sin to righteousness, from wrath to acceptance. But these you reject. If you should ever be lost, you will have finally rejected Christ, and to the extent that you are not this morning saved.

O my poor fellow creature, you are now rejecting Christ; you are as good as saying, "Christ died, but not for me; Christ shed his blood to save men, but I will not be saved in his way. Let him die. I count his death a trifle, and his blood a vanity; I would sooner perish than be saved by him."

This is what you in effect are saying. I know the words make you shudder; you would not venture to utter them, but that is your feeling. You will not have this man to reign over you; you will not bow the knee and kiss the Son; you will still be an adversary to God, and would sooner be destroyed than be saved through the atonement of Christ. Well now, if you reject the only way, what wonder, if having rejected that, there remains no hope? Besides, remember there is no other sacrifice for sin. Scripture expressly tells us that *there remaineth no more sacrifice for sins* (Hebrews 10:26).

Do you think that Jesus will come a second time to die? Shall those divine hands be stretched again to the wood? You reject him now. If he died again you would reject him. Shall the head again be pierced with thorns? Shall the side again be torn with the spear? Why sinner, if you refuse to have him now, you would refuse him if he could die a second time. But that cannot be. He has offered an atonement once and for all, and now forever he sits down at the right hand of the majesty on high. No second atonement, no second redemption shall ever be offered for the sin of men.

Besides, remember there is no Holy Spirit in the pit. The blessed Spirit is here today, and often has he contended with some of you. Do you remember when you trembled like Felix? Do you not remember the time when, like Agrippa, you were almost persuaded? But still all this was put away; conscience was hushed; the Spirit of God was quenched. Well, that Spirit can contend with you again, and if he comes forth in his irresistible strength, if your heart be like a flint, he can break it; and if like iron, he can melt it. But once in the pit, the Holy Spirit never comes there. That blessed dove shuns the place of wrath, and over souls given up to destruction, never will his life-giving wings be known to brood. If so, then you cannot be born again, and cannot enter heaven; you cannot be sanctified, and unsanctified spirits cannot have a share in the skies.

So then, it is clear enough that you cannot possibly pass from hell to heaven. Ah, this will be a judgment upon you, a solemn judgment upon you for many things. You do not like the house of God; you shall be shut out of it. You do not love the Sabbath; you are shut out from the eternal Sabbath. The voice of sacred song had no charm in it for you; you shall not join it. The face of God you never loved; you shall never see it. The name of Jesus Christ was never melodious in your ears; you shall never hear it. Jesus Christ was preached to you, but you rejected him; his blood you trod beneath your feet. The way to heaven was freely set open before you, but you would not come unto him so that you might have life. There is a road from earth to heaven. Sinner, though you have gone into the depths of sin, if you have been the most infamous and most outrageous of offenders, there is a road for you to heaven yet. The harlot, the thief, the profane, and the drunkard may yet find mercy through the grace of Jesus, but

> There are no acts of pardon passed
>   In that cold grave to which we haste;
> But darkness, death, and long despair
>   Reign in eternal silence there.

God bless the solemn remarks we make, and he shall have the glory.

But now, once again to change the subject for a few minutes, I have to notice in the third place, that while no persons can pass that bridge-less chasm, so no things can either. Nothing can come from hell to heaven. Rejoice you saints in light, triumph in your God for this – no temptation of Satan can ever vex you when once you are landed on the golden shore; you are beyond bowshot of the archenemy; he may howl and bite his iron hands, but his howlings cannot terrify and his bitings cannot disturb. No longer shall you be vexed with the filthy conversation of the ungodly. Lot shall never hear another foul word. You shall not have to say, *Woe is me, that I sojourn in Mesech, that I dwell in the tents of Kedar!* (Psalm 120:5).

> No light discourse shall reach your heart,
> Nor trifles vex your ear.

You shall be shut out from everything that belongs to hell. And remember, you shall be in heaven, so secure that the wrath of God that makes hell shall never light on you. Your Savior carried it, and not a drop of it shall fall upon your persons. No present pains shall be in heaven, they are for the lost; no pains of body, no distractions of mind. You shall have no sin; sin cannot pass from them to you; you shall be perfect like your Lord, without spot or wrinkle, or any such thing.

> Your inward foes shall all be slain,
> Nor Satan vex your peace again.

You shall have no fears for the future. You shall know that your bliss is eternal. This shall always be the honey of your honeycomb – that it lasts forever. Millions of years you shall gaze into the face of your beloved; throughout endless ages you shall bask in the sunlight of his smile. This is joy, I say, to the Christian; if he will but think it over, it will reconcile him to the hardest strokes of temporary tribulation, and make him rejoice in the hardest toil of this mortal struggle. Courage, man; it is but a day or two of wrestling, and then the immortal crown; an hour or two of fighting, and then the everlasting rest. It seems to me that I see today the angels leaning from the battlements of the celestial palace, and as they observe you, like armed men cutting your way to the gates thereof, they cry to you,

> Come in, come in,
> Eternal glory you shall win.

Will you sheathe your swords? Will you stop the conflict? No; press on and let your true Jerusalem blades cut through soul and spirit, and divide joint and marrow, until you reach the summit, and the eternal glory shall be yours.

Again, we change the strain for a fourth point, and this a terrible one. Since nothing can come from hell to heaven, so nothing heavenly can ever come to hell. There are rivers of life at God's right hand – those streams can never leap in blessed waterfalls to the lost. No, Lazarus is not permitted to dip the tip of his finger in water to administer the cooling drop to the fire-tormented tongue. Not a drop of heavenly water can ever cross that chasm.

See then, sinner, that heaven is *rest*, perfect rest – but there is no rest in hell. It is labor in the fire, but no ease, no peace, no sleep, no calm, no quiet. It is everlasting storm; eternal hurricane; unceasing tempest. In the worst disease, there are some respites: spasms of agony, but then pauses of rest. There is no pause in hell's torments. The dreadful music of the eternal moan has not so much as a single stop in it. It is on, on, on, with crash of battle, and dust and blood, and fire and vapor of smoke.

Heaven, too, is a place of *joy*; there happy fingers sweep celestial chords; there joyous spirits sing hosannas day without night. But there is no joy in hell; for music there is the groan; for joy there is the pang; for sweet fellowship there is the binding-up in bundles; for everything that is blissful there is everything that is sorrowful. No, I could not exaggerate, that would be impossible; I cannot come up to the sad facts; therefore, there I leave them. Nothing of the joy of heaven can ever come to hell.

Heaven is the place of *sweet communion* with God –

> There they behold his face,
>   And never, never sin;
> There from the rivers of his grace,
>   Drink endless pleasures in.

There is no communion with God in hell. There are prayers, but they are unheard; there are tears, but they are unaccepted; there are cries for pity, but they are all an abomination unto the Lord. God desires not the death of any; he would rather that he should turn unto him and live, but if that grace be refused,

> The Lord, in vengeance dressed,
> Shall lift his hand and swear,
> You that despised my promised rest
> Shall have no portion there.

Tell me what heaven is, if you will, and I must say of any description that you give of its joys, that there is none of them in Tophet, for heaven's blessings cannot cross from the celestial regions to the infernal prison house. No, it is sorrow without relief, misery without hope, and here is the pang of it – it is death without end. There is only one thing that I know of in which heaven is like hell – it is eternal. "The wrath *to come,* the wrath *to come,* the wrath *to come,*" forever and forever spending itself, and yet never being spent.

And now, would to God I could speak with you as my heart desires; for this is my only opportunity, since, as I have already said, I can do this no more if I be saved and if you be lost. Spare me, then, two or three minutes while I close this poor discourse of mine, by trying to reason with those of you who are unconverted. I have had little to say to God's people this morning. I may comfort them in the evening, but this morning I have to deal with you who fear not God.

Many of you now present are unconverted. I will never flatter you by preaching to you as though you were all Christians. The Lord my God knows there is many a heart here that never was broken; there is many a spirit here that never trembled before the majesty of infinite justice, and never kissed the outstretched scepter of a crucified Redeemer. You know this, some of you; you know you are *in the gall of bitterness, and in the bond of iniquity* (Acts 8:23). I do not mean you alone who live in open sin; but I mean you who are amiable, excellent, and admirable in your posture and conduct, but yet the love of God is not in you.

There is no fault to be found with your outward character, maybe, but you have not been born again; you have never passed from death unto life. And remember, sirs, there is the same hell for the most excellent as for the most abominable, unless you fly to Christ – *For other foundation can no man lay than that is laid, which is Jesus Christ;* and if you believe not in him, then you shall die in your sins, *for there is none other name under heaven given among men, whereby we must be saved.* Come, then, let me plead with you, and I will ask you a question – Do you believe all this? Do you believe that there is a hell? Do you believe that there is a heaven to be lost? If you profess that you do not so believe, I will be done with you. God bring you to a better mind.

But what did you come here for? Why do you profess to be a Christian if you reject the Christian's inspired Book? Become an infidel and be honest. For my part, modern infidelity never gives me any alarm; I would rather as soon see you outwardly infidels, as to hear you pretend to be Christians, and yet disbelieve what that Book teaches. I like honesty, and it seems to me that when a man honestly says, "I shall not make a profession of believing what I do not believe," that there is at least one virtue in him, and we may hope that others may find soil to grow in. But you who profess to be religious, and attend your church or your chapel, and yet do not believe the revelation of God, what can I say to you, but that your damnation will be most just?

I think I hear many of you say, "Believe it, sir, oh! we never doubted it; we learned it in our earliest childhood, we have heard it always, and we never ventured to doubt it." Ah! well then, I ask you, Are you in your sober senses to believe that there is a hell, and not seek to escape from it? Do you believe there is a wrath to come, and that it may fall upon you in the next minute, for you may be dead and never leave this house of prayer, and yet do you sit easy in your pews, or are you mad? Has sin so impaired you with its foul intoxication that you cannot think? For if you can think, and there be an angry God who will punish with the awful force of his omnipotence, how is it that you can be at ease in Zion?

Let me ask you another question. If these things be so, have you used your senses in giving a preference to the pleasures of this life beyond the joys of heaven; in following the pleasures of today, when you know they will be followed with the miseries of eternity? Do not mistake. I do not mean to say that a Christian is without pleasures. We have the highest and purest pleasures that mortal or immortal can know; we have not the pleasures of sin, but we have higher, more delightful, and deeper pleasures. But this is what I mean: Will you spend yourselves in sinful pleasure? Will you occupy your time with lust, or drunkenness, or with the frivolities of fashionable life, and do you think that these are worth the expense that they will cause?

"Oh," said one to me, who holds a high position in society, as I talked with him long; after having preached earnestly the gospel, he took me by the button, and he said, "it does seem to me to be an awful thing, that I, knowing as I do what will be my lot if I live and die as I am, should still act as I do. When you are with me," said he, "and I listen to a solemn address, I think there shall come a change over me; I will serve God. But O sir, you do not know the temptations of my life; you do not know how it is when I get into the midst of splendors and vanities, and perhaps mingle with men who ridicule all thoughts of religion. It all goes, and I am such a fool that I sell my soul – sell my soul for it."

Oh! there are such fools here today, who sell their souls for a little sin – one or two whirls in the world's mad dance, and then the devil is your partner, and your merriment is over. I ask you to use your reason, and judge whether it be worth your while to gain the whole world and lose your own soul.

I shall put it to you in another way. How is it that you do not lay hold of Christ, since this is the only time when there is a probability that Christ can be laid hold of? I will tell you why it is. You do not love Christ, you love sin. Or else you are too proud to come to Christ; you think yourselves good enough, and you think that Christ is not for such as you are, but only for great sinners and the lowest of the low. O sirs, is your pride such a fine thing, that you will be damned in order to maintain its dignity? Throw your pride down, come as a sinner must come, and lay hold of Jesus Christ. Or if it be your sin that hinders, may God the Holy Spirit help you to pluck out the right eye and cast off a right arm sooner than having two eyes and two arms to be cast into hellfire.

"But," says one, "how may I lay hold on Christ?" May the blessed Spirit enable you to do it. Here it is: Trust Jesus Christ and you shall be saved. Conscious that you deserve his wrath, trembling because of his terrible law, look to Jesus. There hangs a bleeding Savior. It seems to me that these eyes can see him bleeding there. God eternal, he by whom the heaven of heavens were made, and the earth and the fullness thereof, takes upon himself the form of man and hangs upon the tree of the curse.

> See from his head, his hands, his feet,
>   Sorrow and love flow mingled down!
> Did e'er such love and sorrow meet,
>   Or thorns compose so rich a crown!

There is life in a look at that Crucified One; there is life at this moment for you. Will you glance at him with a tearful eye and say, "Jesus, slaughtered, martyred, murdered for my sake, I do believe in you. Here at your feet I throw myself, all guilty, polluted, foul; let your blood drop on me; turn your eye upon me; say to me, *I have loved thee with an everlasting love: therefore with lovingkindness have I drawn thee*" (Jeremiah 31:3). Come, and welcome, sinner – come. I have but preached the law to you out of love. God knows how these hard things, as I speak them, make my heart bleed blood. O that you would believe in Jesus; he is freely preached to you – accept him.

May the Spirit of God lead you now to accept him. These are no hard terms, no stern conditions of a bloodthirsty tyrant; he does but say, "*Bow the knee* and *kiss the Son* (Genesis 41:43; Psalm 2:12). Come, and welcome, sinner – come." Young man, will you be saved or not? You sinner, yonder, with your gray head, signifying the approach of death, will you believe in Christ or not? It may be this is your last time – you shall never hear the gospel faithfully and affectionately pressed home upon you again. Will you have Jesus to be yours?

Spirit of God, lead that heart to say, "Yes, Lord, I will"; and as the acceptance is heard on earth, may it be registered in heaven, and may salvation come to that man's heart this day. The Lord bless you all, every one of you; and when he gathers his people together, may I and you, every one of us, be found at his right hand, to see his smiling face.

Chapter 7

A Preacher from the Dead

And he said unto him, If they hear not Moses and the proph-
ets, neither will they be persuaded, though one rose from the
dead. (Luke 16:31)

M an is very reluctant to think ill of himself. The most of mankind
are very prone to indulge in apologies for sin. They say, "If we
had lived in better times, we would have been better men; if we had
been born into this world under happier guidance, we would have been
holier; and if we had been placed in more excellent circumstances, we
would have been more inclined to the right." The mass of men, when
they seek the cause of their sin, seek it anywhere but in the right place.
They will not blame their own nature for it; they will not find fault with
their own corrupt heart, but they will lay the blame anywhere else. Some
of them find fault with their peculiar position.

"If," says one, "I had been born rich, instead of being poor, I would
not have been dishonest." "Or if," says another, "I had been born in
middle-class life, instead of being rich, I would not have been exposed
to such temptations to lust and pride as I am now; but my very condition is so adverse to piety, that I am compelled by the place I hold in
society to be anything but what I ought to be."

Others turn around and find fault with the whole of society. They say
that the whole organism of society is wrong; they tell us that everything

in government, everything that concerns the state, everything that melts men into commonwealths is all so bad that they cannot be good while things are what they are. They must have a revolution, they must upset everything; and then they think they could be holy!

Many, on the other hand, throw the blame on their training. If they had not been so brought up by their parents, if they had not been so exposed in their youth, they would not have been what they are. It is their parents' fault; the sin lay at their father's or their mother's door. Or it is their personality. Hear them speak for themselves: "If I had such a temper as So-and-so, what a good man I would be! But with my headstrong disposition it is impossible. It is all very well for you to talk to me; but men have different turns of mind, and my turn of mind is such that I could not by any means be a serious character"; and so he throws the blame on his nature.

Others go a deal further and throw the blame on the ministry. "If," they say, "at one time the minister had been more earnest in preaching, I would have been a better man. If it had been my privilege to sit under sounder doctrine and hear the Word more faithfully preached, I would have been better." Or else they lay it at the door of professors of religion, and say, "If the church were more consistent, if there were no hypocrites and no formalists, then we would reform!"

Ah! sirs, you are putting the saddle on the wrong horse, you are laying the burden on the wrong back; the blame is in your hearts, and nowhere else. If your hearts were renewed you would be better; but until that is done, if society were remodeled to perfection, if ministers were angels, and professors of religion were a celestial hierarchy, you would be none the better; but having less excuse for your sin, you would be doubly guilty, and you would perish with a more terrible destruction. But yet men will always be holding to it that if things were different, they would be different too, whereas the difference must be made in themselves, if they begin in the right place.

Among other whims that have occurred to the human mind, such a one as that of my text may sometimes have arisen. "If," said the rich man in hell, "one should arise from the dead, if Lazarus should go from heaven to preach, my hardened brethren would repent." And some have been apt to say, "If my aged father, or some revered patriarch could rise from the dead and preach, we would all of us turn to God." That is another way of casting the blame in the wrong quarter. We shall endeavor, if we can, to refute such a supposition as that this morning, and affirm most strenuously the doctrine of the text, that *if they hear not Moses and the prophets, neither will they be persuaded, though one rose from the dead.* Let us proceed with this subject.

Suppose a preacher should come from another world to preach to us; we must naturally suppose that he came from heaven. Even the rich man did not ask that he or any of his companions in torment might go out of hell to preach. Spirits that are lost and given up to unutterable wickedness could not visit this earth; and if they did, they could not preach the truth, nor lead us on the road to heaven that they had not walked themselves. The advent of a damned spirit upon earth would be a curse, a blemish, a withering blast; we need not suppose that such a thing ever did or could occur. The preacher from another world, if such could come, must come from heaven. He must be a Lazarus who had lain in Abraham's bosom, a pure, perfect, and holy being.

Now, imagine for a moment that such a one had descended upon earth; suppose that we heard tomorrow a sudden piece of news – that a revered spirit, who had been a long time buried, had all of a sudden burst his burial clothes, lifted up his coffin lid, and was now preaching the Word of Life. Oh! what a rush there would be to hear him preach! What place in this wide world would be large enough to hold his massive congregations? How you would rush to listen to him! How many thousands of portraits would be published of him, representing him in the dread winding-sheet of death, or as an angel fresh from heaven.

Oh! how this city would be stirred, and not this city only, but also this whole land! Nations far remote would soon hear the news; and every ship would be freighted with passengers, bringing men and women to hear this wonderful preacher and traveler who had returned from the point unknown. And how you would listen! And how solemnly you would gaze at that unearthly specter. And how your ears would be attentive to his every word! His faintest syllable would be caught and published everywhere throughout the world – the utterances of a man who had been dead and was alive again. And we are very apt to suppose, that if such a thing should happen, there would be numberless conversions, for surely the congregations thus attracted would be immensely blessed.

Many hardened sinners would be led to repent; hundreds of faltering ones would be made to decide, and great good would be done. Ah! stop; though the first part of the fairy dream would occur, yet the last would not. If someone should rise from the dead, still would sinners no more repent through his preaching than through the preaching of any other. God might bless such preaching to salvation, if he pleased; but in itself there would be no more power in the preaching of the sheeted dead, or of the glorified spirit, than there is in the preaching of feeble man today. Though one should rise from the dead, they would not repent.

But yet, many men would suppose that advantages would arise from the resurrection of a saint, who could testify to what he had seen and heard. Now, the advantages, I suppose, could only be three. Some would say there would be an advantage *in the strength of evidence that such a man could give to the truth of Scripture;* for you would say, "If a man did actually come from the pearly-gated city of Jerusalem, the home of the blessed, then there would be no more dispute about the truth of revelation. That would be settled."

Some would suppose that he could tell us more than Moses and the prophets had told us, and that there would be *an advantage in the instruction that he could confer,* as well as in the evidence that he would bear.

And thirdly, there may be some who suppose that it would be an advantage gained *in the manner in which such a one would speak.* "For surely," they say, "he would speak with great eloquence, with a far mightier power, and with a deeper feeling than any common preacher who had never beheld the earnestness of another world." Now, these three points one after another we think we will settle them.

First, it is thought that if one did come from the dead to preach, there would be a confirmation of the truth of the gospel, and a testimony borne at which jeering infidelity would stand aghast in silence. Stop; we will see about that. We do not think so. We believe that the resurrection of one dead man today, to come into this hall and preach, would be no confirmation of the gospel to any person present here who does not believe it already.

If, my friends, the testimony of one man who had been raised from the dead were of any value for the confirming of the gospel, *would not God have used it before now?* This shall be my first argument. It is undoubtedly true that some have risen from the dead. We find accounts in Holy Scripture of some men who by the power of Christ Jesus, or through the instrumentality of prophets, were raised from the dead; but you will note this memorable fact, that they never any of them spoke one word that is recorded, by way of telling us what they saw while they were dead. I shall not enter into any discussion as to whether their souls slept during the time of their death, or whether they were in heaven or not. That would be a discussion without profit, only causing disputes, which could yield no fruit. I only say, it is memorable that there is not a record of any one of them having given any description of what they saw while they were dead.

Oh, what secrets might he have told out, who had lain in his grave for four days! Do you not suppose that his sisters questioned him? Do you not think that they asked him what he saw – whether he had stood before the burning throne of God, and been judged for the things done in his body, and whether he had entered into rest? But however they may have asked, it is certain he gave no answer; for had he given an answer we would have known it now; tradition would have cherished the record.

And do you remember when Paul once preached a long sermon, even until midnight, there was a young man in the third loft named Eutychus, who fell asleep, and fell down, and was taken up dead? Paul came down and prayed, and Eutychus was restored to life. But did Eutychus get up and preach after he had come from the dead? No; the thought never seems to have struck a single person in the assembly. Paul went on with his sermon, and they sat and listened to him, and did not care one fig about what Eutychus had seen; for Eutychus had nothing more to tell them than Paul had.

Of all the number of those who by divine might have been brought again from the shades of death, I repeat the assertion: we have not one secret told; we have not one mystery unraveled by them all. Now, God knows best; we will not compare our surmises to divine decision. If God decided that resurrection men should be silent, it was lest it should be that their testimony would have been of little worth or help to us, or else it would have been borne.

But again, I think it will strike our minds at once, that if this very day a man should rise from his tomb and come here to affirm the truth of the gospel, *the infidel world would be no more near believing than it is now.* Here comes Mr. Infidel Critic. He denies the evidences of the Bible, evidences that so clearly prove its authenticity, that we are obliged to believe him to be either blasphemous or senseless, in that he does so, and we leave him to his choice between the two. But he dares to deny the truth of Holy Scripture and will have it that all the miracles whereby it is attested are untrue and false.

Do you think that one who had risen from the dead would persuade such a man as that to believe? What? When God's whole creation having been ransacked by the hand of science, has only testified to the truth of revelation – when the whole history of buried cities and departed nations has but preached out the truth that the Bible was true – when every strip of land in the far-off East has been an exposition and a confirmation of the prophecies of Scripture? If men are yet unconvinced, do you suppose that one dead man rising from the tomb would convince them? No; I see the critical blasphemer already armed for his prey. Listen to him: "I am not quite sure that you ever were dead. Sir, you profess to be risen from the dead; I do not believe you. You say you have been dead and have gone to heaven; my dear man, you were in a trance. You must bring proof from the church register that you were dead." The proof is brought that he was dead.

"Well, now you must prove that you were buried." It is proved that he was buried, and it is proved that some church officer in old times did take up his dry bones and cast his dust in the air. "That is very good. Now I want you to prove that you are the identical man that was buried."

"Well, I am, I know I am. I tell you as an honest man I have been to heaven, and I have come back again."

"Well then," says the infidel, "it is not consistent with reason. It is ridiculous to suppose that a man who was dead and buried could ever come to life again, and so I don't believe you; I tell you so straight to your face."

That is how men would answer him; and instead of having only the sin of denying many miracles, men would have to add to it the guilt of denying another, but they would not be so much as a tenth of an inch nearer to conviction. And certainly, if the wonder were done in some far-off land, and only reported to the rest of the world, I can suppose that the whole infidel world would exclaim, "Simple childish tales and such traditions have been current elsewhere; but we are sensible men, we do not believe them." Although a churchyard should come to life, and stand up before the infidel who denies the truth of Christianity, I declare I do not believe there would be enough evidence in all the churchyards in the world to convince him.

Infidelity would still cry for something more. It is like *the horse-leach . . . crying, Give, give* (Proverbs 30:15). Prove a point to an infidel, and he wants it proved again; let it be as clear as noonday to him from the testimony of many witnesses, yet he does not believe it. In fact, he does believe it, but he pretends not to do so and is an infidel in spite of himself. But certainly, the dead man's rising would be of little worth for the conviction of such men.

But remember, my dear friends, that the most numerous class of unbelievers is a set of people who never think at all. There are a great number of people in this land that eat and drink, and do everything else except think; at least, they think enough to take their shop shutters down in the morning, and put them up at night; they think enough to know a little about the rising of the funds, or the rate percent of interest, or something like how articles are selling, or the price of bread; but their brains seem to be given to them for nothing at all, except to meditate upon bread and cheese. To them religion is a matter of very small concern. They dare say the Bible is very true, they dare say religion is all right; but it does not often trouble them much.

They suppose they are Christians, for were they not christened when they were babies? They must be Christians – at least they suppose so; but they never sit down to inquire what religion is. They sometimes go to church and chapel and elsewhere, but it does not signify much to them. One minister may contradict another, but they do not know; they dare say they are both right. One minister may fall foul of another in almost every doctrine; it does not matter, and they pass over religion with the strange idea – "God Almighty will not ask us where we went to, I dare say." They do not exercise their judgments at all. Thinking is such hard work for them that they never trouble themselves at all about it.

Now, if a man were to rise from the dead tomorrow, these people would never be startled. Yes, yes, they would go and see him once, just as they go and see any other curiosity such as the living skeleton or Tom Thumb. They would talk about him a good deal, and say, "There's a man risen from the dead," and possibly some winter's evening they might read one of his sermons; but they would never give themselves trouble to think whether his testimony was worth anything or not.

No, they are such blocks that they never could be stirred; and if the ghost were to come to any of their houses, the most they would feel would be that they were in a fearful fright. But as to what he said, that would never exercise their sluggish brains and never stir their stony senses. Though one should rise from the dead, the great mass of these people never would be affected.

And besides, my friends, *if men will not believe the witness of God, it is impossible that they should believe the witness of man.* If the voice of God from the top of Sinai and his voice by Moses in the book of the Law, if his voice by the diverse prophets in the Old Testament, and especially his own word by his own Son, who has brought immortality to light by the gospel, cannot convince men, then there is nothing in the world that can of itself accomplish the work. No; if *God* speaks once, but man regards him not, we need not wonder that we have to preach many a time without being regarded; and we should not harbor the thought that some men who had risen from the dead would have a greater power to convince than the words of God.

If this Bible be not enough to convert you, apart from the Spirit (and certainly it is not), then there is nothing in the world that can, apart from his influence. And if the revelation which God has given of his Son Jesus Christ in this blessed Book, if the Holy Scripture be not in the hands of God enough to bring you to the faith of Christ, then, though an angel from heaven, then, though the saints from glory, then, though God himself should descend on earth to preach to you, you would go on unsaved and unblessed. *If they hear not Moses and the prophets, neither will they be persuaded, though one rose from the dead.* That is the first point.

It is imagined, however, that if one of *the spirits of just men made perfect* would come to earth, even if he did not produce a most satisfactory testimony to the minds of skeptics, he would yet be able to give abundant information concerning the kingdom of heaven. "Surely," some would say, "if Lazarus had come from the bosom of Abraham, he could have unfolded a tale that would have made our hair stand upright, while he talked of the torments of the rich man. Surely, if he had looked from the gates of bliss, he might have told us about the worm that dies not and the fire that never can be quenched: some horrible details, some thrilling words of horror and of terror he might have uttered, which would have unfolded to us more of the future state of the lost than we know now."

"And," says the bright-eyed believer, "if he had come on earth he might have told us of the saints' everlasting rest. He might have pictured to us that glorious city that has the Lord God for its eternal light, the streets that are of gold, and its gates of pearl. Oh! how sweetly would he have sung upon the bosom of Christ, and known the joy of the blessed, because he had been

> Up where eternal ages roll;
>   Where solid pleasures never die,
> And fruits immortal feast the soul.

"Surely, he would have brought down with him some handfuls of the clusters of Eshcol; he would have been able to tell us some celestial secrets that would have cheered our hearts, and strengthened us to run the heavenly race, and put on a cheerful courage." Stop; that is a dream too. A spirit of the just descending from heaven could tell us no more that would be of any use to us than we know already. What more could that spirit from heaven tell us of the pains of hell than we do already know? Is not the Bible explicit enough? Did not the lips of Christ dreadfully portray the lake of fire? Did he not, even he who wept over men, did he not in awful language tell us that God would say at last, *Depart from me, ye cursed, into everlasting fire, prepared for the devil and his angels* (Matthew 25:41)?

Do you need more thrilling words than these? *Their worm dieth not, and the fire is not quenched* (Mark 9:44). Do you need more terrible warnings than these – *The wicked shall be turned into hell, and all the nations that forget God* (Psalm 9:17)? Do you want more awful warnings than this – *Who among us shall dwell with everlasting burnings?* (Isaiah 33:14). What! Do you want a fuller declaration than the words of God: *Tophet is ordained of old; . . . the pile thereof is fire and much wood; the breath of the Lord, like a stream of brimstone, doth kindle it*

(Isaiah 30:33)? You cannot need more than Scripture gives of that, even that which you try to run away and escape from; you say the book is too horrible and tells you too much of damnation and hell.

Sirs, if you think there is too much there, and therefore reject it, would you stand for an instant to listen to one who should tell you more? No; you do not wish to know more, nor would it be of any use to you if you did. Do you need more details concerning the judgment, that day of wrath to which each of us is drawing near? Are we not told that the king shall *sit upon the throne of his glory: and before him shall be gathered all nations: and he shall separate them one from another, as a shepherd divideth the sheep from the goats* (Matthew 25:31-33)?

Suppose there were one here who had seen the solemn preparation for the great judicial inquest – one who had stood where the throne is to be planted and had marked the future with a more piercing eye than ours. Yet of what help would it be to us? Could he tell us more than Holy Writ has told us now – at least, anything that would be more profitable? Perhaps he knows no more than we know. And one thing I am sure of: he would not tell us more about the rule of judgment than we know now. Spirit that has returned from another world, tell me, how are men judged? Why are they condemned? Why are they saved?

I hear him say, "Men are condemned because of sin. Read the Ten Commandments of Moses, and you will find the ten great condemnations whereby men are forever cut off." I knew that before, bright Spirit; you have told me nothing! "No," says he, "and nothing can I tell. Because I was hungry, and you gave me no meat; I was thirsty, and you gave me no drink; I was sick, and you visited me not; I was in prison, and you came not unto me; therefore, inasmuch as you did it not unto one of the least of these my brethren, you did it not to me. Depart, you cursed" (see Matthew 25:42-46).

"Why, Spirit, was that the word of the King?"

"It was," says he.

"I have read that too; you have told me no more."

If you do not know the difference between right and wrong from reading the Scripture, you would not know it if a spirit should tell you; if you do not know the road to hell and the road to heaven from the Bible itself, you would never know it at all. No book could be more clear, no revelation more distinct, no testimony more plain. And since without the agency of the Spirit, these testimonies are insufficient for salvation, it follows that no further declaration would benefit. Salvation is ascribed wholly to God, and man's ruin only to man. What more could a spirit tell us than a distinct declaration of the two great truths – *O Israel, thou hast destroyed thyself; but in me is thine help* (Hosea 13:9).

Beloved, we do solemnly say again, that Holy Scripture is so perfect, so complete, that it cannot need the supplement of any declaration concerning a future state. All that you ought to know concerning the future you may know from Holy Scripture. It is not right to say with Young,

> My hopes and fears start up alarmed,
> And o'er life's narrow verge look down,
> On what? A bottomless abyss,
> A dread eternity.

It is not right to say that, as if it were all we know. Blessed be God, the saint does not look down upon a bottomless abyss; he looks up to the celestial *city which hath foundations, whose builder and maker is God* (Hebrews 11:10). Nor do even the wicked look down upon an unknown abyss, for to them it is clearly revealed. Though *eye hath not seen, nor ear heard* (1 Corinthians 2:9) the tortures of the lost, yet has Holy Scripture sufficiently told us of them to make it a well-mapped road, so that when they meet with death, and hell, and terror, it shall be no new thing; for they heard of it before, and it was distinctly revealed to them. Nothing more could we know that would be of any use. Tattlers, idle curiosity people, and such like, would be mightily delighted with such a man.

Ah! what a precious preacher he would be to them, if they could get him all the way from heaven, and get him to tell all its secrets out! Oh, now would they love him – how would they delight in him! "For," say they, "he knows a great deal more than anybody else; he knows a great deal more than the Bible tells us; he knows a great many little details, and it is wonderful to hear him explain them!" But there the matter would end. It would be merely the gratification of curiosity; there would be no conferring of blessing, for if to know more of the future state would be a blessing for us, God would not withhold it; there can be no more told to us. If what you know would not persuade you, *neither will [you] be persuaded, though one rose from the dead* (Luke 16:31).

Yet some say, "Surely, if there were no gain in matter, yet there would be a gain in manner. Oh, if such a spirit had descended from the spheres, how he would preach! What celestial eloquence would flow from his lips! How majestically would he word his speech! How mightily would he move his hearers! What marvelous words would he utter! What sentences that might startle us from our feet and make us quiver with their thrilling influence. There would be no dullness in such a preacher; it would be no weariness to hear him; there would be no lack of affection in him, and surely no lack of earnestness; we might well be pleased to hear him every day, and never weary with his wonderful speech. Such a preacher earth has never heard. Oh, if he would but come! How would we listen!" Stop! That too is a dream.

I do believe that Lazarus from Abraham's bosom would not be so good a preacher as a man who has not died, but whose lips have been touched with a live coal from off the altar. Instead of his being better, I cannot see that he would be quite so good. Could a spirit from the other world speak to you more solemnly than Moses and the prophets have spoken? Or could they speak more solemnly than you have heard the Word spoken to you at diverse times already?

O sirs, some of you have heard messages that have been as solemn as death and as serious as the grave. I can recall to some of your memories seasons when you have sat beneath the sound of the Word, wondering and trembling all the while. It seemed as if the minister had taken to himself bow and arrows and was making your conscience the butt at which his shafts were leveled. You have not known where you were; you have been so grievously frightened and struck with terror that your knees did knock together, and your eyes ran with tears. What more do you want than that? If that solemn preaching of some mighty preacher whom God had inspired for the time – if that did not save you, what can save you, apart from the influence of the Spirit?

And oh! you have heard more solemn preaching than that. You had a little daughter once. That child of yours had been to the Sunday school; she came home, and was sick unto death. You watched her night and day, and the fever grew upon her, and you saw that she would die.

You have not forgotten yet how your little daughter Mary preached to you a sermon that was solemn indeed: just before she departed, she took your hand in her little hand, and she said, "Father, I am going to heaven; will you follow me?"

That was a solemn sermon to you. What more could the sheeted dead have said? You have not forgotten yet, how when your father lay dying – (a holy man of God he had been in his day, and served his Master well) – you with your brothers and sisters stood around the bed, and he addressed you one by one.

Woman! you have not forgotten yet, despite all your sin and wickedness since then, how he looked you in the face and said, "My daughter, it would have been better for you that you had never been born than that you should be a despiser of Christ and a neglecter of his salvation." And you have not forgotten how he looked when with solemn tears in his eyes he addressed you and said, "My children, I charge you by death and by eternity, I charge you, if you love your own souls, despise not the gospel of Christ; forsake your follies, and turn unto God and live." What preacher do you want better than that? What voice more solemn than the voice of that of your own parent upon the confines of eternity? And you have not yet quite thoroughly escaped from the influence of another solemn scene.

You had a friend, a so-called friend; he was a traitor, one who lived in sin and rebelled against God with a high hand and an outstretched arm. You remember his deathbed, when he lay near to death that terrors got hold of him; the flames of hell began to get their grip on him before he had completely departed. You have not yet forgotten his shrieks, his screams; you have not yet quite gotten from your vision in your dreams that hand through which the fingernails were almost pierced in agony, and that face, contorted with dreadful twitchings of dismay. You have not completely escaped yet from that horrid yell with which the spirit entered the realm of darkness and forsook the land of the living. What more of a preacher do you want? Have you heard this preaching, and yet have you not repented? Then truly, if after all this you are hardened, neither would you be persuaded though one rose from the dead.

Ah! but you say, you want someone to preach to you more feelingly. Then, sir, you cannot have that in the preacher you desire. A spirit from heaven could not be a feeling preacher. It would be impossible for Lazarus, who had been in Abraham's bosom, to preach to you with emotion. As a perfect being, of course he must be supremely happy. Imagine this morning a supremely happy being preaching to you about repentance and the wrath of God. Do you not see him? There is a placid smile ever upon his brow; the light of heaven gilds his face; he is talking about the torments of hell, it was the place for sighs and groans; but he cannot sigh; his face is just as placid as ever. He is speaking of the torments of the wicked, and it was the time for tears; but he cannot weep, for that would be incompatible with blessedness.

The man is preaching of dreadful things with a smile upon his face; there is summer on his brow, and winter on his lips – heaven in his eyes, and hell in his mouth. You could not bear such a preacher; he would seem to mock you. Alas, it needs a man to preach, a man like yourselves, who is capable of feeling. There needs to be one who, when he preaches of Christ, smiles on his hearers with love – who, when he tells of terror, cowers in his own spirit while he utters the wrath of God. The great power of preaching, next to the power of God's Spirit, lies in the preacher's feeling it. We shall never do much good in preaching unless we feel what we utter. *Knowing therefore the terror of the Lord, we persuade men* (2 Corinthians 5:11).

Now, a glorified spirit from heaven could not feel these things; he could show but little emotion. True, he could speak of the glories of heaven; and how his face would grow brighter, and brighter, and brighter, as he told the wonders of that upper world! But when he came to cry, *Flee from the wrath to come* (Matthew 3:7), the voice would sound as sweet when he spoke of death and judgment as when he spoke of glory; and that would make sad disharmony, the sound not answering to the sense – the modulations of his voice being unfit to express the idea upon the mind. Such a preacher could not be a powerful preacher, even though he came again from the dead.

And one thing we may say: he could not preach more closely home to you than you have had the truth preached to you. I shall not say that you have had preaching put very close to you from the pulpit. I have endeavored to be very personal sometimes; I have not shunned to point some of you out in the congregation, and given you a word of rebuke, such as you could not mistake; nor if I knew that any of you were indulging in sin would I spare you. I bless God that I am not afraid to be a personal preacher, and to shoot the arrow at each separate man when he needs it. But, nevertheless, I cannot preach home to you as I would. You are all thinking your neighbor is intended, when it is yourself. But you have had a personal preacher once.

There was a great preacher called at your house one day; his name was Cholera and Death. A terrible preacher was he! With grim words and hard accent he came and laid his hand upon your wife; and then he put his other hand on you, and you grew cold and almost stiff. You remember how he preached to you then. He made your conscience ring again and again; he would not let you lie still; he cried aloud concerning your sin and your iniquity; he brought all your past life to light, and set all your evil conduct in review. From your childhood even up until then he led you through all your wanderings, and then he took the whip of the law and began to plow your back with furrows. He frightened you with *the wrath to come.*

You sent for the minister. You bade him to pray; you thought you prayed yourself; and after all that, that preacher went away, and he had come on a fruitless errand, for no good had been done to you. You had been a little startled and a little stirred, but you are today what you were then, unsaved and unconverted. Then, sir, you would not be converted, though one rose from the dead. You have been wrecked at sea; you have been cast into the jaws of the grave by fever; you have been nearly struck to death by accident; and yet, with all this personal preaching, and with Mr. Conscience thundering in your ears, you are today unconverted.

Then learn this truth, that no outward means in the world can ever bring you to the footstool of divine grace and make you a Christian, if Moses and the prophets have failed. All that can be done now is this: God the Spirit must bless the Word to you; otherwise conscience cannot awaken you, reason cannot awaken you, powerful appeals cannot awaken you, and persuasion cannot bring you to Christ.

Nothing will ever do it except God the Holy Spirit. Oh! do you feel that you are drawn this morning? Does some sweet hand draw you to Christ, and does some blessed voice say, "Come to Jesus, sinner; there is hope for you"? Then that is God's Spirit. Bless him for it! He is drawing you by the hands of love and the cords of a man.

But oh! if you be undrawn and left to yourself, you will surely die. Brethren and sisters in the faith, let us lift up our prayers to God for sinners, that they may be drawn to Christ – that they may be led to come, all guilty and burdened, and look to Jesus to be lightened, and that they may be persuaded, by the coming power of the Spirit, to take Christ to be their "all in all," knowing that they themselves are "nothing at all." O God the Holy Spirit, bless these words, for Jesus Christ's sake. Amen and Amen.

Chapter 8

The Importunate Widow

And he spake a parable unto them to this end, that men ought always to pray, and not to faint; saying, There was in a city a judge, which feared not God, neither regarded man: and there was a widow in that city; and she came unto him, saying, Avenge me of mine adversary. And he would not for a while: but afterward he said within himself, Though I fear not God, nor regard man; yet because this widow troubleth me, I will avenge her, lest by her continual coming she weary me. And the Lord said, Hear what the unjust judge saith. And shall not God avenge his own elect, which cry day and night unto him, though he bear long with them? I tell you that he will avenge them speedily. (Luke 18:1-8)

Remember that our Lord did not only infuse prayer with great earnestness, but he was also himself a brilliant example of it. It always gives force to a teacher's words when his hearers well know that he carries out his own instructions. Jesus was a prophet mighty both in deed and in word, and we read of him: *Jesus began both to do and teach* (Acts 1:1).

In the exercise of prayer, "cold mountains and the midnight air" witnessed that he was as great a doer as a teacher. When he exhorted his disciples to continue in prayer, and to *pray without ceasing,* he only bade them to follow in his steps. If any one of all the members of the mystical body might have been supposed to need no prayer, it would certainly have been our Covenant Head, but if our Head abounded in prayer, much more ought we, the inferior members.

He was never defiled with the sins that have debased and weakened us spiritually; he had no inbred lusts to struggle with. But if the perfectly pure One drew near so often unto God, how much more incessant in prayer ought we to be! So mighty, so great, and yet so prayerful! O you weak ones of the flock, how forcibly does the lesson come home to you! Imagine, therefore, the discourse of this morning is not preached to you by me, but comes fresh from the lips of One who was the great master of secret prayer, the highest paragon and pattern of private prayer, and let every word have the force about it as coming from such a One.

Turn we at once to our text, and in it we shall notice, first, *the end and design of the parable;* secondly, we shall have some words to say upon *the two actors in it,* whose characters are intentionally so described as to give force to the reasoning; and then, thirdly, we shall dwell upon *the power that in the parable is represented as triumphant.*

First, then, consider our Lord's design in this parable – *Men ought always to pray, and not to faint.*

But can men pray always? There was a sect in the earlier days of Christianity who were foolish enough to read the passage literally, and to attempt praying without ceasing by continual repetition of prayers. They of course separated themselves from all worldly concerns, and in order to fulfill one duty of life they neglected every other duty. Such madmen might well expect to reap the due reward of their follies. Fortunately, there is no need in this age for us to deny such an error; there is far more necessity to cry out against those who, under the pretense of praying always, have no settled time for prayer at all, and so run to the opposite extreme.

Our Lord meant by saying men ought always to pray that *they ought to be always in the spirit of prayer,* always ready to pray. Like the old knights, always in warfare, not always on their steeds dashing forward with their lances in rest to dislodge an adversary, but always wearing their weapons where they could readily reach them, and always ready to encounter wounds or death for the sake of the cause that they championed. Those grim warriors often slept in their armor; so even when we sleep, we are still to be in the spirit of prayer, so that if perhaps we wake in the night, we may still be with God. Our soul, having received the divine centripetal influence that makes it seek its heavenly center, should be evermore naturally rising towards God himself.

Our heart is to be like those beacons and watchtowers that were prepared along the coast of England when the invasion of the Armada was hourly expected, not always blazing, but with the wood always dry, and the match always there, the whole pile being ready to blaze up at the appointed moment. Our souls should be in such a condition that spontaneous prayer should be very frequent with us. No need to pause in business and leave the counter and fall down upon the knees; the spirit should send up its silent, short, swift petitions to the throne of grace.

When Nehemiah wanted to ask a favor of the king, you will remember that he found an opportunity to do so through the king's asking him, *Why is thy countenance sad?* (Nehemiah 2:2); but before he gave him an answer, he said, *I prayed to the God of heaven* (Nehemiah 2:4). Instinctively perceiving the occasion, he did not leap forward to embrace it, but he halted just a moment to ask that he might be enabled to embrace it wisely and fulfill his great design therein. So, you and I should often feel, "I cannot do this until I have asked a blessing on it." However impulsively I may spring forward to gain an advantage, nevertheless my spirit, under the influence of divine grace, should hesitate until it has said, *If thy presence go not with me, carry [me] not up hence* (Exodus 33:15).

A Christian should carry the weapon of all-prayer like a drawn sword in his hand. We should never sheathe our prayers. Never may our hearts be like an unlimbered gun, with everything to be done to it before it can thunder on the foe; but it should be like a piece of cannon, loaded and primed, only requiring the fire so that it may be discharged. The soul should be not always in the exercise of prayer, but always in the energy of prayer; not always actually praying, but always intentionally praying.

Further, when our Lord says *men ought always to pray,* he may also have meant that *the whole life of the Christian should be a life of devotion to God.*

Prayer and praise, with sins forgiven,
Bring down to earth the bliss of heaven.

To praise God for mercies received both with our voices and with our actions, and then to pray to God for the mercies that we need, devoutly acknowledging that they come from him, these two exercises in one form or other should make up the sum total of human life. Our life psalm should be composed of alternating verses of praying and of praising until we get into the next world, where the prayer may cease, and praise may swallow up the whole of our immortality. "But," says one, "we have our daily business to attend to." I know you do, but there is a way of making business a part of praise and prayer.

You say, *Give us this day our daily bread* (Matthew 6:11), and that is a prayer as you utter it; you go off to your work, and as you toil, if you do so in a devout spirit, you are actively praying the same prayer by your lawful labor. You praise God for the mercies received in your morning hymn; and when you go into the duties of life, and there exhibit those graces that reflect honor upon God's name, you are continuing your praises in the best manner. Remember that with Christians, to labor is to pray, and that there is much truth in the verse of Coleridge – "He prayeth best who loveth best."

To desire my fellow creatures' good and to seek after it, to desire God's glory, and so to live as to promote it, is the truest of devotion. The devotion of the cloisters is by no means equal to that of the man who is engaged in the battle of life; the devotion of the nunnery and the monastery is at best the heroism of a soldier who shuns the battle. But the devotion of the man in business life, who turns all to the glory of God, is the courage of one who seeks the thickest of the fray, and there stands aloft the grand old standard of Jehovah-Nissi. You need not be afraid that there is anything in any lawful calling that need make you desist from vital prayer; but oh! if your calling is such that you cannot pray in it, you had better leave it.

If it be a sinful calling, an unholy calling, then of course, you cannot present that to God; but any of the ordinary distractions of life are such that if you cannot sanctify them, it is a lack of sanctity in yourself, and the fault lies with you. Men ought *always* to pray. It means that when they are using the lapstone or the chisel, when the hands are on the plow handles or on the spade, when they are measuring out the goods, when they are dealing in stocks, whatever they are doing, they are to turn all these things into a part of the sacred pursuit of God's glory. Their common garments are to be ceremonial clothes, their meals are to be sacraments, their ordinary actions are to be sacrifices, and they themselves are to be a royal priesthood, a peculiar people zealous for good works.

A third meaning which I think our Lord intended to convey to us was this: men ought always to pray; that is, *they should persevere in prayer.* This is probably his first meaning. When we ask God for mercy once, we are not to consider that now we are not further to trouble him with it, but we are to come to him again and again. If we have asked of him seven times, we ought to continue until seventy times seven. In secular mercies there may be a limit, and the Holy Spirit may bid us to ask no more. Then must we say, "The Lord's will be done."

If it be anything for our own personal advantage, we must let the spirit of submission rule us, so that after having sought the Lord three times, we shall be content with the promise, *My grace is sufficient for thee* (2 Corinthians 12:9), and no longer ask that the thorn in the flesh should be removed. But in spiritual mercies, and especially in the united prayers of a church, there is no taking a denial. Here, if we would prevail, we must persist; we must continue incessantly and constantly, and know no pause to our prayer until we win the mercy to the fullest possible extent. *Men ought always to pray.*

Week by week, month by month, year by year, the conversion of that dear child is to be the father's main plea. The bringing in of that unconverted husband is to lie upon the wife's heart night and day until she gets it. She is not to take even ten or twenty years of unsuccessful prayer as a reason why she should cease; she is to set God no times nor seasons, but so long as there is life in her and life in the dear object of her concern, she is to continue still to plead with the mighty God of Jacob.

The pastor is not to seek a blessing on his people occasionally, and then in receiving a measure of it to desist from further intercession; but he is to continue vehemently without pause, without restraining his energies, to cry aloud and spare not until the windows of heaven be opened, and a blessing be given too large for him to house.

But, brethren, how many times we ask of God, and have not because we do not wait long enough at the door! We knock a time or two at the gate of mercy, and since no friendly messenger opens the door, we go our ways. Too many prayers are like boys' runaway knocks: the knock is given, and then the giver is away before the door can be opened.

O for grace to stand foot to foot with the angel of God, and never, never, never relax our hold; feeling that the cause we plead is one in which we must be successful, for souls depend on it, the glory of God is connected with it, and the state of our fellow man is in jeopardy. If we could have given up in prayer our own lives and the lives of those dearest to us, nevertheless the souls of men we *cannot* give up; we must urge and plead again and again until we obtain the answer.

> The humble suppliant cannot fail
> To have his wants supplied,
> Since he for sinners intercedes
> Who once for sinners died.

I cannot leave this part of the subject without observing that our Lord would have us learn that *men should be more frequent in prayer.* Not only should they always have the spirit of prayer, and make their whole lives a prayer, and persevere in any one object that is dear to their souls, but there should also be a greater frequency of prayer among all the saints. I gather that from the parable: *lest by her continual coming she weary me.* Prayerfulness will scarcely be kept up long unless you set apart times and seasons for prayer. There are no times laid down in Scripture except by the example of holy men, for the Lord trusts much to the love of his people and to the spontaneous motions of the inner life.

He does not say, "Pray at seven o'clock in the morning every day," or "pray at night at eight, or nine, or ten, or eleven"; but he says, *Pray without ceasing.* Yet every Christian will find it exceedingly useful to have his regular times for retreating, and I doubt whether any notable piety can be maintained without these seasons being very carefully and scrupulously observed.

We read in the old traditions of James the apostle, that he prayed so much that his knees grew hard through his long kneeling. And it is recorded by Fox, that Latimer, during the time of his imprisonment, was so much upon his knees that frequently the poor old man could not rise to his meals, and had to be lifted up by his servants.

When he could no longer preach, and was imprisoned within stone walls, his prayers went up to heaven for his country, and we in these times are receiving the blessing. Daniel prayed with his windows open daily and at regular intervals. *Seven times a day,* says one, *do I praise thee* (Psalm 119:164). David declared that at *evening, and morning, and at noon* (Psalm 55:17) would he wait upon God. O that our intervals of prayer were not so distant one from the other; would God that on the pilgrimage of life, the wells at which we drink were more frequent. In this way should we continue in prayer.

Our Lord means, to sum up the whole, that *believers should exercise a universality of petition* – we ought to pray at all times. There are no orthodox hours in the Christian's day or week. We should pray from cockcrowing to midnight, at such times as the Spirit moves us. We should pray in all conditions, in our poverty and in our wealth, in our health and in our sickness, in the bright days of festival and in the dark nights of lamentation. We should pray at the birth and pray at the funeral, we should pray when our soul is glad within us by reason of abundant mercy, and we should pray when our soul draws near unto the gates of death by reason of heaviness. We should pray in all transactions, whether secular or religious.

Prayer should sanctify everything. The Word of God and prayer should come in over and above the common things of daily life. Pray over a bargain, pray over going into the shop and coming out again. Remember in the days of Joshua how the Gibeonites deceived Israel because Israel did not inquire of the Lord, and do not be deceived by a deceptive temptation, as you may well be if you do not daily come to the Lord and say, "Guide me. Make straight a plain path for my feet, and lead me in the way everlasting."

You shall never err by praying too much; you shall never make a mistake by asking for God's guidance too often. But you shall find this to be the gracious illumination of your eyes, if in the turning of the road where two paths meet that seem to be equally right, you shall stay a moment and cry unto God, "Guide me, O thou great Jehovah." *Men ought always to pray.* I have enlarged upon it from this pulpit; go you and express it in your daily lives.

In enforcing this precept, our Lord gives us a parable in which there are two actors, with the characteristics of the two actors being such as to add strength to his precept.

In the first verse of the parable there is *a judge*. Now, herein is the great advantage to us in prayer. Brethren, if this poor woman prevailed with a judge whose office is stern, unbending, and untender, how much more ought you and I to be urgent in prayer and hopeful of success when we have to petition a Father! Far different is a father than a judge. The judge must necessarily be impartial and stern, but the father is necessarily partial to his child, and compassionate and tender to his own offspring. Does she prevail over a judge, and shall we not prevail with our Father who is in heaven? And does she continue in her desperate need to weary him until she wins what she desires, and shall not we continue in the agony of our desires until we get from our heavenly Father whatsoever his Word has promised?

In addition to being a judge, he was *devoid of all good character*. In both branches he failed. He *feared not God*. Conscience was seared in him; he had no thoughts of the great judgment seat before which judges must appear. Though possibly he had taken an oath before God to judge impartially, yet he forgot his oath, and crushed justice under his foot. *Neither did he regard man.* As for the commendation of his fellow creatures, which is very often a power even with naturally bad men, either to restrain them from overt evil, or else to constrain them to righteousness, this principle had no effect upon him.

Now, if the widow prevailed over such a wretch as this, if the iron of her demands broke the iron and steel of this man's callousness, how much more may we expect to be successful with him who is righteous, and just, and good, the Friend of the needy, the Father of the fatherless, and the Avenger of all such as are oppressed! O let the character of God as it rises before you in all its majesty of truthfulness and faithfulness, blended with loving-kindness and tenderness and mercy, excite in you an inexhaustible intensity of prayer, making you resolve with this poor woman that you will never cease to pray until you win your suit.

The judge was a man so unutterably bad that he *even confessed his badness to himself* with great contentment too. Without the slightest tinge of remorse, he said within himself, *Though I fear not God, nor regard man.* There are few sinners who will go to this length. They may neither fear God nor regard men, yet still they will indulge in their minds some semblance of that which is virtuous, and cheat themselves into the belief that at least they are not worse than others. But with this man there was no self-deception. He was as cool about this acknowledgement as the Pharisee was concerning the opposite: *God, I thank thee, that I am not as other men are* (Luke 18:11).

To what a brazen irrelevance must this man have come, to what an extent must he have hardened his mind, that knowing himself to be such, he yet climbed the judgment seat, and sat there to judge his fellow man! Yet the woman prevailed with this monster in human form, who had come to take pleasure in his own wickedness and gloated in the badness of his own heart. Over this man compulsion prevailed – how much more over him who spared not his own Son, but freely delivered him up for us all; how much more over him whose name is love, whose nature is everything that is attractive and encouraging, to such as seek his face! The worse this judge appears, and he could scarcely have been painted in blacker colors, the more does the voice of the Savior seem to say to us, *Men ought always to pray, and not to faint.*

Note with regard to the character of this judge, that he was one who *consciously cared for nothing but his own ease.* When at last he consented to do justice, the only motive that moved him was, *Lest by her continual coming she weary me.* "She *stun* me" might be the Greek word – a kind of slang, I suppose, of that period, meaning lest "she batter me," "she bruise me," and as some translate it: "blacken my face with her incessant, constant batterings." That was the kind of language he used: a short, quick sentence of indignation at being bothered, as we should say, by such a case as this. The only thing that moved him was a desire to be at ease, and to take things comfortably.

O brethren, if she could prevail over such a one, how much more shall we succeed with God whose delight it is to take care of his children, who loves them even as the apple of his eye!

This judge was *practically unkind and cruel to her,* yet the widow continued. For awhile, he would not listen to her, though her household, her life, and her children's comfort were all hanging upon his will; he left her by a passive injustice to suffer still. But our God has been practically kind and gracious to us; up to this moment he has heard us and granted our requests. Set this against the character of the judge, and surely every loving heart that knows the power of prayer will be moved to incessant demands.

We must, however, pass on now to notice the other actor in the scene – *the widow;* and here everything reveals itself again the same way, to induce the church of God to be compelling. She was apparently *a perfect stranger to the judge.* She appeared before him as an individual in whom he took no interest. He had possibly never seen her before; who she was and what she wanted was of no concern to him. But when the church appears before God, she comes as Christ's own bride; she appears before the Father as one whom he has loved with an everlasting love. And shall he not avenge his own elect, his own chosen, his own people? Shall not their prayers prevail with him when a stranger's demands won a suit of an unwilling judge?

The widow appeared at the judgment seat *without a friend.* According to the parable, she had no advocate, no powerful pleader to stand up in the court and say, "I am the patron of this humble woman." If she prevailed, she must prevail by her own fervency and her own intensity of purpose. But when you and I come before our Father, we come not alone, for

> He is at the Father's side,
> The Man of love, the Crucified.

We have a Friend who *ever liveth to make intercession for [us].* O Christian, urge your appeal with holy boldness, press your case, for the blood of Jesus speaks with a voice that must be heard. Be not therefore faint in your spirit but continue instant in your prayer.

This poor woman came *without a promise to encourage her,* no, with the reverse – with much to discourage her. But when you and I come before God, we are commanded to pray by God himself, and we are promised that if we ask it shall be given to us, and if we seek we shall find. Does she win without the sacred weapon of the promise, and shall we not win who can set the battering rams of God's own Word against the gates of heaven, a battering ram that shall make every timber in those gates quiver? O brethren, we must not pause nor cease for a moment while we have God's promise to back our plea.

The widow, in addition to having no promise whatever, was even *without the right of constant access.* She had, I suppose, a right to cry out in order to be heard at ordinary times when judgment was administered, but what right had she to dog the judge's footsteps, to waylay him in the streets, to hammer at his private door, to be heard calling at nightfall, so that he, sleeping at the top of his house, was awakened by her cries? She had no permission so to request urgently, but we may come to God at all times and all seasons. We may cry day and night unto him, for he has bidden us to pray without ceasing. What, without a permit is this woman so incessant! And with the sacred permissions that God has given us, and the encouragement of abounding loving-kindness, shall we cease to plead?

She, poor soul, every time she prayed, *provoked the judge;* lines of anger were on his face. I doubt not he foamed at the mouth to think he should be wearied by a person so insignificant; but with Jesus, every time we plead, we please him rather than provoke him. The prayers of the saints are the music of God's ears.

> To him there's music in a groan,
>   And beauty in a tear.

We, speaking after the manner of men, bring a gratification to God when we intercede with him. He is vexed with us if we restrain our petitions; he is pleased with us when we draw near constantly. Oh then, as you see the smile upon the Father's face, children of his love, I beg you to faint not, but continue still without ceasing to plead for the blessing.

Once more, this woman had a suit in which *the judge could not himself be personally interested;* but ours is a case in which the God we plead with is more interested than we are; for when a church asks for the conversion of souls, she may justly say, *Arise, O God, plead thine own cause* (Psalm 74:22). It is for the honor of Christ that souls should be converted; it brings glory to the mercy and power of God when great sinners are turned from the error of their ways; consequently, we are pleading for the judge with the judge, for God we are pleading with God. Our prayer is practically *for* Christ as *through* Christ, that his kingdom may come, and his will may be done.

I must not forget to mention that in this woman's case *she was only one.* She prevailed though she was only one, but shall not God avenge his own elect, who are not *one,* but tens of thousands? If there be a promise that if two or three are agreed it shall be done, how much more if in any church hundreds meet together with unanimous souls anxiously desiring that God would fulfill his promise? These pleas cast chains around the throne of God! How they do, as it were, hem in omnipotence! How they constrain the Almighty to arise out of his place and come in answer to his people and do the great deed that shall bless his church and glorify himself.

You see, then, whether we consider the judge, or consider the widow, each character has points about it which tend to make us see our duty and our privilege to pray without ceasing.

The third and last point is the power that, according to this parable, triumphed.

This power was not the woman's eloquence. "I pray thee, *avenge me of mine adversary.*" These words are very few. They have the merit of being very expressive, but he that would study oratory will not gather many lessons from them. "I pray thee, *avenge me of mine adversary.*" Just eight words. You observe there is no plea, there is nothing about her widowhood, nothing urged about her children, nothing said about the wickedness of her adversary, nothing concerning the judgment of God upon unjust judges, nor about the wrath of God upon unjust men who devour widows' houses – nothing of the kind. "I pray thee, *avenge me of mine adversary.*"

Her success, therefore, did not depend upon her power in rhetoric, and we learn from this that the prevalence of a soul or of a church with God does not rest upon the effective speaking of its words, or upon the eloquence of its language. The prayer that mounts to heaven may have but very few of the tail feathers of adornment about it, but it must have the strong wing feathers of intense desire; it must not be as the peacock, gorgeous for beauty, but it must be as the eagle, for soaring aloft, if it would ascend up to the seventh heavens.

When you pray in public, as a rule, the shorter the better. Words are cumbersome to prayer. It often happens that an abundance of words reveals a scarcity of desires. Verbiage is generally nothing better in prayer than a miserable fig leaf with which to cover the nakedness of an unawakened soul.

Another thing is quite certain, namely, that the woman *did not prevail through the merits of her case.* It may have been a very good case, there is nothing said about that. I do not doubt the rightness of it; but still, the judge did not know nor care whether it was right or wrong; all he cared about was that this woman troubled him. He does not say, "She has a good case, and I ought to listen to it." No, he was too bad a man to be moved by such a motive; but rather, "she wearies me," that is all; "I will attend to it."

So, in our suit – in the suit of a sinner with God, it is not the merit of his case that can ever prevail with God. You have no merit. If you are to win, another's merit must stand instead of yours, and on your part it must not be merit but misery; it must not be your righteousness but your compulsion that is to prevail with God.

How this ought to encourage those of you who are laboring under a sense of unworthiness! However unworthy you may be, continue in prayer. Black may be the hand, but if it can but lift the knocker, the gate will open. Alas, though you have a paralysis in that hand; though, in addition to that paralysis, you be leprous, and the white leprosy be on your forehead, yet if you can but tremblingly lift up that knocker and let it fall by its own weight upon that sacred promise, you shall surely get an audience with the King of Kings. It is not eloquence, it is not merit, that wins with God; it is nothing but compulsion.

Note with regard to this woman that the judge said first that she troubled him; next he said that she came continually, and then he added his fear lest *she weary me.* I think the case was somewhat after this fashion. The judge was sitting one morning on his bench, and many were the persons coming before him asking for justice, which he was dealing out with the impartiality of a villain, giving always his best word to him who brought the heaviest bribes; when presently a poor woman uttered her complaint. She had tried to be heard several times, but her voice had been drowned by others; but this time it was more shrill and sharp, and she caught the judge's eye. "My lord, *avenge me of mine adversary.*" He no sooner sees from her poverty-stricken dress that there are no bribes to be had, than he replies, "Hold your tongue! I have other business to attend to."

He goes on with another suit in which the fees are more attractive. Still he hears the cry again, "My lord, I am a widow, *avenge me of mine adversary.*" Vexed with the renewed disturbance, he bade the usher to put her out, because she interrupted the silence of the court and stopped the public business. "Take care that she does not get in again tomorrow," said he. "She is a troublesome woman." Long before the next day had come, he found out the truth of his opinion. She waited until he left the court, dogged his footsteps, and followed him through the streets, until he was glad to get through his door, and bade the servants to fasten it lest that noisy widow should come in, for she had constantly attacked him with the cry, *Avenge me of mine adversary.*

He is now safely within the doors, and bids the servants to bring in his meal. They are pouring water on his hands and feet, and his lordship is about to enjoy his meal, when a heavy knock is heard at the door, followed by an outcry, pushing, and a scuffle. "What is it?" says he. "It is a woman outside, a widow woman, who wants your lordship to see justice done to her." "Tell her I cannot attend to her, she must be gone." He seeks his rest at nightfall on the housetop, when he hears a heavy knock at the door, and a voice comes up from the street beneath his residence: "My lord, *avenge me of mine adversary.*"

The next morning his court is open, and, though she is forbidden to enter, like a dog that will enter somehow, she finds her way in, and she interrupts the court continually with her plea, "My lord, *avenge me of mine adversary.*" Ask her why she is thus urgent, and she will tell you her husband is dead, and he left a little plot of land. It was all they had, and a cruel neighbor who looked with greedy eyes upon that little plot has taken it as Ahab took Naboth's vineyard, and now she is without any meal or any oil for the little ones, and they are crying for food.

Oh, if their father had been alive, how he would have guarded their interests, but she has no helper, and the case is a glaring one; and what is a judge for if he is not to protect the injured? She has no other chance, for the creditor is about to take away her children to sell them into bondage. She cannot bear that. "No," she says, "I have but one chance; it is that this man would speak up for me and do me justice, and I have made up my mind he shall never rest until he does so. I am resolved that if I perish, the last words on my lips shall be, 'Avenge me of mine adversary.'" So, the court is continually interrupted.

Again, the judge shouts, "Put her out! Put her out! I cannot conduct the business at all with this crazy woman here continually repeating in my ears a shriek of 'Avenge me of mine adversary.'" But it is sooner said than done. She lays hold of the pillars of the court so as not to be dragged out, and when at last they get her in the street, she does but wait for her chance to enter again. She pursues the judge along the highways, and she never lets him have a minute's peace.

"Well," says the judge, "I am worried out of my very life. I care not for the widow, nor her property, nor her children. Let them starve; what are they to me? But I cannot stand this; it will weary me beyond measure. I will see to it." It is done, and she goes her way. Nothing but her compulsion prevails.

Now, brethren, you have many other weapons to use with God in prayer, but our Savior bids you not to neglect this supreme, all-conquering instrument of compulsion. God will be more easily moved than this unjust judge, only be you as compelling as this widow was. If you are sure it is a right thing for which you are asking, plead now, plead at noon, plead at night, plead on; with cries and tears spread out your case, order your arguments, back up your pleas with reasons, urge the precious blood of Jesus, set the wounds of Christ before the Father's eyes, bring out the atoning sacrifice, point to Calvary, enlist the crowned Prince, the Priest who stands at the right hand of God, and resolve in your very soul that if Zion does not flourish, if souls be not saved, if your family be not blessed, if your own zeal be not revived, yet you will die with the plea upon your lips, and with the compelling wish upon your spirits.

Let me tell you that if any of you should die with your prayers unanswered, you need not conclude that God has disappointed you. With one story I will finish. I have heard that a certain godly father had the unhappiness of being the parent of some five or six most graceless sons. All of them as they grew up steeped themselves in infidel passions and led lewd lives. The father who had been constantly praying for them, and was a pattern of every virtue, hoped at least that in his death he might be able to say a word that would move their hearts. He gathered them to his bedside, but his unhappiness in dying was extreme, for he lost the light of God's countenance, and was troubled with doubts and fears, and the last dark thought that haunted him was, "Instead of my death being a testimony for God, which will win my dear sons, I die in such darkness and gloom that I fear I shall confirm them in their infidelity, and lead them to think that there is nothing in Christianity at all."

The effect was the reverse. The sons came around the grave at the funeral, and when they returned to the house, the eldest son thus addressed his brothers: "My brothers, throughout his lifetime, our father often spoke to us about religion, and we have always despised it, but what a sermon his deathbed has been to us! For if he who served God so well and lived so near to God found it so hard a thing to die, what kind of death may we expect ours to be who have lived without God and without hope?" The same feeling possessed them all, and thus the father's death had strangely answered the prayers of his life through the grace of God.

You cannot tell but what, when you are in glory, you should look down from the windows of heaven and receive a double heaven in beholding your dear sons and daughters converted by the words you left behind.

I do not say this to make you cease pleading for their immediate conversion, but to encourage you. Never give up prayer, never be tempted to cease from it. So long as there is breath in your body, and breath in their bodies, continue still to pray, for I tell you that he will avenge you speedily though he endure long with you. God bless these words for Jesus' sake. Amen.

Chapter 9

The Search for Faith

Nevertheless when the Son of man cometh, shall he find faith on the earth? (Luke 18:8)

It is absolutely certain that God will hear the prayers of his people. From beneath the altar souls cry unto him day and night to vindicate the cause of Christ, the cause of truth and righteousness, and to cast down his adversary; these prayers shall be answered speedily. Here on earth, sparse though the prayers may be, yet there is a remnant according to the election of grace who cease not to beg urgently the almighty God to make bare his arm, and display the majesty of his Word. Though for wise and gracious purposes the answer to those prayers may be delayed, yet it is absolutely certain.

Shall not God avenge his own elect, which cry day and night unto him, though he keeps their case long in hand? Assuredly he will; for those prayers are inspired by the Spirit, who knows the mind of God; they are for the glory of God and of his Christ, and they are presented by our Great High Priest. Longsuffering keeps back the advent and the judgment for a while; for the Lord is not willing that any should perish, but that all should come to repentance; but he will not forever delay the long-expected end.

The Lord Jesus himself gives us this personal assurance: *I tell you that he will avenge them speedily.* No doubt remains when Jesus says, *I tell you.* The Lord will come, and, according to his own reckoning, he will come *quickly*. His reckoning is according to the chronology of heaven, and this the heirs of heaven ought gladly to accept; it is good that we keep celestial time even now.

Brethren, let not your hearts fail you as to the ultimate issue of the present conflict. *The Lord shall reign for ever and ever* (Exodus 15:18). Hallelujah! The idols he shall utterly abolish. Antichrist shall be overthrown; like a millstone cast into the sea, he shall fall and be no more. The heathen shall be our Lord's inheritance, and the uttermost parts of the earth shall be his possession. He must reign until all enemies shall be put under his feet. If the present contest should be continued century after century, be not weary. It only seems long due to your impatience, while it is a short work for God. So grand a volume of the book as this, which contains the history of redemption, that it may well require a long time for its unrolling, and to such poor readers as we are, the spelling of it out word by word may seem an endless task; but we shall yet come to its close, and then we shall find that, like the book of Psalms, it ends in hallelujahs.

The matter to be questioned is not what God will do, but what men will do. Faithfulness is established in the very heavens, but what of faithfulness upon the earth? The part that God allots to us is that we believe his Word, for so shall we be established. It is the child's part to trust his father; it is the disciple's part to accept the teaching of his Master. Alas! how little there is of it at this moment! Knowing the feebleness of the faith of those around him, and foreseeing that future generations would partake of the same folly, the Savior gave utterance to this memorable question: *When the Son of man cometh, shall he find faith on the earth?* God is faithful, but are men faithful? God is true, but do we believe him? This is the point, and it is upon this that I shall speak this morning as the Holy Spirit shall help me.

I notice with regard to our text, first, that it is remarkable if we consider the person mentioned as searching for faith. *When the Son of man cometh, shall he find faith on the earth?*

When Jesus comes, he will look for precious faith. He has more regard for faith than for all else that earth can yield him. Our returning Lord will care nothing for the treasures of the rich or the honors of the great. He will not look for the abilities we have manifested, nor the influence we have acquired; but he will look for our faith. It is his glory that he is *believed on in the world* (1 Timothy 3:16), and to that he will have respect. This is the jewel for which he is searching. This heavenly merchantman counts faith to be the pearl of great price – faith is precious to Jesus as well as to us.

The last day will be occupied with a great scrutiny, and that scrutiny will be made upon the essential point – where is there faith, and where is there no faith? *He that believeth . . . shall be saved; but he that believeth not shall be damned.* A search warrant will be issued for our houses and our hearts, and the question will be: Where is your faith? Did you honor Christ by trusting his Word and his blood, or did you not? Did you glorify God by believing his revelation and depending upon his promise, or did you not? The fact that our Lord, at his coming, will seek for faith should cause us to think very highly of faith. It is no mere act of the intellect; it is a grace of the Holy Spirit that brings glory to God and produces obedience in the heart.

Jesus looks for it because he is the proper object of it, and it is by means of it that his great end in his first advent is carried out. Dear friends, imagine for a minute that our Savior is searching for faith now. *His eyes behold, his eyelids try, the children of men* (Psalm 11:4). This is the gold he seeks after amid the quartz of our humanity. This is the object of his royal quest – Do you believe in the Lord Jesus Christ?

When our Lord comes and looks for faith, *he will do so in his most sympathetic character.* Our text does not say, When the Son of *God* cometh, but rather, *When the **Son of man** cometh, shall he find faith on the earth?* (emphasis added). It is peculiarly as the Son of Man that Jesus will sit as a refiner, to discover whether we have true faith or not. He also as the Son of Man displayed faith in God. In the epistle to the Hebrews it is mentioned as one of the points in which he is made like unto his brethren, that he said, *I will put my trust in him* (Hebrews 2:13). The life of Jesus was a life of faith – faith that cried, *My God, my God* (Matthew 27:46), even when he was forsaken.

His was, on a grander scale than ours, the battle of faith in the great Father, waged against all the rebellious influences that were in array against him. He knows what fierce temptations men experience, for he has felt the same. He knows how need tests the faithful, and what faith is needed to be able to say, *Man shall not live by bread alone, but by every word that proceedeth out of the mouth of God* shall man live (Matthew 4:4).

He knows how elevation tests the soul, for he once stood on the pinnacle of the temple, and heard the infernal whisper, *Cast thyself down: for . . . He shall give his angels charge concerning thee* (Matthew 4:6). He knows what faith means in contradistinction to a false confidence that misreads the promise and forgets the precept altogether. He will not err in judgment and accept brass for gold. He knows what it is to be tempted with the offer of honor and gain: *All these things will I give thee,* said the fiend, *if thou wilt fall down and worship me* (Matthew 4:9).

He knows how faith puts all the glory of the world away with its one brave and prompt utterance: *Get thee hence, Satan: for it is written, Thou shalt worship the Lord thy God, and him only shalt thou serve* (Matthew 4:10). Beloved, when Jesus comes as the Son of Man he will recognize our weaknesses, he will remember our trials; he will know the struggle of our hearts, and the sorrow that an honest faith has cost us. He is best qualified to put the true price upon tested faith, self-denying faith, long-enduring faith. He will discern between the men who presume, and the men who believe; the men who dote upon vain delusions, and those who follow the plain path of God's own Word.

Further, I would have you note well that *the Son of Man is the most likely person to discover faith if it is to be found.* Not a grain of faith exists in all the world except that which he has himself created. If you have faith, my brother, the Lord has dealt with you; this is the mark of his hand upon you. By faith he has brought you out of your death in sin, and the natural darkness of your mind. *Thy faith hath saved thee* (Luke 7:50), for it is the candlestick that holds the candle by which the chamber of your heart is enlightened. Your God and Savior has put this faith in you.

Now, if faith in every instance is our Lord's gift, he knows where he has given it. If it is the work of God, he knows where he has produced it, for he never forsakes the work of his own hands. If that faith be only as a grain of mustard seed, and if it be hidden away in the obscurest corner of the earth, yet the loving Jesus spies it out, for he has an intimate concern in it, since he is its author and finisher. Our Lord is also the sustainer of faith, for faith is never independent of him upon whom it relies.

The greatest believer would not believe for another moment unless grace were constantly given him to keep the flame of faith burning. Beloved friend, if you have had any experience of the inner life at all, you know that he that first made you live must keep you alive, or else you will go back to your natural death. Since faith from day to day feeds at the table of Jesus, then *he* knows where it is. It is well for us that we have one looking for faith who, on account of his having created and sustained it, will be at no loss to discern it.

Besides, *faith always looks to Christ.* There is no faith in the world worth having but what looks to him, and through him to God, for everything. On the other hand, Christ always looks to faith; there never yet was an eye of faith but what it met the eye of Christ. He delights in faith: it is his joy to be trusted; it is a great part of the reward of his death that the sons of men should come and shelter in him. If faith looks to Christ, and Christ looks to faith, then he is sure to find it out when he comes, and that makes the text so very striking: *When the Son of man cometh, shall **he** find faith on the earth?* (emphasis added).

The Son of Man will give a wise and generous judgment in the matter. Some brethren judge so harshly that they would tread out the sparks of faith, but it is never so with our gracious Lord; he does not quench the smoking flax, nor despise the most trembling faith. The question becomes most emphatic when it is put thus. The tender and gentle Savior, who never judges too severely, when he comes, shall even he find faith on the earth?

What a sad and humbling question it is! He who is no morose critic but a kind interpreter of character, he who makes great allowances for feebleness, he that carries the lambs of faith in his bosom and gently leads the weak ones – when even he shall come to make a kindly search, will he be able to find faith on the earth? Unbelief is rampant indeed, when he who is omniscient can scarcely find a grain of faith amid the mass of doubt and denial! Ah me! that ever I should have to explain the question, *When the Son of man cometh, shall he find faith on the earth?*

Once more, I want to put this question into a striking light by dwelling on *the time of the scrutiny. When the Son of man cometh, shall he find faith on the earth?* Look you, brethren; the ages are accumulating proofs of the truth of Christianity, and the search takes place when this process has reached its climax. Whatever may be said about the present torrent of doubt, which no doubt is exceedingly strong, yet the reason for doubt grows weaker and weaker every year. Every mound of earth in the East contributes a fresh testimony to the accuracy of the Word of God. Stones are crying out against the unbelief of skeptics.

Moreover, all the experiences of all the saints, year after year, are swelling the stream of testimony to the faithfulness of God. You that are growing gray in his service know how every year confirms your confidence in the eternal truths of your God and Savior. I know not how long this allotment of longsuffering will last; but certainly, the longer it continues the more mischievously wicked does unbelief become. The more God reveals himself to man in ways of Providence, the more detestable is it on man's part to misrepresent his solemn witness.

But yet, my brethren, at the winding-up of all things, when revelation shall have received its utmost confirmation, even then faith will be such a rarity on the earth that it is a question if the Lord himself will find it. You have, perhaps, a notion that faith will go on increasing in the world; that the church will grow purer and brighter; and that there will be a wonderful degree of faith among men in the day of our Lord's appearing. Our Savior does not tell us so, but he puts forth the question of our text about it. Even concerning the dawn of the golden age he asks, *When the Son of man cometh, shall he find faith on the earth?*

I want you to notice *the breadth of the region of search.* He does not say, Shall he find faith among philosophers? When had they any faith? He does not confine his scrutiny to an ordained ministry or a visible church; but he takes a wider sweep – *Shall he find faith **on the earth*** (emphasis added), as if he would search from throne to cottage, among the learned and among the ignorant, among public men and obscure individuals; and, after all, it would be a question of whether among them all, from the pole to the equator, and again from the equator to the other pole, he would find faith at all. Alas, poor earth, to be so void of faith! Is there none in her vast continents, or on the lone islands of the sea? May it not be found in some of the countless ships upon the deep? What! Not upon the earth? Not with Jesus himself to look for it?

I have tried to set forth the question as distinctly as I can, so that it may have due effect upon your minds. It sounds through the chambers of my soul like the ring of many a lively hope and pleasant imagination. Lord, what is man that centuries of mercy can scarcely produce a single fruit of faith among a whole world of the sons of Adam? When thousands of summers and autumns have come and gone, shall there be no harvest of faith upon the earth, except a few heads of wheat, thin and withered by the east wind?

Let us somewhat change the run of our thoughts. Having introduced the question as a remarkable one, we will next notice that it is exceedingly instructive in connection with the parable of which it is part. It is wrong to use the Bible as if it were a box full of separate links, and not a chain of connected truth. Some pick sentences out of it as a crow picks worms out of a plowed field. If you tear words from their connection, they may not express the mind of the Spirit at all. No book, whether written by God or man, will stand to be torn limb from limb without being horribly mutilated.

Public speakers know the unfairness of this to themselves, and Holy Scripture suffers even more. The connection settles the drift and directs us to the true meaning – a meaning that may be very different from that which it seems to bear when torn from its surroundings. Let us carefully note that this passage occurs in connection with the parable of the urgent widow pleading with the unjust judge, for it is to be interpreted in connection with it.

Therefore, it means, first of all, when the Son of Man comes, shall he find upon the earth *the faith that prays compellingly,* as this widow did? Now, the meaning is dawning upon us. We have many upon the earth who pray; but where are those whose continual coming is sure to prevail? I thank God that the prayer meetings of this church are well sustained by praying men and women, but where are the Jacob-like wrestlers? I am afraid it cannot even be said of many churches that their prayer meetings are at all what they should be; for among many, the gathering for prayer is despised, and men say, "It is only a prayer meeting!" as if that were not the very crown and queen of all the assemblies of the church, with the sole exception of that of the breaking of bread.

Brethren, I will not judge with severity, but where are those who offer effective, fervent, much-prevailing prayer? I know that there are many here who do not neglect private and family devotions, and who pray constantly for the prosperity of the church of Jesus Christ, and for the salvation of souls. But even to you I put the question: if the Son of Man were now to come, how many would he find among us who pray with a distinct, vehement, and irresistible compulsion of faith? In the olden days, there was a John Knox, whose prayers were more terrible to the adversary than whole armies, because he pleaded in faith; but where shall we find a Knox at this hour?

Every age of revival has had its men mighty in prayer – where are ours? Where is the Elijah on the top of Mount Carmel who will bring down the rain upon these parched fields? Where is the church that will pray down a Pentecost? I will not belittle my brethren in the ministry, nor speak little of deacons and elders and other distinguished servants of my Lord; but still, my brothers and sisters, taking us all around, how few of us know what it is to pray the heaven-overcoming prayer that is needful for this crisis! How few of us go again, and again, and again to God, with tears, and cries, and heartbreak, pleading as for our own lives for the increase of Zion, and the saving of the ungodly! If the Son of Man comes, will he find much of such praying faith among our own churches? Ah me! that I should have to ask such a question; but I do ask it, hanging my head in shame.

The urgent widow waited with strong resolve, and never ceased through sullen doubt. If the judge had not yet heard her, she was sure he must hear her, for she had made up her mind that she would plead until he did. A waiting faith is rare. Men can believe for a time, but to hold out through the long darkness is another matter. Some soldiers are good at a rush, but they cannot form a square, and stand fast hour after hour.

When the Son of Man comes, will he find many who can believe in a delaying God, and plead a long-dated promise – waiting, but never wearying? When we have a revival, and everybody is crying "Hosannah!" certain eager folk are sure to be in the front; but when the popular voice growls out its "Crucify him!" where are they? Where are even Peter, and John, and the rest of the disciples?

Go, learn to plead on when no answer comes, and to press on when rejected; this is the test of faith. It is so easy to be a believer when everybody believes; but to be a believer when nobody believes, and to be nonetheless a firm believer because nobody believes with you, this is the mark of the man valiant for truth and loyal to Jesus.

Brethren, is it, after all, a matter of counting heads? Can you not dare to be in the right with two or three? Can you not be like rocks that defy the raging waves? Can you not let the billows of popular misbelief wash over you, and break and crash, and break and crash in vain? If these things move you, where is your faith? When the Son of Man comes, how many will he find on the earth whose faith stands not in men, but in the witness of God?

The widow staked her all upon the result of her pleading with the judge. She had not two strings to her bow, she had but one resort in her trouble: the judge must hear her. She would lose her little property, and her children would die of starvation if he did not hear her. He must hear her; about that she had no two opinions. What we want at the present moment is the man that believes God, and believes the gospel, and believes Christ, and does not care two pins about anything else. We need those who will stake reputation, hope, and life itself upon the truthfulness of God and the certainty of the everlasting gospel. To such the revelation of God is not one among many truths, it is the one and only saving truth.

Alas! we have nowadays to deal with foxes with holes to run to in case they are too closely hunted. Oh, to be done with all glory but glorying in the cross! For my part, I am content to be a fool if the old gospel be folly. What is more, I am content to be lost if faith in the atoning sacrifice will not bring salvation. I am so sure about the whole matter, that if I were left alone in the world as the last believer in the doctrines of grace, I would not think of abandoning them, nor even toning them down to win a convert. My all is staked on the truthfulness of God: *Let God be true, but every man a liar* (Romans 3:4).

When the Son of man cometh, shall he find faith on the earth, such as he deserves at our hands? Do we believe in Jesus practically, in matter-of-fact style? Is our faith fact, and not fiction? If we have the truth of faith, have we the degree of faith which we might have? Just think of this: *If ye have faith as a grain of mustard seed, ye shall say unto this mountain, Remove hence to yonder place; and it shall remove* (Matthew 17:20). What does this mean?

Brethren, are we not off the rails? Do we even know what faith means? I begin sometimes to question whether we believe at all. What signs follow our believing? When we think what wonders faith could have done, when we consider what marvels our Lord might have worked among us if it had not been for our unbelief, are we not humiliated?

Have we ever cut ourselves clear of the shackle of self-trustfulness? Have we ever launched out into the deep in clear reliance upon the eternal God? Have we ever left the visible for the invisible? Have we clung to the naked promise of God and rested upon the bare arm of omnipotence, which in and of itself is more than sufficient for the fulfillment of every promise? O Lord, where are we? Where shall we find an oasis of faith amid this wilderness of doubt? Where shall we find an Abraham? Is not the question an instructive one when set in connection with the parable that teaches us the power of compelling prayer?

In the next place, our text seems to me to be suggestive in view of its very form. It is put as a question: *When the Son of man cometh, shall he find faith on the earth?* I think it warns us *not to dogmatize about what the latter days will be.* Jesus puts it as a question. Shall he find faith on the earth? If you say "No," my dear friend, I shall be very much inclined to take the other side, and warmly plead the affirmative. I remember how Elijah said that he only was left, and yet the Lord had reserved unto himself seven thousand men that had not bowed the knee to Baal. Nations that know not Christ shall run to him, and *the kings of Sheba and Seba shall offer gifts* (Psalm 72:10).

I venture to hope that when the Son of Man comes he will find faith on the earth, but if you vehemently assert that it will be so, I shall be driven to advance the negative side with much apprehension that it may prove true. When our Lord was here before, he found little enough of faith; and he has distinctly told us that when he shall come the second time, men will be as they were in the days of Noah: *They did eat, they drank, they married wives, they were given in marriage, until the day that Noah entered into the ark* (Luke 17:27). I am inclined to take neither side. Let it remain a question, as our Lord has put it.

This question leads us to much holy fear as to the matter of faith. If our gracious Lord raises the question, the question ought to be raised. They say that some of us are old fogies, because we are jealous for the Lord of Hosts. They say that we are nervous and fidgety, and that our fears are the result of advancing age.

Yes, at fifty-three I am supposed to be semi-imbecile with years. If I were of their way of thinking, I do not suppose that this would occur to them. We fall into a pessimism – I think that is the word they use; I do not know much about such terms. Surely the Savior was not nervous. None will dare to accuse him of foolish anxiety; but yet he puts it, *When the Son of man cometh, shall he find faith on the earth?* As far as my observation goes, it is a question that might suggest itself to the most hopeful persons at this time; for *many processes are in vigorous action that tend to destroy faith.*

The Scriptures are being criticized with a familiarity that shocks all reverence, and their very foundation is being attacked by persons who call themselves Christians. A chilling criticism has taken the place of a warm, childlike, loving confidence. As one has truly said, "We have now a temple without a sanctuary." Mystery is discarded so that reason may reign. Men have eaten of the fruit of the Tree of the Knowledge of Good and Evil until they think themselves gods. Revealed truth is not now a doctrine to be believed, but a proposition to be discussed. The loving woman at Jesus' feet is cast out to make room for the traitor kissing Christ's cheek. Like Belshazzar, our men of modern thought are drinking out of the vessels of the Lord's sanctuary in honor of their own deities.

The idea of childlike faith is mocked, and he is regarded as the most honest man who can doubt the most, and pour the most contempt upon the authority of the divine Word. If this continues, we may well say, *When the Son of man cometh, shall he find faith on the earth?* In some places the greatest fountain of infidelity is the Christian pulpit. If this is the case – and I am sure it is so – what must become of the churches, and what must come to the outlying world? Will Jesus find faith in the earth when he comes?

In addition to many processes that are in action to exterminate faith, *are there not influences that dwarf and stunt it?* Where do you find great faith? Where is the preaching or the teaching that is done in full faith in what is preached and taught? It is no use flogging other people; let us come home to ourselves.

My brothers and sisters, where is our own faith? It seemed almost a novelty in the church when it was stated long ago that Mr. George Müller walked by faith in regard to worldly things. To feed children by faith in God, he was looked upon as a pious freak. We have come to a pretty pass, have we not, when God is not to be trusted about common things? Abraham walked with God about daily life; but nowadays, if you meet with a man who walks with God as to his business, and trusts God as to every item and detail of his domestic affairs, persons look at him with a degree of suspicious wonder. They think he has grace in his heart, but they also suspect that he has a bee in his bonnet, or he would not act in that sort of way. Oh yes, we have an imagined faith; but when it comes to the stern realities of life, where is our faith?

My brethren, why are you so full of worldly care? Why are you so anxious, if you have faith in God? Why do you display in worldly things almost as much distrust as worldly men? From where comes this fear? this murmuring? this worry? O my Savior, if you were to come, we could not defend ourselves for our wretched mistrust, our foolish dread, our lack of loving reliance upon you. We do not trust you as you ought to be trusted; and if this be the case among those who are such great debtors to your loving faithfulness, where will you find faith on earth? Where is that unstaggering faith that commits itself to prevailing prayer, and so rises above the petty miseries of the hour, and the fears of a threatening future?

Do you not think that this, put in a question as it is, *invites us to intense watchfulness over ourselves?* Do you not think it should set us scrutinizing ourselves as our Lord will scrutinize us when he comes? You have been looking for a great many things in yourself, my brother; let me implore you to look to your faith. What if love grows cold! I am sorry for it, but, after all, the frost must have begun in your faith. You are not so active as you used to be, and that is to be greatly regretted; but the streams run low because the wellhead is not so full as it was accustomed to being; your faith is failing. Oh, that your soul was fed upon divine realities! Oh, that you had a vivid consciousness of the certainty of God's presence and power!

When faith is strong, all the other graces are vigorous. The branches flourish when the root sucks up abundant nutrients; and when faith is in a healthy state, all the rest of the spiritual man will be vigorous also. Brethren, guard well your faith. My fear is that when Christ comes, if he delays much longer, he will find many of us faint because of our long waiting, and because of the disappointments that arise out of the slow spread of the gospel. The nations continue in unbelief. O Lord, how long? Because we have not accomplished all that we hoped to have done, we are apt to grow weary.

Or perhaps when he comes he will find us sleeping for sorrow, like the disciples in the garden when he came to them three times and found their eyes very heavy. We may get to feel so sad that the gospel does not conquer all mankind, that we may fall into a swoon of sadness, a dullness of despair, and so be asleep when the Bridegroom comes.

I fear, most of all, that when Jesus comes, he may find that the love of many has grown cold because iniquity abounds. Warmhearted saints keep each other warm, but cold also is contagious. When sin abounds, saints may be able to stand against it; and yet it has a sad tendency to chill their faith. If the Master comes and finds us lukewarm, it will be a calamity indeed. The question stirs a bitter anguish in my soul. I trust it moves you also.

It is a question. I cannot answer it, but I open wide the doors of my heart to let it enter and test me. It acts like a fan in the Lord's hand to purge the floor. It sweeps away my self-confidence and leads me to watch and pray, so that I enter not into the temptation of giving up my faith. I pray that we may stand fast when others slide, so that when the Lord comes we may be found accepted by him.

I will close with this remark: my text is very impressive in respect to personal duty. *When the Son of man cometh, shall he find faith on the earth?* Let faith have a home in *our* hearts, if it is denied a lodging everywhere else. If *we* do not trust our Lord, and trust him much more than we have ever done, we shall deserve his gravest displeasure. It will be an indulgence of naughtiness for us to doubt; for to some of us conversion was a clear, sharp, and distinct fact.

The change made in our characters was so manifest that the devil himself could not make us doubt it. We know that the misery we suffered under a sense of sin was no fiction, and that the peace we received through faith in Jesus was no dream. Why do we doubt? Since conversion some of us have been led in a strange way, and every step of it has shown us that the Lord is good and true, and ought to be trusted without limitation. We have been sorely sick, and full of pain, and anguish, and depression of spirit, and yet we have been upheld, and sustained, and brought through. In great labors we have been strengthened, in great undertakings we have been supported.

Some of you have been very poor, or your business has been declining, and emergencies have been frequent, and yet all these have proved the truth of God. Do not these things make it the more incumbent upon you to trust him? Others of you have suffered sad bereavements: you have lost, one after another, the supports of your comfort; but when you have gone to God, he has heard your prayers, and has been better to you than father, husband, or friend. It is down in your diary in black and white that his mercy endures forever; and you have said to yourself many times, "I shall never doubt again after this."

Brethren, it ought to us to be impossible to mistrust, and natural to confide; and yet I fear it is not so. If after all this watering we grow so little faith, we may not wonder that our Lord said, *When the Son of man cometh, shall he find faith on the earth?*

Some of us have been so familiar with dying beds, we have seen so many pass away in holy calm, and even with transporting triumph, that for us to doubt is disrespectful to the memories of the saints. For us to doubt would be treachery to the Lord who has favored ourselves also with visits of his love. We may doubt the dearest ones we have, and that would be cruel; but we had better do that than cast any suspicion upon him who has manifested himself to us as he does not to the world. I speak not to you all, but I speak to those whom the Lord has specially favored, to whom he has revealed his secrets, and made known his covenant; for these to question his faithfulness is wickedness.

What shall I say of his own elect, if they do not believe him? If it were possible for you to leave your faith, you would crucify your Lord afresh. He must not be thus wounded in the house of his friends. No; go where you will, O unbelief, you shall not find willing lodging in my heart. From my spirit you shall be banished as a detested traitor; for my Beloved is true, and I will lean upon him.

I think I hear you say, "We are resolved upon it; we are called to have faith in our Lord, even if no one else believes him." Then look to it that you do not fail in these evil times. If you would keep your faith, settle it in your minds that the Holy Scriptures are inspired by the Holy Spirit, and so is our infallible rule of faith. If you give up that foundation, you cannot exhibit faith worthy of the name. It is as clear as the sun in the heavens that a childlike faith in God as he is revealed is not possible for the man who doubts the revelation. You must accept the revelation as infallible, or you cannot unquestioningly believe in the God revealed in that respect. If you once give up inspiration, the foundations are removed, and all building is laborious trifling. How are the promises the support of faith if they are themselves questionable?

God can only be known by his own light, and if we cannot trust the light, where are we? Next, settle it in your soul as to the Holy Spirit's dealings with yourself. He has renewed you in the spirit of your mind. At least, I ask the question – Has he or has he not? You were converted by a divine agency from your lost estate of sin, and brought by the same divine agency into newness of life: were you or were you not?

Unless you are quite certain about this, it is not possible for you to rise to any height of faith. You must know that God has come into contact with your soul, or else what have you to believe? Next to that belief, you must know your full pardon and sure justification through the blood and righteousness of Jesus Christ your Lord.

Believe in the precious blood; whatever else you doubt, believe in the merit of the great sacrifice of Calvary. Rejoice in your own acceptance through the sacrifice, seeing your whole faith rests therein. O brothers, our eternal hopes cannot be built on speculation; we need revelation. We cannot fight the battles of life with probabilities; we need certainties for such a conflict. If God has not revealed fixed truth, you may go and think and dream; but if he has given us a clear revelation, let us believe it, and cease to imagine and invent.

O sirs, if you must speculate, risk your silver and your gold; but I beg you to lay aside all ideas of speculating in reference to your souls. I want absolute certainties and unquestionable truths to bear me up when death's cold flood is rising up to my loins.

Divine truths, as they are written in the Book and brought home to the heart by the Holy Spirit, are sure-standing ground for that faith that Jesus looks for. He looks for it in vain when men no longer accept his work as undoubted fact. Again, if you would have strong faith, never relax your confidence in the effectualness of prayer. This is essential to my text; for the widow used no other weapon than prayer in her demands with the judge. She would not have persevered as she did in her pleadings if she had not felt morally certain that in the long run she would prevail. Brethren, believe that God hears your prayers, and that he will answer them.

As for me, I do not need any argument to prove the influence of prayer with God. I have tried it, and do try it, until it is no longer an experiment. The man that habitually eats bread knows that he is nourished by it; the man that habitually lives by prayer to God knows that God hears him. It would be absurd to offer him evidence for or against the statement. If a person were to argue with me that there was no sun in the heavens, I am afraid I would laugh outright. If anyone said that he did not believe me to be alive, I do not know in what way I could prove it to him. Would it be lawful to kick him, by way of argument?

When a man says, "I do not believe in prayer," I answer, "What if you do not? You are the only loser." That God answers prayer is a living certainty to me, and I can say no more and no less. If you do not believe in prayer, assuredly the Lord will not find in you the faith of which our text speaks. If you regard it as a pious exercise that refreshes the devout but has no power whatever with God – well then, if all are of your mind, then the Son of Man will find no faith on the earth. Do not talk about believing; you know nothing of the matter.

If you do believe, believe up to the hilt. Plunge into this sea of holy confidence in God, and you shall find waters to swim in. He that believes what he believes shall see what he shall see. No man was ever yet found guilty of believing in God too much. Among the high intelligences of heaven no creature was ever rebuked for being too ready to believe when dealing with the word of the Most High. Let us believe implicitly and explicitly. Let us believe without measure and without reserve. Let us hang our all upon the truth of God. Let us aspire also to walk with God in the heavenlies, and become the King's remembrancers. Let us seek grace to become urgent pleaders of a sort that cannot be denied, since their faith overcomes heaven by prayer.

Oh, that I might have in my church many a prevailing Israel! Some here know what it is to be up early in the morning to besiege the throne of grace with all the power of believing prayer. How much I owe to these dear ones, eternity alone will declare! Oh, that we had many more intercessors, who would bear sinners on their hearts day and night, before the Lord, and, like their Savior, would never rest until the Lord built up his church!

Alas, for the rarity of such conquering faith! I question whether there are not Christian people here who have never heard a certain text that I am about to quote; and I am sure there are others who will shudder when they hear it. *Thus saith the Lord, . . . concerning the work of my hands command ye me* (Isaiah 45:11). "Surely that cannot be Scripture!" cries one. But it is so.

Turn to Isaiah 45:11, and read it both in the Authorized and the Revised Versions. Can a man command the Lord? Yes, to believing men he puts himself at their call; he bids them to command his help, and use it as they will. Oh, that we could rise to this! Is there such faith among us? If there is not, may our Lord Jesus, by his Spirit, work it in us for his own glory! Amen.

Chapter 10

A Message for the Worst Man on Earth

And the publican, standing afar off, would not lift up so much as his eyes unto heaven, but smote upon his breast, saying, God be merciful to me a sinner. (Luke 18:13)

It was the fault of the Pharisee that, though he went up into the temple to pray, he did not pray; there is no prayer in all that he said. It is one excellence of the publican that he went up to the temple to pray, and he did pray; there is nothing but prayer in all that he said. *God be merciful to me a sinner* is a pure, unadulterated prayer throughout. It was the fault of the Pharisee that when he went up to the temple to pray, he forgot an essential part of prayer, which is confession of sin. He spoke as if he had no sins to confess, but many virtues to parade.

It was a chief excellence in the devotion of the publican that he did confess his sin; alas, that his utterance was full of confession of sin: from beginning to end it was an acknowledgment of his guilt, and an appeal for grace to the merciful God. The prayer of the publican is admirable for its fullness of meaning. An expositor calls it *a holy telegram;* and certainly, it is so compact and so condensed, so free from excess words, that it is worthy to be called by that name. I do not see how he could have expressed his meaning more fully or more briefly. In the original Greek the words are even fewer than in the English. Oh, that men would learn to pray with less of language and more of meaning!

What great things are packed away in this short petition! God, mercy, sin, the atoning sacrifice, and forgiveness.

He speaks of great matters, and trifles are not thought of. He has nothing to do with fasting twice in the week, or the paying of tithes, and such second-rate things; the matters he expounds are of a higher order. His trembling heart moves among staggering things that overcome him, and he speaks in tones consistent with that. He deals with the greatest things that can ever be: he pleads for his life, his soul. Where could he find themes more weighty, more vital to his eternal interests? He is not playing at prayer, but pleading in awful earnest.

His prayer prospered well with God, and he speedily won his suit with heaven. Mercy granted to him full justification. The prayer so pleased the Lord Jesus Christ, who heard it, that he stooped to become a portrait painter, and took a sketch of the petitioner. I say the prayer in itself was so pleasing to the gracious Savior that he tells us how it was offered: *Standing afar off, [he] would not lift up so much as his eyes unto heaven, but smote upon his breast.* Luke, who, according to tradition, was somewhat of an artist as well as a physician, takes great care to place this picture in the national portrait gallery of men saved by sovereign grace.

Here we have the portrait of a man who called himself *the* sinner, who may yet be held up as a pattern to saints. I am glad to have the divine sketch of this man, that I may see the bodily form of his devotion. I am gladder still to have his prayer, that we may look into the very soul of his pleading. My heart's desire this morning is that many here may seek the mercy of the Lord as this publican did, and go down to their houses justified. I ask no man to use the same words. Let no man attach a superstitious value to them.

Alas, this prayer has been used flippantly, and foolishly, and almost looked upon as a sort of charm! Some have said, "We may live as we like, for we have only to say, 'God be merciful to me' when we are dying, and all will be well."

This is a wicked misuse of gospel truth; yes, it turns it into a lie. If you choose thus to pervert the grace of the gospel to your own destruction, your blood must be on your own heads. You may not have space given you in which to breathe out even this brief sentence; or if you have, the words may not come from your heart, and so you may die in your sins.

I pray you, do not thus presume upon the patience of God. But if with the publican's heart we can take the publican's attitude, if with the publican's spirit we can use the publican's words, then there will follow a gracious acceptance, and we shall go home justified. If such be the case, there will be grand times today, for angels will rejoice over sinners reconciled to God and made to know in their own souls the boundless mercy of the Lord.

In preaching upon the text, I shall endeavor to bring out its innermost spirit. May we be taught of the Spirit, so that we may learn four lessons from it!

The first is this – the fact of sinnership is no reason for despair. None of you need to say, "I am guilty, and therefore I may not approach God; I am so greatly guilty that it would be too daring a thing for me to ask for mercy." Dismiss such thoughts at once. My text and a thousand other arguments forbid despair.

For, first, *this man who was a sinner still dared to approach the Lord.* According to our version, he said, *God be merciful to me **a** sinner* (emphasis added), but a more accurate rendering is that which the Revised Version puts in the margin – "*the* sinner." He meant to say that he was emphatically *the* sinner. The Pharisee yonder was *the* saint of his age, but this publican who stood afar off from the holy place was *the* sinner. If there was not another sinner in the world, he was one; and in a world of sinners he was a prominent offender – the sinner of sinners. Emphatically he applies to himself the guilty name. He takes the chief place in condemnation, and yet he cries, "God be merciful to me *the* sinner."

Now, if you know yourself to be a sinner, you may plead with God; but if you mourn that you are not only a sinner, but also *the* sinner, with the definite article, the sinner above all others, you may still hope in the mercy of the Lord. The worst, the most profane, the most horrible of sinners may venture, as this man did, to approach the God of mercy. I know that it looks like a daring action; therefore you must do it by faith. On any other footing but that of faith in the mercy of God, you who are a sinner may not dare to approach the Lord lest you be found guilty of presumption.

But with your eye on mercy you may be bravely trustful. Believe in the great mercy of God, and though your sins be abundant, you will find that the Lord will abundantly pardon; though they blot your character, the Lord will blot them out; though they be red like crimson, yet the precious blood of Jesus will make you whiter than snow.

This story of the Pharisee and the publican is intended as an encouraging example to you. If this man who was *the* sinner found forgiveness, so also shall you if you seek it in the same way. One sinner has succeeded so well, why should not you? Come and try for yourself, and see if the Lord does not prove in your case that his mercy endures forever.

Next, remember that you may not only find encouragement in looking at the sinner who sought his God, but also in the God whom he sought. Sinner, *there is great mercy in the heart of God.* How often did that verse ring out as a chorus in the temple song –

> For his mercy shall endure
> Ever faithful, ever sure!

Mercy is an especially glorious attribute of Jehovah, the living God. He is *the Lord God, merciful and gracious* (Exodus 34:6). He is *slow to anger, and plenteous in mercy* (Psalm 103:8). Do you not see how this should cheer you? Sinners are needful if mercy is to be indulged. How can the Lord display his mercy except to the guilty? Goodness is for creatures, but mercy is for sinners. Towards unfallen creatures there may be love, but there cannot be mercy. Angels are not suitable recipients of mercy; they do not require it, for they have not transgressed.

Mercy comes into exercise after the law has been broken, and not until then. Among the attributes it is the last that found an object for itself. So to speak, it is the Benjamin, and the darling attribute of God: *He delighteth in mercy* (Micah 7:18). Only to a sinner can God be merciful. Do you hear this, you sinner? Be sure that you catch it! If there be boundless mercy in the heart of God, and it can only exercise itself towards the guilty, then you are the man to have it, for you are a guilty one. Come, then, and let his mercy wrap around you like a garment this day, and cover all your shame. Does not God's delight in mercy prove that sinnership is no reason for despair?

Moreover, *the conception of salvation implies hope for sinners.* That salvation that we preach to you every day is glad tidings for the guilty.

Salvation by grace implies that men are guilty. Salvation means not the reward of the righteous, but the cleansing of the unrighteous. Salvation is meant for the lost, the ruined, and the undone; and the blessings that it brings of pardoning mercy and cleansing grace must be intended for the guilty and the polluted. *They that are whole need not a physician* (Luke 5:31); the physician has his eye upon the sick. Charity is for the poor, bread is for the hungry, pardon is for the guilty.

O you who are guilty, you are the men whom mercy seeks after! You were in God's eye when he sent his Son into the world to save sinners. From the very first inception of redemption to the completion of it, the eyes of the great God were set on the guilty, and not on the deserving. The very name of Jesus tells us that *he shall save his people from their sins* (Matthew 1:21).

Let me further say, that inasmuch as that salvation of God is a great one, it must have been intended to meet great sins. O sirs, would Christ have shed the blood of his heart for some trifling, forgivable sins that your tears could wash away? Do you think God would have given his dear Son to die as a mere luxury?

If sin had been a small matter, a little sacrifice would have sufficed. Do you think that the divine atonement was made only for small offenses? Did Jesus die for little sins, and leave the great ones unatoned for? No, the Lord God measured the greatness of our sin, and found it as high as heaven, as deep as hell, and as broad as the infinite, and therefore he gave so great a Savior.

He gave his only begotten Son, an infinite sacrifice, an unmeasurable atonement. With such throes and pangs of death as never can be fully described, the Lord Jesus poured out his soul in unknown sufferings, that he might provide a great salvation for the greatest of sinners. See Jesus on the cross, and learn that *all manner of sin and of blasphemy shall be forgiven unto men* (Matthew 12:31).

The fact of salvation, and of a great salvation, ought to drive away the very notion of despair from every heart that hears of it. Salvation – that is for me, for I am lost. A great salvation – that is for me, for I am the greatest of sinners. Oh, hear my word this day! It is God's word of love, and it rings out like a silver bell. O my beloved friends, I weep over you, and yet I feel like singing all the time, for I am sent to proclaim salvation from the Lord for the very worst of you.

The gospel is especially, definitely, and distinctly addressed to sinners. Listen to it: *This is a faithful saying, and worthy of all acceptation, that Christ Jesus came into the world to save sinners; of whom I am chief* (1 Timothy 1:15). *I am not come to call the righteous, but sinners to repentance* (Matthew 9:13). *The Son of Man is come to seek and to save that which was lost* (Luke 19:10).

The gospel is like a letter directed in a clear and legible hand; and if you will read its direction, you will find that it runs thus: "To the sinner." O sinners, to you is the word of this salvation sent. If you are a sinner, you are the very man for whom the gospel is intended; and I do not mean by this a merely complimentary nominal sinner, but an out-and-out rebel, a transgressor against God and man. O sinner, seize upon the gospel with joyful willingness, and cry unto God for mercy at once!

'Twas for *sinners* that he suffer'd
   Agonies unspeakable;
Canst thou doubt thou art a sinner?
   If thou canst – then hope, farewell.

But, believing what is written –
   "All are guilty" – "dead in sin,"
Looking to the Crucified One,
   Hope shall rise thy soul within.

If you will think of it again, there must be hope for sinners, for *the great commands of the gospel are most suitable to sinners.* Hear, for instance, this word: *Repent ye therefore, and be converted, that your sins may be blotted out* (Acts 3:19). Who can repent but the guilty? Who can be converted but those who are on the wrong track and therefore need to be turned?

The following text is evidently addressed to those who are good for nothing: *Let the wicked forsake his way, and the unrighteous man his thoughts: and let him return unto the Lord, and he will have mercy upon him; and to our God, for he will abundantly pardon* (Isaiah 55:7). The very word *repent* indicates that it is addressed to those who have sinned; let it beckon you to mercy.

Then you are bidden to believe in the Lord Jesus Christ. Now, salvation by faith must be for guilty men; for the way of life for the innocent is by perseverance in good works. The law says, *This do, and thou shalt live* (Luke 10:28). The gospel talks of salvation by believing, because it is the only way possible for those who have broken the law and are condemned by it. Salvation is of faith so that it might be by grace. Believe and live! Believe and live! Believe and live! This is the jubilee note of the trumpet of free grace. Oh, that you would know the joyful sound, and thus be blessed! Oh, that you who are sinful would hear the call as addressed to you in particular! You are up to your necks in the mire of sin, but a mighty hand is stretched out to deliver you. *Repent ye, and believe the gospel* (Mark 1:15).

If you want any other argument – and I hope you do not – I would put it thus: *Great sinners have been saved.* All sorts of sinners are being saved today. What wonders some of us have seen! What wonders have been worked in this tabernacle! A man was heard at a prayer meeting pleading in louder tones than usual; he was a sailor, and his voice was pitched to the tune of the roaring billows. A lady whispered to her friend, "Is that Captain F?"

"Yes," said the other, "why do you ask?"

"Because," said she, "the last time I heard that voice, its swearing made my blood run cold; the man's oaths were beyond measure terrible. Can it be the same man?"

Someone observed, "Go and ask him."

The lady timidly said, "Are you the same Captain F that I heard swearing in the street, outside my house?"

"Well," he said, "I am the same person, and yet, thank God, I am not the same!" O brethren, *such were some of [us]: but [we] are washed, but [we] are sanctified* (1 Corinthians 6:11)! Wonders of grace to God belong. I was reading the other day a story of an old shepherd who had never attended a place of worship; but when he had grown gray, and was near to dying, he was drawn by curiosity into the Methodist chapel, and all was new to him. Hard-hearted old fellow as he was, he was seen to have shed tears during the sermon. He had obtained a glimpse of hope. He saw that there was mercy even for him. He laid hold on eternal life at once.

The surprise was great when he was seen at the chapel, and greater still when, on the Monday night, he was seen at the prayer meeting; yes, and heard at the prayer meeting, for he fell down on his knees and praised God that he had found mercy. Do you wonder that the Methodists shouted, "Bless the Lord"? Wherever Christ is preached, the most wicked of men and women are made to sit at the Savior's feet, *clothed, and in [their] right mind[s]* (Mark 5:15). My friend, why should it not be so with you? At any rate, we have full proof of the fact that sinnership is no reason for despair.

I must now advance to my second observation: A sense of sinnership confers no right to mercy. You will wonder why I mention this self-evident truth, but I must mention it because of a common error that does great mischief. This man was very conscious of his sin insomuch that he called himself "the sinner"; but he did not declare his sense of sin as any reason why he should find mercy. There is an ingenuity in the heart of man, nothing less than devilish, by which he will, if he can, turn the gospel itself into a yoke of bondage.

If we preach to sinners that they may come to Christ in all their anguish and misery, one cries, "I do not feel myself to be a sinner as I ought to feel it. I have not felt those convictions of which you speak, and therefore, I cannot come to Jesus." This is a horrible twist of our meaning. We never meant to insinuate that convictions and doubts and despondencies conferred upon men a claim to mercy and were necessary preparations for grace. I want you, therefore, to learn that a sense of sin gives no man a right to grace.

If a deep sense of sin entitled men to mercy, *it would be a turning of this parable upside down.* Do you dream that this publican was, after all, a Pharisee differently dressed? Do you imagine that he really meant to plead, "God be merciful to me because I am humble and lowly"? Did he say in his heart, "Lord, have mercy upon me because I am not a Pharisee, and am deeply despondent on account of my evil ways"? This would prove that he was in his heart of hearts a Pharisee.

If you make a righteousness out of your feelings, you are just as much out of the true way as if you made a righteousness out of your works. Whether it be work or feeling, anything that is relied upon as a claim for grace is an antichrist. You are no more to be saved because of your conscious miseries than because of your conscious merits; there is no virtue either in the one or in the other. If you make a Savior of convictions, you will be lost as surely as if you made a Savior out of ceremonies. The publican trusted in divine mercy and not in his own convictions, and you must do the same.

To imagine that an awful sense of sin constituted a claim upon mercy would be *like giving a premium to great sin*. Certain seekers think, "I have never been a drunkard, or a swearer, or impure, and I almost wish I had been, that I might feel myself to be the chief of sinners, and so might come to Jesus." Do not wish anything so atrocious; there is no good in sin in any shape or way. Thank God if you have been kept from the grosser forms of vice. Do not imagine that repentance is easier when sin is grosser: the reverse is true. Do believe that there is no advantage in having been a horrible offender. You have sins enough; to be worse would not be better.

If good works do not help you, certainly bad works would not. You that have been moral and excellent should cry for mercy, and not be so silly as to dream that greater sins would help you to readier repentance. Come as you are, and if your heart be hard, confess it as one of your greatest sins. A deeper sense of sin would not entitle you to the mercy of God; you can have no title to mercy but that which mercy gives you. Could your tears forever flow, could your grief no respite know, you would have no claim upon the sovereign grace of God, who will have mercy on whom he will have mercy.

Then, dear friends, remember, if we begin to preach to sinners that they must have a certain sense of sin and a certain measure of conviction, *such teaching would turn the sinner away from God in Christ to himself.* The man begins at once to say, "Have I a broken heart? Do I feel the burden of sin?" This is only another form of looking to self. Man must not look to himself to find reasons for God's grace. The remedy does not lie in the seat of the disease, it lies in the physician's hand. A sense of sin is not a claim, but a gift of that blessed Savior who is exalted on high to give repentance and remission of sins.

Beware of any teaching that makes you look to yourself for help, but cling to that doctrine that makes you look alone to Christ. Whether you know it or not, you are a lost, ruined sinner, only fit to be cast into the flames of hell forever. Confess this, but do not ask to be driven mad by a sense of it. Come to Jesus just as you are, and do not wait for a preparation made out of your own miseries. Look to Jesus, and to him alone.

If we fall into the notion that a certain sense of sin has a claim upon God, *we shall be putting salvation upon other grounds than that of faith*, and that must be a false ground. Now, the ground of salvation is – *God so loved the world, that he gave his only begotten Son, that whosoever believeth in him should not perish, but have everlasting life* (John 3:16).

A simple faith in the Lord Jesus Christ is the way of salvation; but to say, "I shall be saved because I am horribly convicted of sin, and driven to desperation," is not to speak like the gospel, but to rave out of the pride of an unbelieving heart. The gospel is that you believe in Christ Jesus, that you get right out of yourself, and depend alone on him.

Do you say, "I feel so guilty"? You are certainly guilty, whether you feel it or not; and you are far more guilty than you have any idea of. Come to Christ because you are guilty, not because you have been prepared to come by looking at your guilt. Trust nothing of your own, not even your sense of need. A man may have a sense of disease a long time before he will get healing out of it.

The looking glass of conviction reveals the spots on our face, but it cannot wash them away. You cannot fill your hands by putting them into your empty pocket and feeling how empty it is; it would be far wiser to hold them out and receive the gold that your friend so freely gives you. *God be merciful to me a sinner* is the right way to put it, and not, "God be merciful to me because I sufficiently feel my sinnership, and most fittingly bemoan it."

My third observation is this: The knowledge of their sinnership guides men to right action. When a man has learned from the Holy Spirit that he is a sinner, then by a kind of instinct of the new life, he does the right thing in the right way. This publican had not often been to the temple, and had not learned the orthodox way of behaving. It is easy to learn how we all do it nowadays in our temples – take off your hat, hold it in front of your face, and read the maker's name and address. Then sit down, and at the proper moment, bend forward and cover your eyes, and furthermore, stand up when the rest of the congregation does so. People get to do this just as if they were wound up by machinery; yet they do not pray when they are supposed to be praying, nor bow before the Lord when worship is being offered.

This publican is out of rank; he does not follow the rule of conduct; he has gestures of his own. First, instead of coming forward he stands afar off. He does not dare to come where that most respectable person, the Pharisee, is displaying himself, for he does not feel worthy. He leaves space between himself and God, an opening for a Mediator, room for an Advocate, place for an Intercessor to intercede between himself and the throne of the Most High. Wise man is he therefore to stand afar off, for by this means he could safely draw near in the person of Jesus. Furthermore, he would not lift so much as his eyes unto heaven. It seems natural to lift up your hands in prayer, but he would not even lift his eyes.

The uplifting of the eyes is very proper, is it not? But it was still more proper for "the sinner" not to lift his eyes. His downcast eyes meant much. Our Lord does not say that he *could* not lift up his eyes, but that he *would* not. He could look up, for he did in spirit look up as he cried, *God be merciful to me;* but he would not, because it seemed improper for eyes like his to peer into the heavens where dwells the holy God. In the meanwhile, the repentant publican kept striking his breast. The original does not say that he struck his breast once, but he struck and struck again. It was a continuous act. He seemed to say, "Oh, this wicked heart!" And he would strike it.

Again and again he expressed his intense grief by this Oriental gesture, for he did not know how else to set forth his sorrow. His heart had sinned, and he struck it; his eyes had led him astray, and he made them look down to the earth; and as he himself had sinned by living far off from God, he banished himself far from the manifest Presence. Every gesture and posture is significant, and yet all came spontaneously. He had no book of directions on how to behave himself in the house of God; his sincerity guided him. If you want to know how to behave yourselves as repentant ones, be repentant ones. The best rules of conduct of worship are those that are written on broken hearts.

I have heard of a minister who was said to cry in the wrong place in his sermons, and it was found afterwards that he had written in the margin of his manuscript: "Weep here." His audience could not see the reason for his artificial moisture. It must have had a ludicrous effect. In religion everything artificial is ridiculous, or worse; but grace in the heart is the best "master of ceremonies." He who prays correctly with his heart will not err much with foot, and hand, and head. If you would know how to approach God, confess yourself a sinner, and so take your true place before the God of truth. Throw yourself on divine mercy, and thus place God in his true position as your judge and Lord.

Observe that this man, even under the weight of conscious sin, was led correctly; for *he went straightaway to God.* A sense of sin without faith drives us from God, but a sense of sin with faith draws us immediately to God. He came to God alone; he felt that it would be of no benefit to confess his fault to a mortal, or to look for forgiveness from man. He did not resort to the priest of the temple, but to the God of the temple. He did not ask to speak to the good and learned man, the Pharisee, who stood on the same floor with him. His inquiry room was the secret of his own soul, and he inquired of the Lord. He ran straightaway to God, who alone was able to help; and when he opened his mouth, it was, *God be merciful to me a sinner.*

That is what you have to do, my dear friend, if you would be saved: you must go distinctly and immediately to God in Christ Jesus. Forget all things else, and say, with the returning prodigal, *I will arise and go to my father.* None but God can help us out of our low estate. No mercy but the mercy of God can serve our purpose, and none can give us *that* mercy but the God of mercy. Let every broken-down sinner come to his God, whom he has offended.

The publican did not look around on his fellow worshippers; he was too much absorbed in his own grief of heart. Specially is it noteworthy that he had no remarks to make upon the Pharisee. He did not denounce the pride, or the hypocrisy, or the hard-heartedness of the professor who so offensively looked down upon him. He did not return contempt for contempt, as we are all too apt to do. No; he dealt with the Lord alone in the deep sincerity of his own heart, and it was well. My friend, when will you do the same? When will you cease to rebuke others, and reserve your severity for yourself, and your critical observations for your own conduct?

When he came to God it was *with a full confession of sin – God be merciful to me a sinner.* His very eyes and hands joined with his lips in acknowledging his iniquities. His prayer was wet with the dew of repentance.

He poured out his heart before God in the most free and artless manner; his prayer came from the same fountain as that of the prodigal when he said, *Father, I have sinned,* and that of David when he cried, *Against thee, thee only, have I sinned, and done this evil in thy sight* (Psalm 51:4). The best praying is that which comes from the lowliest heart.

Then he appealed to mercy only. This was wise. See how rightly he was guided. What had he to do with justice, since it could only condemn and destroy him? Like a naked sword, it threatens to sheathe itself in my heart; how can I appeal to justice? Neither power nor wisdom, nor any other quality of the great God could be resorted to; only mercy stretched out her wing. The prayer, *God be merciful,* is the only prayer that you can pray who have been greatly guilty. If all your lives you have spurned your Savior, all you can do now is to cast yourselves upon the mercy of God.

The original Greek permits us to see that this man had an eye to the atonement. I do not say that he fully understood the doctrine of atonement, but still his prayer was: "God be appeased to me the sinner." He had seen the morning and the evening lamb, and he had heard of the sin offering; and though he might not have known all about atonement, pardon, and substitution, yet as far as he did know, his eye was turned that way. "O God, be appeased, accept a sacrifice, and pardon me."

If you know your sin, you will be wise to plead the atonement that God has set forth for human sin. May the Spirit of God constrain you to trust in Jesus now! The new year is already gliding away; its second month is slipping from under us; how many months are to go before you, a guilty sinner, will come and ask mercy of God, the infinitely gracious One? Great God, let this day be the day of your power!

I now close with my last topic, which is this – The believing confession of sinnership is the way of peace. *God be merciful to me a sinner* was the prayer, but what was the answer? Listen to this: *This man went down to his house justified rather than the other* (Luke 18:14).

In a few sentences let me sketch this man's progress. He came to God only as a sinner, nakedly as a sinner. Observe that he did not say, "God be merciful to me a *repentant* sinner." He was a repentant sinner, but he did not plead his repentance; and if you are ever so repentant and convinced of sin, do not mention it as an argument, lest you be accused of self-righteousness.

Come as you are, as a sinner, and as nothing else. Exhibit your wounds. Bring your spiritual poverty before God, and not your supposed wealth. If you have a single penny of your own, get rid of it. Perfect poverty alone will discharge you from your bankruptcy. If you have a moldy crust in the cupboard of self-righteousness, no bread from heaven will be yours. You must be nothing and nobody if God is to be your all in all.

This man does not cry, "God be merciful to me the repentant one," but "*Be merciful to me a sinner.*" He does not even say, "God be merciful to me the *reformed* sinner." I have no doubt he did reform and give up his evil ways, but he does not plead that reformation. Reformation will not take away your sinnership; therefore, do not speak as if it could do so. What you are to be will make no atonement for what you have been. Come, therefore, simply as a sinner, not as a changed and improved sinner. Do not come because you *are* washed, but to be washed!

The publican does not say, "God be merciful to me a *praying* sinner." He was praying, but he does not mention it as a plea, for he thought very little of his own prayers. Do not plead your prayers; you might as well plead your sins. God knows that your prayers have sin in them.

Why, man, your very tears of repentance need washing! When your prayers are most sincere, what are they but the wailings of a condemned creature who cannot give a single reason why he should not be executed. Feel and admit that you deserve condemnation, and come to God as a sinner. Off with your despicable finery; I mean your *filthy rags* (Isaiah 64:6). Do not trick yourself out in the weeds of your own repentance, much less in the fig leaves of your own resolutions, but come to God in Christ Jesus in all the nakedness of your sin, and everlasting mercy will cover both you and your sins.

Next, notice that this man did nothing but appeal to mercy. He said, *God be merciful to me.* He did not attempt to excuse himself, and say, "Lord, I could not help it. Lord, I was not worse than other publicans. Lord, I was a public servant, and only did what every other tax collector did." No, no, he is too honest to forge excuses. He is a sinner, and he admits it. If the Lord should condemn him out of his own mouth, and send him to hell, he cannot help it; his sin is too evident to be denied. He lays his head on the block, and humbly pleads, *God be merciful to me a sinner.*

Neither does this publican offer any *promises* of future correction as a compensation. He does not say, "Lord, be merciful for the past, and I will be better in the future." Nothing of the sort; *be merciful to me a sinner* is his one and only request.

So would I have you cry, "O God, be merciful to me! Although I am even now condemned, and deserve to be hopelessly damned by your justice, yet have mercy upon me, have mercy on me now." That is the way to pray; and if you pray in that way God will hear you. He does not offer to *pay* anything; he does not propose any form of self-paid ransom; he does not present to God his tears, his abstinence, his self-denial, his generosity to the church, his liberality to the poor, or anything else, but he simply begs the Lord to be appeased, and to be merciful to him because of the great sacrifice. Oh, that all of you would at once pray in this fashion!

Now, I want to cheer your hearts by noticing that this man, through this prayer and through this confession of sin, experienced a remarkable degree of acceptance. He had come up to the temple condemned; he *went down to his house justified.* A complete change, a sudden change, a happy change was worked upon him. Heavy heart and downcast eyes were exchanged for glad heart and hopeful outlook. He came into that temple with trembling, he left it with rejoicing. I am sure his wife noticed the difference. What had come over him? The children began to observe it also. Poor father used to sit alone, and heave many a sigh; but all of a sudden he is so happy; he even sings psalms of David out of the latter end of the book. The change was very marked.

Before dinner he says, "Children, we must give God thanks before we eat this meal." They gather around and wonder at dear father's happy face as he blesses the God of Israel. He says to his friends, "Brethren, I am comforted; God has had mercy upon me. I went to the temple guilty, but I have returned justified. My sins are all forgiven me. God has accepted an appeasement on my behalf." What good would come of such a happy testimony! This was a very sudden change, was it not? It was effected in a moment.

The process of spiritual reviving is not a matter of hours, but of a single second of time. The processes that lead up to it, and spring out of it, are long, but the actual reception of life must be instantaneous.

Not in every case would you be able to put your finger upon that second of time, but the passage from death unto life must be instantaneous.

There must be a moment in which the man is dead, and another moment in which he is alive. I grant you, life would be very feeble at first; still, there must be a time in which it was not there at all; and again, there must have been an instant in which it begins. There can be no middle condition between dead and alive. Yet a man may not know *when* the change took place.

If you were going to the Cape you might cross the equator at dead of night, and know nothing about it, but still you would cross it. Some poor landsmen have thought that they would see a blue line right across the waves; but it is not perceptible, although it is truly there. The equator is quite as real as if we could see a golden belt around the globe. Dear friends, I want you to cross the line this morning! Oh, that you might go out of this house saying, "Glory, glory, hallelujah! God has had mercy upon me." Though you feel this morning that you would not give twopence for your life, yet if you come to God through Jesus Christ, you shall go away blessing God not only that you are alive, but also that you shall live forever, happy in his love.

Once more, this man went away with a witness such as I pray we may all have. He was justified. "But," you add, "how do I know he was justified?" Listen to these words. Our blessed Lord says, **I tell you,** *this man went down to his house justified rather than the other* (emphasis added). *I tell you.* Jesus, our Lord, can tell. Into our ear he tells it. He tells it to God and the holy angels, and he tells it to the man himself. The man who has cried from his heart, *God be merciful to me a sinner* is a justified man. When he stood and confessed his sin, and cast himself wholly upon the divine mercy, that man was unburdened, so that he went down to his house justified.

We are all going down to our houses. Oh, that we might go down justified! You are going home; I want you to go home to God, who is the true home of the soul. *[He] went down to his house justified,* and why should you not do the same? Perhaps, my hearer, you have never been to the tabernacle before. Possibly, my friend, you are one of those gentlemen who spend Sunday mornings in their shirtsleeves at home reading the weekly paper. You have come here this morning quite by accident. Blessed be God! I hope you will go home justified. The Lord grant it!

Perhaps you always come here, and have occupied a seat ever since the tabernacle was built, and yet you have never found mercy. Oh, that you might find mercy this morning! Let us seek this blessing. Come with me to Jesus. I will lead the way. I pray you say with me this morning – *God be merciful to me a sinner.* Rest on the great atonement: trust in Jesus Christ's atoning blood. Cast yourself upon the Savior's love, and you shall go down to your house justified. Is it a poor cottage? Is it less than that – a back room up three pairs of stairs? Are you very, very poor, and have you been out of work for a long time?

Never mind. God knows all. Seek his face. It will be a happy Sunday for you if you this day begin a new life by faith in Jesus. You shall have joy, peace, and happiness if you seek and find mercy from the great Father. I think I see you trudging home, having left your load behind you, but embraced with songs of praise unto our God. So be it. Amen and Amen.

Chapter 11

Confession and Absolution

And the publican, standing afar off, would not lift up so much as his eyes unto heaven, but smote upon his breast, saying, God be merciful to me a sinner. (Luke 18:13)

Most of the heroes of our Savior's stories are selected to illustrate traits of character entirely dissimilar to their general reputation. What would you think of a moral writer of our own day, should he endeavor in a work of fiction, to set before us the gentle virtue of benevolence by the example of a Sepoy (a native of India employed as a soldier by a European power)? And yet, Jesus Christ has given us one of the finest examples of charity in the case of a Samaritan. To the Jews, a Samaritan was as proverbial for his bitter animosity against their nation as the Sepoy is among us for his treacherous cruelty, and as much an object of contempt and hatred; but Jesus Christ, nevertheless, chose his hero from the Samaritans, that there should be nothing external to adorn him, but that all the adorning might be given to the grace of charity.

Thus, too, in the present instance, our Savior, being desirous of setting before us the necessity of humiliation in prayer, has not selected some distinguished saint who was famed for his humility, but he has chosen a tax gatherer, probably one of the most extortionate of his class, for the Pharisee seems to hint as much; and I doubt not he cast his eye scornfully at this publican when he observed, with self-gratulation, *God, I thank thee, that I am not as other men are, extortioners, unjust, adulterers, or even as this publican* (Luke 18:11). Still, our Lord, in order that we might see that there was nothing to predispose in the person, but that the acceptance of the prayer might stand out, set even in a brighter light by the black foil of the publican's character, has selected this man to be the pattern and model of one who should offer an acceptable prayer unto God.

Note that, and you will not be surprised to find the same characteristic exhibited very frequently in the parables of our Lord Jesus Christ. As for this publican, we know but little of his previous career, but we may, without risking any serious error, conjecture somewhat near the truth. He may have been, and doubtless he was a Jew, piously brought up and religiously trained, but, perhaps like Levi, he ran away from his parents, and finding no other trade exactly suited to his vicious taste, he became one of that corrupt class who collected the Roman taxes, and, ashamed to be known as Levi any longer, he changed his name to Matthew, lest anyone should recognize in the degraded cast of the publican, the man whose parents feared God and bowed their knees before the Lord. It may be that this publican had in his youth forsaken the ways of his fathers, and given himself up to lasciviousness, and then found this unworthy occupation to be most compatible with his vicious spirit. We cannot tell how often he had ground the faces of the poor, or how many curses had been spilled upon his head when he had broken into the heritage of the widow and had robbed the friendless, unprotected orphan.

The Roman government gave a publican far greater power than he ought to have possessed, and he was never slow to use the advantage for his own enrichment. Probably half of all he had was a robbery, if not more, for Zacchaeus seems to hint as much in his own instance, when he says, *Behold, Lord, the half of my goods I give to the poor; and if I have taken any thing from any man by false accusation, I restore him fourfold* (Luke 19:8). It was not often that this publican troubled the temple. The priests very seldom saw him coming with a sacrifice; it would have been an abomination, and he did not bring it.

But so it happened, that the Spirit of the Lord met with the publican, and made him think upon his ways, and their peculiar wickedness. He was full of trouble, but he kept it to himself, pent up in his own bosom; he could scarcely rest at night, nor go about his business by day, for day and night the hand of God was heavy upon him. At last, unable to endure his misery any longer, he thought of that house of God at Zion, and of the sacrifice that was daily offered there. "To whom, or where should I go," said he, "but to God? And where can I hope to find mercy, but where the sacrifice is offered?" No sooner said than done, he went; his unaccustomed feet bent their steps to the sanctuary, but he was ashamed to enter.

Yonder Pharisee, holy man as he appeared to be, goes up unblushingly to the court of the Israelites. He goes as near as he dares to the very precincts, within which the priesthood alone might stand, and he prays with boastful language.

But as for the publican, he chooses for himself some secluded corner where he shall neither be seen nor heard. And now he is about to pray, not with uplifted hands as yonder Pharisee, not with eyes turned up to heaven with a holy gaze of hypocrisy, but fixing his eyes upon the ground, the hot tears streaming from them, not daring to lift them up to heaven. At last his stifled feelings found utterance; yet that utterance was a groan, a short prayer that must all be comprehended in the scope of a sigh: *God be merciful to me a sinner.* It is done; he is heard; the angel of mercy registers his pardon; his conscience is at peace; he goes down to his house a happy man, justified rather than the Pharisee, and rejoicing in the justification that the Lord has given to him.

Well then, my business this morning is to invite, to urge, to plead with you to do what the publican did, so that you may receive what he obtained. There are two particulars upon which I shall endeavor to speak solemnly and earnestly: the first is *confession*; the second is *absolution*.

Brethren, let us imitate the publican, first of all in his confession. There has been a great deal of public excitement during the last few weeks and months about the confessional (a place where a priest hears confessions). As for that matter, it is perhaps a mercy that the outward and visible sign of Roman Catholicism in the Church of England has discovered to its sincere friends the inward and spiritual evil that had long been lurking there. We need not imagine that the confessional, or priestcraft, of which it is merely an offshoot, in the Church of England is any novelty: it has long been there. Those of us who are outside her borders have long observed and mourned over it, but now we congratulate ourselves on the prospect that the Church of England herself will be compelled to discover her own evils; and we hope that God may give her grace and strength to cut the cancer out of her own breast before she shall cease to be a Protestant church, and God shall cast her away as a despised thing.

This morning, however, I have nothing to do with the confessional. Silly women may go on confessing as long as they like, and foolish husbands may trust their wives, if they please, to such men as those. Let those that are fools show it; let those that have no sense do as they please about it; but as for myself, I should take the greatest care that neither I nor mine have anything to do with such things. Leaving that, however, we come to personal matters, endeavoring to learn, even from the errors of others, how to act rightly ourselves.

Note the publican's confession; *to whom was it presented? God be merciful to me a sinner.* Did the publican ever think about going to the priest to ask for mercy, and confessing his sins? The thought may have crossed his mind, but his sin was too great a weight upon his conscience to be relieved in any such way, so he very soon dismissed the idea. "No," says he, "I feel that my sin is of such a character that none but God can take it away; and even if it were right for me to go and make the confession to my fellow creature, yet I should think it must be utterly unhelpful in my case, for my disease is of such a nature that none but an almighty Physician ever can remove it." So, he directs his confession and his prayer to one place, and to one alone – *God be merciful to me a sinner.*

And you will note in this confession to God that it was *secret.* All that you can hear of his confession is just those two words – *a sinner.* Do you suppose that was all he confessed? No, beloved, I believe that long before this, the publican had made a confession of all his sins privately, upon his knees in his own house before God. But now, in God's house, all he has to say for man to hear is, "I am a sinner."

And I counsel you, if ever you make a confession before man, let it be a general one but never a particular one. You ought to confess often to your fellow creatures that you have been a sinner, but to tell any man in what respect you have been a sinner is but to sin over again, and to help your fellow creature to transgress. How filthy must be the soul of that priest who makes his ear a common sewer for the filth of other men's hearts. I cannot imagine even the devil to be more depraved than the man who spends his time in sitting with his ear against the lips of men and women who, if they do truly confess, must make him an expert in every sin, and school him in iniquities that he otherwise never could have known.

Oh, I charge you, never pollute your fellow creature; keep your sin to yourself, and to your God, for he cannot be polluted by your iniquity. Make a plain and full confession of it before him; but to your fellow creature, add nothing to the general confession – "I am a sinner!"

This confession that he made before God was *spontaneous*. There was no question put to this man as to whether he was a sinner or not, or as to whether he had broken the seventh commandment, or the eighth, or the ninth, or the tenth. No, his heart was full of repentance, and it melted out in this breathing – *God be merciful to me a sinner.*

They tell us that some people never can make a full confession unless a priest helps them by questions. My dear friends, the very excellence of repentance is lost, and its spell is broken, if there be a question asked. The confession is not true and real unless it be spontaneous. The man cannot have felt the weight of sin who wants somebody to tell him what his sins are. Can you imagine any man with a burden on his back who, before he groaned under it, wanted to be told that he had one there? Surely not. The man groans under it, and he does not want to be told, "There it is on your back"; he knows it is there. And if, by the questioning of a priest, a full and thorough confession could be drawn from any man or woman, it would be totally useless, totally vain before God, because it is not spontaneous.

We must confess our sins because we cannot help confessing them. It must come out because we cannot keep it in. Like fire in the bones, it seems as if it would melt our very spirits unless we gave vent to the groaning of our confession before the throne of God. See this publican; you cannot hear the humble, full confession that he makes; but what you can hear is his simple acknowledgement that he is a sinner, and that comes spontaneously from his lips. God himself does not have to ask him the question, but he comes before the throne, and freely surrenders himself up to the hands of almighty justice, confessing that he is a rebel and a sinner. That is the first thing we have to note in his confession – that he made it to God secretly and spontaneously; and all he said openly was that he was *a sinner.*

Again, *what did he confess?* He confessed, as our text tells us, that he was sinner. Now, how suitable is this prayer for us! For are there lips present here that this confession will not suit – *God be merciful to me a sinner?* Do you say, "The prayer will suit the harlot, when, after a life of sin, rottenness is in her bones, and she is dying in despair – that prayer suits her lips"?

Alas, but my friend, it will suit your lips and mine too. If you know your heart, and I know mine, the prayer that will suit her will suit us also. You have never committed the sins that the Pharisee disowned; you have neither been extortionate, nor unjust, nor an adulterer; you have never been even as the publican. But nevertheless, the word *sinner* will still apply to you, and you will feel it to be so if you are in a right condition. Remember how much *you* have sinned against light. It is true that the harlot has sinned more openly than you, but had she such light as you have had? Do you think she had such an early education and such training as you have received? Did she ever receive such checkings of conscience and such guardings of Providence, as those that have watched over your career?

This much I must confess for myself – I do, and must feel a peculiar heinousness in my own sin, for I sin against light, against conscience, and more, against the love of God received, and against the mercy of God promised. Come forward, you greatest among saints, and answer this question – Does not this prayer suit you? I hear you answer, without one moment's pause, "Alas, it suits me now; and until I die, my quivering lips must often repeat the petition, 'Lord, have mercy upon me a sinner.'"

Men and brethren, I implore you to use this prayer today, for it must suit you all. Merchant, have you no sins of business to confess? Woman, have you no household sins to acknowledge? Child of many prayers, have you no offense against father and mother to confess? Have we loved the Lord our God with all our heart, with all our soul, with all our strength; and have we each loved our neighbor as ourself? Oh, let us close our lips as to any boasting, and when we open them, let these be the first words that escape from them: "I have sinned, O Lord; I have broken your commandments; Lord, have mercy upon me a sinner." But observe, is it not a strange thing that the Holy Spirit should teach a man to plead his sinnership before the throne of God?

One would think that when we come before God, we would try to talk a little of our virtues. Who would suppose that when a man was asking for mercy he would say of himself, "I am a sinner"? Why, surely reason would prompt him to say, "Lord, have mercy upon me; there is some good point about me. Lord, have mercy upon me; I am not worse than my neighbors. Lord, have mercy upon me; I will try to be better." Is it not against reason, is it not marvelously above reason, that the Holy Spirit should teach a man to urge at the throne of grace, that which seems to be against his plea, the fact that he is a sinner?

And yet, dear brethren, if you and I want to be heard, we must come to Christ as sinners. Do not let us attempt to make ourselves better than we are. When we come to God's throne, let us not for one moment seek to gather any of the false jewels of our pretended virtues; rags are the garments of sinners. Confession is the only music that must come from our lips. *God be merciful to me a sinner;* that must be the only character in which I can pray to God. Now, are there not many here who feel that they are sinners, and are groaning, sighing, and lamenting, because the weight of sin lies on their conscience?

Brother, I am glad you feel yourself to be a sinner, for you have the key of the kingdom in your hands. Your sense of sinnership is your only title to mercy. Come, I beg you, just as you are. Your nakedness is your only claim on heaven's wardrobe; your hunger is your only claim on heaven's granaries; your poverty is your only claim on heaven's eternal riches. Come just as you are, with nothing of your own except your sinfulness, and plead that before the throne – *God be merciful to me a sinner.* This is what this man confessed, that he was a sinner, and he pleaded it, making the burden of his confession to be the matter of his plea before God.

Now again, *how does he come?* What is the posture that he assumes? The first thing I would have you notice is that he stood *afar off.* What did he do that for? Was it not because he felt himself a separated man? We have often made general confessions in the temple, but there never was a confession accepted, unless it was particular, personal, and heartfelt. There were the people gathered together for the accustomed service of worship, they join in a psalm of praise; but the poor publican stood far away from them. Immediately they unite in the order of prayer, but still he could not go near them. No, he had come there for himself, and he must stand by himself. Like the wounded deer that seeks the deepest glades of the forest where it may bleed and die alone in profound solitude, so did this poor publican seem to feel he must be alone. You notice he does not say anything about other people in his prayer. *God be merciful to me,* he says. He does not say, "one of a company of sinners," but *a sinner,* as if there were not another sinner in all the world.

Mark this, my friend, that you must feel yourself solitary and alone before you can ever pray this prayer acceptably. Has the Lord ever picked you out in a congregation? Has it seemed to you in this hall as if there were a great black wall round about you, and you were closed in with the preacher and with your God, and as if every shaft from the preacher's bow was leveled at you, and every threatening meant for you, and every solemn rebuke was a rebuke for you? If you have felt this, I will congratulate you. No man ever prayed this prayer correctly unless he prayed alone, unless he said, *God be merciful to me,* as a solitary, lonely sinner. *The publican, standing afar off.*

Note the next thing. He *would not lift up so much as his eyes unto heaven.* That was because he dared not, not because he would not; he would have done it if he had dared to. How remarkable it is that repentance takes all the daring out of men. We have seen fellows very daredevilish before they were touched by sovereign grace, who have become, afterwards, the most trembling and conscientious men with the most tender conscience that one could imagine.

Men who were careless, bragging and defying God, have become as humble as little children, and even afraid to lift their eyes to heaven, though once they sent their oaths and curses there. But why did he not dare to lift up his eyes? It was because he was dejected in his spirit, so oppressed and burdened that he could not look up. Is that your case, my friend, this morning? Are you afraid to pray? Do you feel as if you could not hope that God would have mercy on you; as if the least gleam of hope was more light than you could possibly bear; as if your eyes were so used to the darkness of doubt and despondency that even one stolen ray seemed to be too much for your poor weak vision?

Ah! well, fear not, for happy shall it be for you. You are only following the publican in his sad experience now, and the Lord who helps you to follow him in the confession, shall help you to rejoice with him in the pardon.

Note what else he did. He *smote upon* [struck] *his breast.* He was a good theologian; he was a real doctor of divinity. What did he strike his breast for? Because he knew where the mischief lay – in his breast. He did not strike his brow as some men do when they are perplexed, as if the mistake were in their understanding. Many a man will blame his understanding, while he will not blame his heart, and say, "Well, I have made a mistake; I have certainly been doing wrong, but I am a good-hearted fellow at the bottom." This man knew where the mischief lay, and he struck the right place.

Here on my heart the burden lies.

He struck his breast as if he were angry with himself. He seemed to say, "Oh! that I could strike you, my ungrateful heart, all the harder, because you have loved sin rather than God." He did not do confession, and yet it was a kind of confession upon himself when he struck his breast again and again, and cried, "Alas! Alas! woe is me that I should ever have sinned against my God. *God be merciful to a sinner.* Now, can you come to God like this, my dear friend?

Oh, let us all draw near to God in this fashion. You have enough, my brother, to make you stand alone, for there have been sins in which you and I have stood each of us in solitary guilt. There are iniquities known only to ourselves, which we never told to the partner of our own bosom, not to our own parents or brothers, nor yet to the friend with whom we took sweet counsel. If we have sinned thus alone, let us go to our chambers, and confess alone, the husband apart, and the wife apart, the father apart, and the child apart. Let us each one wail for himself.

Men and brethren, cease accusing one another. Cease from the bickerings of your faultfinding, and from the slanders of your envy. Rebuke yourselves and not your fellows. Tear your own hearts, and not the reputation of your neighbors. Come, let each man now look to his own case, and not to the case of another; let each cry, "Lord, have mercy upon *me,* as here I stand alone, a sinner." And do you not have good reason to cast down your eyes? Does it not seem sometimes too much for us ever to look to heaven again? We have blasphemed God, some of us, and even invoked curses on our own limbs and eyes; and when those things come back to our memory, we may well be ashamed to look up.

Or if we have been preserved from the crime of open blasphemy – how often have you and I forgotten God! how often have we neglected prayer! how have we broken his Sabbaths and left his Bible unread! Surely these things, as they flash across our memory, might constrain us to feel that we cannot lift up so much as our eyes towards heaven. And as for striking our breast, what man is there among us that need not do it? Let us be angry with ourselves, because we have provoked God to be angry with us. Let us be in wrath with the sins that have brought ruin upon our souls; let us drag the traitors out, and put them at once to a comprehensive death. They deserve it well, for they have been our ruin; let us be their destruction. He struck his breast and said, *God be merciful to me a sinner.*

There is one other feature in this man's prayer that you must not overlook. *What reason had he to expect that God would have any mercy upon him?* The Greek explains more to us than the English does, and the original word here might be translated – "God be *propitiated* to me a sinner." There is in the Greek word a distinct reference to the doctrine of atonement. It is not the Unitarian's prayer – "God be merciful to me"; it is more than that – it is the Christian's prayer – "God be propitiated towards me, a sinner." There is, I repeat it, a distinct appeal to the atonement and the mercy seat in this short prayer.

Friend, if we would come before God with our confessions, we must take care that we plead the blood of Christ. There is no hope for a poor sinner apart from the cross of Jesus. We may cry, "God be merciful to me," but the prayer can never be answered apart from the victim offered, the Lamb slain from before the foundation of the world. When you have your eye upon the mercy seat, take care to have your eye upon the cross too. Remember that the cross is, after all, the mercy seat; that mercy never was enthroned until she did hang upon the cross crowned with thorns. If you would find pardon, go to dark Gethsemane, and see your Redeemer sweating, in deep anguish, and gouts of gore. If you would have peace of conscience, go to Gabbatha, the pavement, and see your Savior's back flooded with a stream of blood. If you would have the last best rest for your conscience, go to Golgotha; see the murdered victim as he hangs upon the cross, with hands and feet and side all pierced, as every wound is gaping wide with misery extreme. There can be no hope for mercy apart from the victim offered – even Jesus Christ the Son of God.

Oh, come; let us one and all approach the mercy seat, and plead the blood. Let us each go and say, "Father, I have sinned; but have mercy upon me, through your Son." Come, drunkard, give me your hand; we will go together. Harlot, give me your hand too, and let us likewise approach the throne. And you, professing Christians, come also, and be not ashamed of your company. Let us come before his presence with many tears, none of us accusing our fellows, but each one accusing himself; and let us plead the blood of Jesus Christ, which speaks peace and pardon to every troubled conscience.

Careless man, I have a word for you before I am done on this point. You say, "Well, that is a good prayer, certainly, for a man who is dying. When a poor fellow has the cholera, and sees black death staring him in the face, or when he is terrified and thunderstruck in the time of storm, or when he finds himself amidst the terrible confusion and alarm of a perilous catastrophe or a sudden accident, while drawing near to the gates of death, it is only right that he should say, 'Lord, have mercy upon me.'"

Ah, friend, the prayer must be suitable to you then, if you are a dying man; it must be suitable to you, for you know not how near you are to the borders of the grave. Oh, if you did but understand the frailty of life, and the slipperiness of that poor support on which you are resting, you would say, "Alas for *my* soul! if the prayer will suit me dying, it must suit me now; for I am dying, even this day, and know not when I may come to the last gasp." "Oh," says one, "I think it will suit a man that has been a very great sinner." Correct, my friend, and therefore, if you knew yourself, it would suit you. You are quite correct in saying that it won't suit any but great sinners; and if you don't feel yourself to be a great sinner, I know you will never pray it. But there are some here that feel themselves to be what you ought to feel and know that you are. Such will, constrained by grace, use the prayer with an emphasis this morning, putting a tear upon each letter, and a sigh upon each syllable, as they cry, *God be merciful to me a sinner.*

But observe, my friend; you may smile contemptuously on the man that makes this confession, but he shall go from this house justified, while you shall go away still in your sins, without a hope, without a ray of joy to cheer your unpurified spirit.

Having thus briefly described this confession, I come more briefly still to notice the pardon that God gave. Pardon from the lips of man I do believe is little short of blasphemy. There is in the Book of Common Prayer of the Church of England a pardon that is essentially Roman Catholic, which I should think must be almost a verbatim extract from the Romish missal (Roman Catholic book used at mass). I do not hesitate to say that where was never anything more blasphemous printed in Holywell Street than the pardon that is to be pronounced by a clergyman over a dying man; and it is positively frightful to think that any persons calling themselves Christians should rest easy in a church until they have done their utmost to get that most excellent book thoroughly reformed and revised, and to get the Roman Catholicism purged out of it.

But there is such a thing as pardon, my friends, and the publican received it. He *went down to his house justified rather than the other.* The other had nothing of peace revealed to his heart; this poor man had all, and he went to his house justified. It does not say that he went to his house having eased his mind; that is true, but there is more: he went to his house *justified.* What does that mean? It so happens that the Greek word used here is the one that the apostle Paul always employs to set forth the great doctrine of the righteousness of Jesus Christ – even the righteousness that is of God by faith.

The fact is, that the moment the man prayed the prayer, every sin he had ever done was blotted out of God's book, so that it did not stand on the record against him; and more than that, the moment that prayer was heard in heaven, the man was reckoned to be a righteous man. All that Christ did for him was cast upon his shoulders to be the robe of his beauty; that moment all the guilt that he had ever committed himself was washed entirely away and lost forever. When a sinner believes in Christ, his sins positively cease to be, and what is more wonderful is that they *all* cease to be, as Kent says in those well-known lines –

Here's pardon for transgressions past,
 It matters not how black their cast,
And, O my soul with wonder view,
 For sins to come here's pardon too.

They are all swept away in one solitary instant; the crimes of many years, extortions, adulteries, or even murder, wiped away in an instant; for you will notice the pardon was instantaneously given. God did not say to the man, "Now you must go and perform some good works, and then I will give you pardon." He did not say as the pope does, "Now you must swelter awhile in the fires of purgatory, and then I will let you out." No, he justified him there and then; the pardon was given as soon as the sin was confessed. "Go, my son, in peace; I have not a charge against you; you are a sinner in your own estimation, but you are none in mine. I have taken all your sins away, and cast them into the depths of the sea, and they shall be mentioned against you no more forever."

Can you tell what a happy man the publican was, when all of a sudden he was changed? If you may reverse the figure used by Milton, he seemed himself to have been a loathsome toad, but the touch of the Father's mercy made him rise to angelic brightness and delight; and he went out of that house with his eye upward, no longer afraid. Instead of the groan that was on his heart, he had a song upon his lips. He no longer walked alone; he sought out the godly and he said, "Come and hear, you who fear God, and I will tell you what he has done for my soul." He did not strike his breast, but he went home to get down his harp, and play upon the strings, and praise his God. You would not have known that he was the same man if you had seen him going out; and all that was done in a minute. "But," says one, "do you think he knew for certain that all his sins were forgiven? Can a man know that?"

Certainly he can. And there are some here who can bear witness that this is true. They have known it themselves. The pardon that is sealed in heaven is resealed in our own conscience. The mercy that is recorded above is made to shed its light into the darkness of our hearts. Yes, a man may know on earth that his sins are forgiven, and may be as sure that he is a pardoned man as he is of his own existence.

And now I hear a cry from someone saying, "And may I be pardoned this morning? and may I know that I am pardoned? May I be so pardoned that all shall be forgotten – I who have been a drunkard, a swearer, or what not? May I have all my transgressions washed away? May I be made sure of heaven, and all that in a moment?"

Yes, my friend, if you believe in the Lord Jesus Christ, if you will stand where you are, and just breathe this prayer out: "Lord, have mercy! God be merciful to me a sinner, through the blood of Christ." I tell you, man, God never did deny that prayer yet; if it came out of honest lips, he never shut the gates of mercy on it. It is a solemn litany that shall be used as long as time shall last, and it shall pierce the ears of God as long as there is a sinner to use it. Come, be not afraid; I implore you, use the prayer before you leave this hall. Stand where you are; endeavor to realize that you are all alone, and if you feel that you are guilty, now let the prayer ascend.

Oh, what a marvelous thing, if from the thousands of hearts present here, so many thousand prayers might go up to God! Surely the angels themselves never had such a day in paradise as they would have today, if every one of us could genuinely make that confession. Some are doing it; I know they are; God is helping them. And sinner, do you stay away? You who have most need to come, do you refuse to join with us?

Come, brother, come. You say you are too vile. No, brother, you cannot be too vile to say, "God be merciful to me." Perhaps you are no viler than we are; at any rate, this we can say – we feel ourselves to be viler than you, and we want you to pray the same prayer that we have prayed. "Ah," says one, "I cannot; my heart won't yield to that; I cannot."

But friend, if God is ready to have mercy upon you, yours must be a hard heart if it is not ready to receive his mercy. Spirit of God, breathe on the hard heart, and melt it now! Help the man who feels that carelessness is overcoming him – help him to get rid of it from this hour. You are struggling against it; you are saying, "Would to God I could pray that I could go back to being a boy or a child again, and then I could; but I have gotten hardened and grown gray in sin, and prayer would be hypocrisy in me."

No, brother, no, it would not. If you can but cry it from your heart, I beg you to say it. Many a man thinks he is a hypocrite when he is not, and is afraid that he is not sincere when his very fear is a proof of his sincerity. "But," says one, "I have no redeeming trait in my character at all." I am glad you think so; still you may use the prayer, *God be merciful to me*. "But it will be a useless prayer," says one.

My brother, I assure you, not in my own name, but in the name of God, my Father and your Father, it shall not be a useless prayer. As sure as God is God, *him that cometh to [Christ he] will in no wise cast out*. Come with me now, I beg you; delay no longer; the bowels of God are yearning for you. You are his child, and he will not give you up. You have run from him these many years, but he has never forgotten you; you have resisted all his warnings until now, and he is almost weary, but still he has said concerning you, *How shall I make thee as Admah? how shall I set thee as Zeboim? mine heart is turned within me, my repentings are kindled together* (Hosea 11:8).

> Come humbled sinner, in whose breast
> A thousand thoughts revolve;
> Come with thy guilt and fear oppressed
> And make this last resolve:
>
> I'll go to Jesus; though my sin
> Hath like a mountain rose,
> I know his courts; I'll enter in,
> Whatever may oppose.
>
> Prostrate I'll lie before his face,
> And there my sins confess;
> I'll tell him I'm a wretch undone,
> Without his sov'reign grace.

Go home to your houses. Let everyone – preacher, deacon, people, you of the church, and you of the world, every one of you, go home, and before you feast your bodies, pour out your hearts before God, and let this one cry go up from all your lips: *God be merciful to me a sinner.*

I pause. Bear with me.

I must detain you for a few moments. Let us use this prayer as our own *now*. Oh, that it might come up before the Lord at this time as the earnest petition of every heart in this assembly! I will repeat it – not as a text, but as a prayer – as my own prayer, as your prayer. Will each one of you take it personally for himself? Let everyone, I beg you, who desires to offer the prayer, and can join in it, utter at its close an audible "Amen."

Let us pray,

"GOD BE MERCIFUL TO ME A SINNER."

[And the people did with deep solemnity say, "AMEN."]

P.S. – The preacher hopes that he who reads this will feel constrained most solemnly to do likewise.

Chapter 12

The Servants and the Pounds

He said therefore, A certain nobleman went into a far country to receive for himself a kingdom, and to return. And he called his ten servants, and delivered them ten pounds, and said unto them, Occupy till I come. (Luke 19:12-13)

We are told the reason for the Savior's delivering this parable at this particular time. He was going up to Jerusalem, and the ignorant and enthusiastic crowd hoped that he might now set up a worldly sovereignty. *They thought that the kingdom of God should immediately appear* (Luke 19:11). Their minds were crowded with mistakes, and the Savior would set them right upon this matter. To banish from their minds the idea of a Jewish empire, in which every Hebrew would be a prince, our Lord told them this story. I use the word *story* deliberately, for his parable was also a fact. He would show them that as yet they were not to be partakers in a kingdom, but were soon to be waiters for an absent Lord who had gone to receive a kingdom, and to return.

In his absence his disciples were to be in the position of servants put in trust with property while their master was gone far away to receive a kingdom, and then to come again. He was now like a nobleman, who may be one among many citizens; but he was going away to a court where he would be invested with royal authority, and he would come back a king. They were to be put in trust with certain pounds until he should return.

I confess I never thoroughly saw the meaning of this parable until I was directed by a distinguished expositor to a passage in Josephus, which, if it be not the key of it, is a wonderfully close example of a class of facts that, no doubt, often occurred in the Roman Empire in our Savior's day. Herod, you know, was king over Judaea; but he was only a subordinate king under the Roman emperor. Caesar at Rome made and unmade kings at his pleasure. When Herod died, he was followed by his son Archelaus, of whom we read in Matthew's account of our Lord's infancy that *when [Joseph] heard that Archelaus did reign in Judaea in the room of his father Herod, he was afraid to go thither* (Matthew 2:22). This Archelaus had no right to the throne until he obtained the sanction of Caesar, and therefore he took ship with certain attendants, and went to Rome, which in those days was a far country, so that he might receive the kingdom, and return.

While he was on the way, his citizens, who hated him, *sent an ambassage after him,* so has the Revised Version correctly worded it; and this ambassage (embassy) bore this message to Caesar: *We will not that this man reign over us* (Luke 19:14 RV). The messengers represented to Caesar that Archelaus was not fit to be king of the Jews. Certain of the pleadings are recorded in Josephus, and they show that barristers nineteen hundred years ago pleaded in much the same style as their brethren of today. The people were weary of the Herods, and preferred anything to their cruel rule. They even asked that Judaea might become a Roman province, and be joined to Syria, rather than they should remain under the hated yoke of the Idumean tyrants. It is evident that in the case of Archelaus his citizens hated him, and said, *We will not have this man to reign over us.* It pleased Caesar to divide the kingdom, and to put Archelaus on the throne as ethnarch, or a ruler with less power than a king.

When he returned, he took fierce revenge upon those who had opposed him, and rewarded his faithful adherents most liberally. This story of what had been done thirty years before would, no doubt, rise up in the recollection of the people when Jesus spoke, for Archelaus had built a palace for himself very near to Jericho, and it may be that under the walls of that palace the Savior used the event as the basis of his parable. Those who lived in our Lord's day must have understood his allusions to current facts much better than we do who live nineteen centuries later. The providence of God provided for that observant Jew, Josephus, to store up much valuable information for us. Read the passage in his history, and you will see that even the details correspond with this parable. There is the story.

The Savior, without excusing Archelaus or commending him in the least degree, simply makes his going to Rome an illustration. Here is a noble personage who is to be a king, but to obtain the throne he must journey to the distant court of a superior power. While he is going, his citizens so hate him that they send an embassy to oppose his claims; for they will not have him for their king. However, he receives the kingdom, and returns to rule it. When he does so, he rewards those who have been faithful to him, and he punishes with overwhelming destruction those who have tried to prevent his reigning. There is the story; let me further interpret it.

The Savior likens himself to a nobleman. He was here on earth a man among men, and truly a nobleman in the midst of his fellow citizens. It was his to become king, king of all the earth. Indeed, he is such by nature and by right, but he must first go, by death, resurrection, and ascension, away to the highest courts, and there from the great Lord of all he must receive for himself a kingdom. It is written, *Ask of me, and I shall give thee the heathen for thine inheritance* (Psalm 2:8); therefore, Jesus must plead his claims before the king, and win his suit. The day is coming when he will return, clothed with glory and honor, to take unto himself his great power and reign; for he must reign until all enemies are put under his feet. When he comes, his enemies will be destroyed, and his faithful servants will be abundantly rewarded.

Let us now draw near to this feast of divine teaching. May the Spirit of God help us to gather practical lessons from this parable!

First, I invite you to notice that there are two sets of persons here. We see the enemies who would not have this man to reign over them, and the servants who had to trade with his money. There are many divisions among men into nationalities, ranks, offices, and characters; but, after all, the deep divisions will always be two – the enemies and the servants of Christ Jesus. You who are not servants are enemies; you who are not enemies must take care that you are servants. I find no class of persons mentioned in the parable but these two, and I feel certain that there are no others on the face of the earth. You are all either enemies or servants of Jesus.

Consider *the enemies*! The person hated was a nobleman. He was a man, but a noble man. What a man is the Lord Jesus! Forgetting his deity for the moment, regard him only as the man Christ Jesus, and what a man! I need not dwell upon the nobility of his birth, of the seed of David; but I would remind you of the nobility of his character, for that is where true nobility resides. In this respect, where is there nobility to be compared to his? Brothers, it would be difficult to find a second to the man Christ within measurable distance of him; even those who copy him most nearly confess, regretfully, that in many things they fall short of his glory. There was nothing petty, mean, or selfish about Jesus of Nazareth. He was altogether the noble man.

He condescended, for gracious purposes, to become a citizen among others; for since we read of his being anointed above his fellows, it is implied that some were his fellows. He was a man among men. He was of the society of carpenters; he was also free of the company of itinerant preachers. He associated with men of the sea, with men that handled the net and the oar. He went in and out among the peasantry, and in his dress and style of living there was nothing to distinguish him from the rest of the citizens. Truly, he was separate from them by his holier character, but the separation was not caused by his unwillingness to come down to them, but by their inability to go up to him.

The citizens hated him, but they hated him without a cause. There is always some cause for dislike in us, but there was none in him. In tone, or manner, or spirit, even the best give some cause of offense; but in him there was nothing that could excuse their hate: it was a malicious rejection of the fittest to reign.

As he claimed to be the King of the Jews, they especially hated his royalty, saying, *We will not have this man to reign over us;* and again, *We have no king but Caesar* (John 19:15). *He came unto his own, and his own received him not* (John 1:11). Yet, my brethren, merely regarding Jesus as a man, if we wanted a king, then he ought to be elected by the universal votes of mankind, openly given by uplifted hands and joyful acclamations. *Lo triumphe!* Mighty Conqueror, reign forever! Prince of the kings of the earth, lover of the sons of men, who did for our sake pour out your precious blood, you deserve to be king of all! The most kingly of men should be king of men.

Yet they hated his royal claims, and this also without cause. Which of them had he oppressed? What revenue did he extort from the people? What law of his was hard or cruel? In what case did he ever judge unrighteously? Yet his citizens hated him. There is that same hatred of Christ in the world today. Do any of you hate him? "No," say you. Yet are not some of you who do not oppose him treating him with greater contempt than if you did oppose him? You pass him by altogether, he is not in all your thoughts; you act as if he were not worthy even to be opposed; you make nothing of him. He is not among the objects for which you live. Sometimes you may speak with a partial admiration of his character, but earnest admiration leads to imitation. If Jesus be a Savior, what worse thing can you do to him than to refuse to be saved by him?

I charge you indifferent ones with being, in the core of your hearts, his worst enemies. Oh, that you would repent of this, and turn unto him, for he is coming again; and when he comes, he will say, *Those mine enemies, . . . slay them before me* (Luke 19:27). The expression is full of terror. To be slain before the eyes of injured love is doubly death. May the Lord by his grace deliver us from so dread a doom!

The other set of persons were *his servants;* the original would justify the translation: his bond servants. Those who were not his enemies were his faithful servants. I suppose that the nobleman had bought them with his money, or that they had been born in his house, or that they had willingly bound themselves by contracts to him. When I said that these were only his slaves, you inwardly said, "Then you who believe in Jesus are his bond servants." Spare us not even the harsher word "slaves." We were never free until we came under bonds to Jesus, and we grow in freedom as we yield to him. Paul said, *I bear in my body the marks of the Lord Jesus* (Galatians 6:17), as if the hot iron of affliction had branded him with the name of Christ.

Yes, we are the property of the Lord Jesus, and not our own. We cannot somehow find words that will in all their fullness express our belonging to Jesus; we wish to sink into Christ, and to become as nothing for his sake. Truly he has called us friends, but we call ourselves his servants. We take a great delight in owning him as Master. We are like David, who said, *Truly I am thy servant;* and then again, *I am thy servant;* and then again, *and the son of thine handmaid.* He was born a servant, born of a mother who was also herself a servant. After all this he added, *Thou hast loosed my bonds* (Psalm 116:16). Servitude to Christ is perfect freedom, and in every respect we have found it so. We never expect to know perfect freedom until he has brought every thought, every conception, imagination, and desire into captivity to himself. We have been bought with his money, and we cost him dearly. We have also been born in his house by a second birth, and we are bound to him by contracts that we have gladly signed and sealed, and are ready to sign and seal again.

> High heaven, that heard the solemn vow,
> That vow renew'd shall daily hear;
> Till in life's latest hour we bow,
> And bless in death a bond so dear.

We are truly thus on the opposite side of his enemies, for we are willingly his servants.

I have thus introduced to you the two classes. Before we go any further, may the Holy Spirit operate upon us, to make us discern to which of these two we belong! If we are enemies, may we become servants from this time forth!

We now advance a step further, and notice the engagements of these servants. Their lord was going away, and he left his ten servants in charge with a little capital, with which they were to trade for him until he returned. He did not tell them how long he would be away; perhaps he did not know himself – I mean the king in the story. Even our Master says, *Of that day and hour knoweth no man, no, not the angels of heaven* (Matthew 24:36). "I am going away," he said. "You are my servants, and I leave you as my servants in the midst of my enemies. Be loyal to me; and, to prove your faithfulness, continue to trade in my name. I shall entrust to each of you a very small sum of money, but it will keep you occupied, and your trading on my account will be your daily protest that you are loyal to me, whatever others may be."

Notice, first, that *this was honorable work*. They were not entrusted with large funds, but the amount was enough to serve as a test. It put them upon their honor. If they were really attached to their master, they would feel that he had placed a confidence in them that they must justify. Slaves are not always to be entrusted with money; in fact, the tendency of bondage has been always to take away from men the quality of trustworthiness. Our bondage to Christ has the opposite effect, because it is no bondage at all. These servants of the master were treated in some respect as partners; they were to have fellowship with him in his property. They were his confidants and trustees. His eye was not watching them, for he had gone into a far country, and he trusted them to be a law unto themselves. They were not to render a daily account, but to be left alone until he returned. Now that is just how the Master has treated us: he has put us in trust with the gospel, and he relies upon our honor. He does not call us at once to an audit, for he is not here. I do not think that systems of church government that involve a measure of the spy system are at all in the characteristic manner of our Lord's mind.

If Christians are what they ought to be, they can be trusted: they are a law unto themselves. The Lord puts you not under certain rules and regulations so as to ordain that you shall give a tenth, though I wish you did give as much at least. He does not say, "You shall subscribe so much at such a time, and work in such a way." No; you are not under law, but under grace. If you love your Master, you will soon discover what to do for him, and you will do it with delight.

The Lord does not lay down rigid rules, and order that at such an hour in the morning you must begin work, and that you must work on for so many hours. No; he says, "Take my pound, and trade with that." Our version, *Occupy till I come,* is a lumbering Latin way of saying, "Trade with that until I come." The Lord has put us on the footing of confidence, appealing to our honor and love. He will not come and look after us today or tomorrow, though he will ultimately have a strict reckoning with us.

Meanwhile he has gone, but he has left us here in the midst of his enemies, to show his enemies that he has some friends, and that he must be a good Master, since even those who acknowledge themselves to be subservient to him rejoice to spend their whole lives in his service. I say he gave them honorable work, and was it not so?

It was work for which he gave them capital. He gave to each of them a pound. "Not much," you will say. No, he did not intend it to be much. They were not capable of managing very much. If he found them faithful in *a very little,* he could then raise them to a higher responsibility. I do not read that any one of them complained about the smallness of his capital, or wished to have it doubled.

Brothers, we need not ask for more talents; we have quite as many as we shall be able to answer for. Preachers need not seek for larger spheres; let them be faithful in those that they now occupy. A brother said to me, "I cannot do much with a hundred hearers," and I replied, "You will find it hard work to give a good account for even a hundred people."

I confess it very quietly, but I have often wished that I had a little congregation, so that I might watch over every soul in it. But now I am doomed to an everlasting dissatisfaction with my work, for what reason am I among so many? I can only feel that I have not even begun to do the hundredth part of what needs to be done in such a church as this. Each one had a pound in his hand, and his lord only said, "Trade with that." He did not expect them to do a wholesale business on so small a stock, but they were to trade as the market would allow. He did not expect them to make more than the pound would fairly bring in, for, after all, he was not a harsh man. "Take that pound," he said, "and do your best. I know the times are bad, for you have to trade among enemies. You could not, perhaps, manage to put out twenty pounds under such circumstances, but you can turn over a pound, and use every shilling of it." Thus he gave them a sufficient capital for his purpose.

My friend, have you that pound anywhere around you? "Alas!" says one, "I have no abilities at all." How is that? Your Lord gave you a pound; what has become of it? You are one of his servants, and if you are doing nothing, you are in an evil condition, and ought to be ashamed. What have you done with that pound? Put your hand in your pocket again. It is not there. Is it in the napkin? – that napkin with which you ought to have wiped the sweat of labor from your brow? Have you got that pound? You say, "It is not much." The Master did not say it was much; on the contrary, he called it *very little;* but have you used that *very little*? This should go home to your consciences. You have been treated as confidential servants, and yet you are not true to your Lord. How is this?

What they had to do with the pound was prescribed in general terms. They were to trade with it, not to play with it. I dare say they were inclined to argue, "Our master's cause is attacked; let us fight for him"; yet he did not say "fight," but *trade*. Peter drew his sword. Oh yes, we are eager combatants, but slow merchants. Many manifest a defiant spirit, and are never more satisfied than when they are in noise and strife. The servants in this parable were not to fight, but to trade, which is a much more cool-blooded and inferior thing in common esteem. We may leave our Lord's enemies to himself; he will end their rebellions one of these days. We are to follow a much lowlier line of things.

No doubt certain of them might have thought that the pound would be useful to purchase them comforts, or even luxuries: one would buy a new coat, and another would bring home a piece of furniture for his house, and others would solemnly say, "We have our families to think of." Yes, but their lord did not say so; the master said, "Trade with that until I come." They were neither to fight with it, nor hoard it, nor spend it, nor waste it, but to trade with it for him.

The pound was not put into their hands for display. They were not to glory over others who had not so much as a penny to bless themselves with; for though they were little capitalists, that capital was their lord's. It is a pity when graces or talents are boasted of as if they were our own. A tradesman who is prospering seldom has much money to show; it is all needed in his business. Sometimes he can scarcely put his hand upon a five-pound note, because his cash is all absorbed; his golden grain is all sown in the field of his trade. Speaking for myself, I cannot find any room for glorying in myself; for if I have either grace or strength, I certainly have none to spare. I have barely enough for the work in hand, and not enough for the service in prospect. Our pound is not to be hung on our watch chain, but is to be traded with.

Trading represents a life that may be called commonplace; but it is very practical, and it has an exceedingly practical effect upon the person engaged in it. This is owing in part to the fact that it is an occupation in which there is great *scope for judgment*. They were not tied down to a special kind of trade. The man who made his one pound into ten chose the best form of business. He sought not that which was most pleasant, but that which was most profitable.

So you are left, dear friends, to choose your own line of service for your Master, only you must trade for him, and for him everything must be done well. At the present time no trading pays better than the mission to the Congo, or to the hill-tribes of India. Large dividends come also from dealings with the poorest of the poor in the slums, and as much from widows and orphans who are in extreme destitution. When men have to lay down their lives for the Lord Jesus, after a life languished away with fever, the returns are amazing. Where the need is greatest our Lord receives the most glory. It is left to you to judge what you can do, how you can do it, and where you will do it. Do that which will most surely win souls, and that which will best establish your Lord's kingdom. Exercise your very best judgment, and get into that line of holy service in which you can bring in the largest revenue for your glorious Master.

The work that he prescribed was *one that would bring them out.* The man who never succeeds in trade, do you know him? I know him. He complains that he has a small head, and usually the complaint is founded on fact. He needs to follow a business in which the bread and butter will be brought to his door already spread; and even then, unless it is cut up into diced pieces on his plate, he will get no breakfast. The man who is to succeed in trade in these times must have confidence, look alive, keep his eyes open, and be all there. Our times are hard, but not so hard as those described in the parable when the faithful servants were trading in the midst of traitors; they had need of sharp wits. Trade develops a man's perseverance, patience, and courage; it tests honesty, truthfulness, and firmness. It is a singularly excellent discipline for character.

When this nobleman gave his servant the pound, it was so that he might see what stuff he was made of. Trade with small capital means personal work and drudgery, long hours and few holidays, and plenty of disappointment and small gains. It means working with might and muscle, and doing the thing with all your heart and mind. In such a manner we are to serve Christ. The word *trade* has a world of meaning in it. I cannot bring it out this morning; but there is no need, for most of you know more about trade than I do, and you can instruct yourselves. You are to trade for the Lord Jesus Christ in a higher and yet more emphatic sense than that in which you have traded for yourselves. With your physical strength, your mental faculties, your substance, your family, with everything – you are to bring glory to God, and honor to the name of Jesus. It is to be your life business to work *for* Jesus and *with* Jesus.

Trading, if it be successfully carried on, is *an engrossing concern,* calling out the whole man. It is a continuous toil, a varied trial, a remarkable test, a valuable discipline, and this is why the nobleman put his bondsmen to it, that he might afterwards use them in still higher service. Brethren, learn what is meant by trading, and then carry on a spiritual trade with all your heart.

At the same time, let us notice that *it was work suitable to their capacity.* Small as the capital was, it was enough for them; for they were no more than bondsmen, not of a high grade of rank or education. Their master gave them only a pound, which did not mean more than three pounds ten shillings of our money. One would not get a large shop, or even a decent stock with that small amount. They could not complain that they were placed in a business that was too heavy for them to manage. They could any of them buy a few goods and hawk them.

The Lord Jesus Christ does not ask you to do more than you can do; he does not break you down with cares beyond your capacity. We have not yet reached the limit of our powers: we can still do more. Jesus is no exacting master; it is only a false and lying servant who will call him *an austere man, . . . reaping that [he] did not sow* (Luke 19:22). He is nothing of the kind. He has given us a light business: our work for him is suited to our limited powers, and he is ready, by his Holy Spirit, to assist us. Let us use well our single pound. Let it be our ambition to make ten of it at the very least; and may the Lord graciously prosper our endeavors, that we may have large interest to present to him when he shall come!

Did you inquire as to how these men were to be supported? Their master did not tell them to live off of his pound. No, they were his servants, and so they lived under his roof, and he provided for all their needs. He had gone on a journey, but his establishment was not given up: the table was still spread, and the children and the servants had *bread enough and to spare.* "Oh," says one, "that alters the case." Just so, but it does not make it different from yours; or, if it does, I am sorry for you. Are you your own provider? Do you cry, "What shall I eat? What shall I drink?" Do you not know that all these things the nations of the earth do seek after?

Whereas Jesus says, *Your heavenly Father knoweth that ye have need of all these things* (Matthew 6:32). As I understand my life, I am to do my Lord's work, and he is to provide for me. He may do this through my own industry, but still it is *his* work to do it, and not mine. If the providence of God is not sufficient to provide for us, then I am sure we cannot provide for ourselves; and if it be sufficient, we shall be wise to cast all our care on the Lord, and live undividedly for his praise.

Remember that text: *Seek ye first the kingdom of God, and his righteousness; and all these things shall be added unto you* (Matthew 6:33). You, as a servant, are not to be entangled with burdensome cares about your own interests, but you are to give your whole thought and life to your Master's service. He will take care of you now, and reward you when he shall come.

Thirdly, to understand this parable, we must remember the expectancy that was always to influence them. They were left as trusted servants until he should return, but that return was a main item in the matter.

They were to believe that *he would return,* and that he would return a king. The citizens did not believe it. They hoped that Caesar would refuse him the throne; but we are to be sure that our noble Master will receive the kingdom. This rebel world does not believe that Jesus ever will be king. The other day we read of the "Eclipse of Christianity." Constantly we see his dominion attacked. They say that it is practically disproved by facts. Is it?

Sirs, excuse me, I am desperately prejudiced, for I am his servant. I owe him my life, my all. I am persuaded that he is and must be King of Kings. I know him so well that I am sure that he will prevail at the court to which he has gone. He is in very high favor there. The last time I saw the face of the great King I obtained that favor through the use of his name. I receive anything I ask for when I mention his name, and so I am sure that he is in wonderful high character above. Why, his Father is the sovereign! I am sure he will not deny the kingdom to his only begotten Son. Jesus will come in his kingdom; I am sure of it. Let us work in the full conviction that our absent Lord will soon be here again, with a glorious diadem upon his brow. When he went away, he took with him the scars of one who died a felon's death; and he will come again with them, but the nail-prints will be no memorials of his shame: they will be as jewels to his hands.

His servants were to regard their absent master as *already king*, and they were so to trade among his enemies that they should never compromise their own loyalty. They were of the king's party, and of no other. It is a very awkward position to be in, to trade among people who are enemies to your king. You need in such a case to be *wise as serpents, and harmless as doves* (Matthew 10:16). This is precisely our position. We have to bring glory to God out of men who hate him; we have to magnify our Lord among men who would, if they could, again crucify him. We have to go in and out among them in such a manner that they can never say that we side with them in their rebellion, or wink at their disloyalty. We cannot be "Hail fellow: well met!" with those whose life is a practical insult to the crown rights of King Jesus. We must above all things prove ourselves loyal to our absent Lord, lest he appoint us our portion among his enemies.

I find that the original would suggest to anyone carefully reading it that they were to regard their master as *already returning*. This should be our view of our Lord's second coming; he is even now on his way to this place. No sooner had he risen from the grave than, practically, our Lord was coming back. Strange paradox! But his ascension into heaven was, in a certain sense, part of his coming back to us; for the way for him, from the cross on earth to the crown of the whole earth, was via the New Jerusalem. He is coming now as fast as wisdom judges it to be right.

I am sure our Savior will not delay a moment beyond what is absolutely needful, for he loves the church, which is his bride, and as her Bridegroom he will not delay the long-expected hour of their meeting, never to part again. *He* is ready; it is the bride that needs to make herself ready. Jesus desires to come; his heart is responsive to our cry when we say, "Come quickly!" He will come sooner than we think. We are bound to feel that he is at this moment on the road; and we are to live as if he might arrive at any moment.

We must trade on till our Lord has come. There must be no retiring from his business, even if we retire from our own; there must be no ceasing because we imagine we have done enough. Our rest will be when he comes, but until then we must trade on.

Let us labor as in his actual presence. How would you act with Jesus at your elbow? Act just so. He sees us as clearly as if his bodily presence were in our midst. Be aroused and inspired by the Redeemer's eye. Thus will you live in this trial state in accordance with the best possible manner.

Now comes the sweet part of the subject. Note well the secret design of the Lord. Did it ever strike you that this nobleman had a very kindly particular purpose towards his servants? Did this nobleman give these men one pound each with the sole intention that they should make money for him? It would be absurd to think so. A few pounds would be no item to one who was made a king. No, no! It was as Mr. Bruce says, "He was not money making, but character making." His purpose was not to gain by them, but to educate them.

First, their being entrusted with a pound each was *a test*. This nobleman said to himself, "When I am a king, I must have faithful servants in power around me. My going away gives me an opportunity of seeing what my servants are made of. I shall thus test their capacity and their industry, their honesty and their zeal. If they prove faithful over a few things, then they will be fit to be trusted with greater matters." The test was only a pound, and they could not make much mischief out of that; but it would be quite sufficient to try their capacity and fidelity, for *he that is faithful in that which is least is faithful also in much* (Luke 16:10). They did not all endure the test, but by its means he revealed their characters.

It was also a *preparation* of them for future service. He would lift them up from being servants to become rulers. They were, therefore, to be put in a place of measurable responsibility, and to be made men by that means. They were to be rulers over a very little – say a pound, and that which came of it, and this would be an education for them. In the process of trading they would be in training to rule. The best way to learn to be a master is to be first a servant, and the reason why some masters are hard and tyrannical is because they do not know the heart of a servant by experience. They know nothing of service, and so they have not the wisdom, and the generosity, and the tenderness that masters should show towards servants. So this nobleman was wise, but he was at the same time testing and training his men.

Besides this, I think he was giving them a little *anticipation* of their future honors. He was about to make them rulers over cities, and so he first made them rulers over pounds. They had been servants, and had taken orders from him every morning; but now they have no master to go to, and they must use their own discretion. They were in effect, in a small sphere, made into little kings. In all that country the citizens had rebelled, but there was a little kingdom of the nobleman's own servants, and these obeyed him, and did their best to maintain his interest in their little way. They were already made free, placed in a measure of authority, and made to know the sweets and the burdens of personal responsibility.

Oh, you that work for God, when you are overseers of others for him, when you win souls for him, and when you conquer adversaries in his name, you are already anticipating your eternal reward. We are fashioning our future position upon the anvil of our lives; for heaven, though it be a state and a place prepared for us by the Lord Jesus, lies also mainly in character. The man is more the source of joy than the streets of gold in which he will walk. If you hide your pound and neglect your Master's service here, you are making for yourselves a dim and hazy future in that grand millennial reign of his. You that commit yourselves to your holy trade, and consecrate yourselves entirely to your Lord shall have large honors when he comes to reign among his ancients gloriously.

For see, when he came to the man who had earned ten pounds, he gave him ten cities. Think of that! There is no proportion between the poor service and the rich reward. A pound is rewarded with a city. The rewards of the millennium will evidently be all of grace, because they are so incomparably beyond anything that the servants' earnings could have deserved. Their Lord was not bound to pay them anything: they were his bond servants; but what he gave them was from his overflowing grace. I do not think that he who brought five pounds was in the least blamed. He may have been just as diligent as the other, but he had less capacity. But how he must have opened his eyes when his master gave him five *cities*. Perhaps he wondered more than the first servant. Imagine if any one of us had been put to trade with a pound upon commission, and had received five cities for a reward. The money earned would not buy the smallest house, and yet it brings in to the worker five cities!

What surprise filled the heart of the recipient of such bounty! It never entered into his heart to envy the brother who had ten cities, for the five were so vast a recompense. He must have been carried away with rapture with the prospect before him. Though there may be degrees of glory, the only difference will be in the capacity of the blessed to contain it. All the vessels will be full, but they will not be all equally large: the man of the ten pounds will simply be a larger vessel, full to the brim; and the man with the five will be less spacious, but quite as full, to his own glad amazement and joyful bewilderment. However, let us go in for winning the ten pounds if we can. For our Lord's sake let us trade in spiritual things with all our hearts.

"But," says one, "where and what will these cities be?" It may be that all this will literally happen during the millennial period, but I do not know. When Christ shall come the dead in Christ will rise first; and we read that *the rest of the dead lived not again till the thousand years were finished* (Revelation 20:5). There may be space during that era for all the special rewards of the gospel dispensation. It may also be, but I do not know, and so I cannot tell you, that we are in future dispensations to fill unto other worlds much the same office as angels fill unto ours. Jesus has made us kings and priests, and we are in training for our thrones. What if in this congregation I am learning to proclaim my Master's glory to myriads of worlds?

Possibly the preacher who is faithful here may yet be made to tell forth his Lord's glory to constellations at a time. What if one might stand upon a central star and preach Christ to worlds on worlds instead of preaching him to these two galleries and to this area! Why not? At any rate, if I should ever gain a voice loud enough to be heard for millions of miles, I would speak none other than those glorious truths that the Lord has revealed in Christ Jesus.

If we are faithful here, we may expect our Master to entrust us with higher service hereafter; only let us see to it that we are able to endure the test, and that we profit by the training. As our account comes out in the very little, so will it be with us on the grand scale of eternity. This puts another face upon the work of this lower sphere. Rulers over ten cities! Rulers over five cities!

Brothers, you are not fit for such dignities if you cannot serve your Lord well in this world with the little he has entrusted to you. If you live wholly to him here, you will be prepared for the glories unspeakable that await all consecrated souls. Let us go in for a devoted life at once! Time is so short, and the things we deal with are comparatively so small! We are soon coming out of the eggshell of time; and when we break loose into eternity, and see the vastness of the divine purposes, we shall be altogether amazed at the service bestowed, which will be the reward of service done. O Lord, make us faithful! Amen.

Chapter 13

Our Own Dear Shepherd

I am the good shepherd, and know my sheep, and am known
of mine. As the Father knoweth me, even so know I the
Father: and I lay down my life for the sheep. (John 10:14-15)

As the passage stands in the Authorized Version, it reads like a number of short sentences with scarcely any apparent connection. Even in that form it is precious; for our Lord's pearls are priceless even when they are not threaded together. But when I tell you that in the Greek the word *and* is several times repeated, and that the translators have had to leave out one of these *ands* to make sense of the passage on their line of translation, you will judge that they are none too accurate in this case. To use many *ands* is after the manner of John; but there is usually a true and natural connection between his sentences. The "and" with him is usually a real golden link, and not a mere sound; we need a translation that makes it so. Observe also that in our version the word *sheep* is put in italics, to show that it is not in the original. There is no need for this alteration if the passage is more closely rendered. Hear, then, the text in its natural form –

I am the good shepherd; and I know mine own, and mine
own know me, even as the Father knoweth me, and I
know the Father; and I lay down my life for the sheep
(John 10:14-15 RV).

This reading I have given you is that of the Revised Version. For that Revised Version I have but little care as a general rule, holding it to be by no means an improvement upon our common Authorized Version. It is a useful thing to have it for private reference, but I trust it will never be regarded as the standard English translation of the New Testament. The Revised Version of the Old Testament is so excellent that I am half afraid it may carry the Revised New Testament upon its shoulders into general use. I sincerely hope that this may not be the case, for the result would be a decided loss.

However, that is not my point. Returning to our subject, I believe that on this occasion, the Revised Version is true to the original. We will therefore follow it in this instance, and we shall find that it makes most delightful and instructive sense. *I am the good shepherd; and I know mine own, and mine own know me, even as the Father knoweth me, and I know the Father; and I lay down my life for the sheep* (RV).

He who speaks to us in these words is the Lord Jesus Christ. To our mind every word of Holy Scripture is precious. When God speaks to us by priest or prophet, or in any way, we are glad to hear. Although when, in the Old Testament, we meet with a passage that begins with *thus saith the Lord,* we feel specially charmed to have the message directly from God's own mouth, yet we make no distinction between this Scripture and that. We accept it all as inspired; and we are not given to dispute about different degrees and varying modes of inspiration, and all that. The matter is plain enough if learned unbelievers did not mystify it; *all scripture is given by inspiration of God, and is profitable for doctrine, for reproof, for correction, for instruction in righteousness* (2 Timothy 3:16).

Still, there is to our mind a peculiar sweetness about words that were actually spoken by the Lord Jesus Christ himself: these are as honey in the comb. You have before you, in this text, not that which comes to you by prophet, priest, or king, but that which is spoken to you by one who is Prophet, Priest, and King in one, even your Lord Jesus Christ. He opens his mouth and speaks to you. You will open your ear and listen to him, if you are indeed his own.

Observe here, also, that we have not only Christ for the speaker, but we have also Christ for the subject. He speaks, and speaks about himself. It would not be proper for you, or for me, to praise ourselves; but there is nothing more lovely in the world than for Christ to commend himself. He is other than we are, something infinitely above us, and is not under rules that apply to us fallible mortals. When he speaks forth his own glory, we feel that his speech is not conceit; no, rather, when he praises himself, we thank him for doing so, and admire the lowly condescension that permits him to desire and accept honor from such poor hearts as ours.

It would be prideful for us to seek the honor of men; it is humility in him to do so, seeing he is so great a One that the esteem of beings so inferior as we are cannot be desired by him for his own sake, but for ours. Of all our Lord's words, those are the sweetest in which he speaks about himself. Even he cannot find another theme that can excel that of himself.

My brethren, who can speak of Jesus but himself? He masters all our eloquence. His perfection exceeds our understanding; the light of his excellence is too bright for us, it blinds our eyes. Our Beloved must be his own mirror. None but Jesus can reveal Jesus. Only he can see himself, and know himself, and understand himself; and therefore none but he can reveal himself. We are most glad that in his tenderness to us he sets himself forth by many choice metaphors, and instructive emblems, by which he would make us know some little bit of that love that passes knowledge. With his own hand he fills a golden cup out of the river of his own infinity, and hands it to us that we may drink and be refreshed.

Take, then, these words as being doubly refreshing, because they come directly from the Well-beloved's own mouth, and contain rich revelations of his own all-glorious self. I feel that I must read them again – *I am the good shepherd; and I know mine own, and mine own know me, even as the Father knoweth me, and I know the Father; and I lay down my life for the sheep* (RV).

In this text there are three matters about which I shall speak. First, I see here *complete character. I am the good shepherd* (RV). He is not a half shepherd, but a shepherd in the fullest possible sense. Secondly, I see *complete knowledge. And I know mine own, and mine own know me, even as the Father knoweth me, and I know the Father* (RV). Thirdly, here is *complete sacrifice.* How preciously that sentence winds up the whole: *And I lay down my life for the sheep* (RV). He goes the full length to which sacrifice can go. He lays down his soul in the place of his sheep – so the words might be not incorrectly translated. He goes the full length of self-sacrifice for his own.

First, then, here is complete character. Whenever the Savior describes himself by any emblem, that emblem is exalted and expanded; and yet it is not able to bear all his meaning. The Lord Jesus fills out every type, figure, and character; and when the vessel is filled there is an overflow. There is more in Jesus, the Good Shepherd, than you can pack away in a shepherd. He is the good, the great, the chief Shepherd; but he is much more.

Emblems to set him forth may be multiplied as the drops of the morning, but the whole multitude will fail to reflect all his brightness. Creation is too small a frame in which to hang his likeness. Human thought is too condensed, human speech is too feeble to set him forth to the full. When all the emblems in earth and heaven shall have described him to their utmost, there will remain a somewhat not yet described. You may square the circle before you can set forth Christ in the language of mortal men. He is inconceivably above our conceptions, unutterably above our utterances.

But notice that he here sets himself forth as a shepherd. Dwell on this for a moment. A shepherd is hardly such a man as we employ in England to look after sheep for a few months until they are large enough to be slaughtered; a shepherd after the Oriental sort, such as Abraham, Jacob, or David, is quite another person.

The Eastern shepherd is generally *the owner* of the flock, or at least the son of their owner, and so he is their proprietor possibly for the future. The sheep are his own. English shepherds seldom, or never, own the sheep; they are employed to take care of them, and they have no other interest in them. Our native shepherds are a very excellent set of men as a rule – those I have known have been admirable specimens of intelligent working-men – yet they are not at all like the Oriental shepherd, and cannot be; for he is usually the owner of the flock that he tends. He remembers how he came into possession of the flock, and when and where each of the present sheep was born, and where he has led them, and what trials he has had in connection with them; and he remembers this with the emphasis that they are his own inheritance.

His wealth consists in them. He very seldom has much of a house, and he does not usually own much land. He takes his sheep over a good stretch of country, which is open common for all his tribe; but his possessions lie in his flocks. Ask him, "How much are you worth?" and he answers, "I own so many sheep." In the Latin tongue, the word for *money* is akin to the word *sheep,* because, to many of the first Romans, wool was their wealth, and their fortunes lay in their flocks.

The Lord Jesus is our Shepherd: we are his wealth. If you ask what is his heritage, he tells you of *the riches of the glory of his inheritance in the saints* (Ephesians 1:18). Ask him what are his jewels, and he replies, *They shall be mine, . . . in that day* (Malachi 3:17). If you ask him where his treasures are, he will tell you, *The Lord's portion is his people; Jacob is the lot of his inheritance* (Deuteronomy 32:9). The Lord Jesus Christ has nothing that he values as much as he does his own people. For their sakes he gave up all that he had, and died naked on the cross. Not only can he say, *I gave . . . Ethiopia and Seba for thee* (Isaiah 43:3), but he can also say he *loved [his] church, and gave himself for it* (Ephesians 5:25). He regards his church as being his own body, *the fulness of him that filleth all in all* (Ephesians 1:23).

The shepherd, as he owns the flock, is also *the caretaker.* He takes care of them always. One of our brethren now present is a fireman; and, since he lives at the fire station, he is always on duty. I asked him whether he was not off duty during certain hours of every day, but he said, "No, I am never off duty." He is on duty when he goes to bed, he is on duty while he is eating his breakfast, he is on duty if he walks down the street. Any time the bell may ring the alarm, he must be in his place, and hasten to the fire.

Our Lord Jesus Christ is never off duty. He has constant care of his people day and night. He has declared it – *For Zion's sake will I not hold my peace, and for Jerusalem's sake I will not rest* (Isaiah 62:1). He can truly say what Jacob did: *In the day the drought consumed me, and the frost by night* (Genesis 31:40). He says of his flock what he says of his garden: *I the Lord do keep it; I will water it every moment: lest any hurt it, I will keep it night and day* (Isaiah 27:3).

I cannot tell you all the care a shepherd has over his flock, because his anxieties are of such a various kind. Sheep have about as many complaints as men. You do not know much about them, and I am not going to enter into details, for the all-sufficient reason that I do not know much about them myself; but the shepherd knows, and the shepherd will tell you that he leads an anxious life. He seldom has all the flock well at one time. One sheep or another is sure to be ailing, and he spies it out, and has eye and hand and heart ready for its help and relief. There are many varieties of complaints and needs, and all these are laid upon the shepherd's heart. He is both possessor and caretaker of the flock.

Then he has to be *the provider* too, for there is not a woolly head among them that knows anything about the finding and selecting of pasture. The season may be very dry, and where there once was grass there may be nothing but a brown powder. It may be that vegetation is only to be found by the side of the rippling brooks, here and there a bit; but the sheep do not know anything about that; the shepherd must know everything for them. The shepherd is the sheep's providence. Both for time and for eternity, for body and for soul, our Lord Jesus supplies all our needs out of his riches in glory. He is the great storehouse from which we derive everything. He has provided, he does provide, and he will provide; and each one of us may therefore sing, *The Lord is my shepherd; I shall not want* (Psalm 23:1).

But, dear friends, we often dream that we are the shepherds, or that we, at any rate, have to find some of the pasture. I could not help saying just now to our friends at our little prayer meeting, "There is a passage in the Psalms that makes the Lord do for us what one would have thought we could have done for ourselves – '*He maketh me to lie down in green pastures.*'" Surely, if a sheep can do nothing else, it can lie down. Yet to lie down is the very hardest thing for God's sheep to do. It is here that the full power of the rest-giving Christ has to come in to make our fretful, worrying, doubtful natures lie down and rest. Our Lord is able to give us perfect peace, and he will do so if we will simply trust in his abounding care. It is the shepherd's business to be the provider; let us remember this, and be very happy.

Moreover, he has to be *the leader.* He leads the sheep wherever they have to go. I have often been astonished at the shepherds in the South of France, which is so much like Palestine, to see where they will take their sheep.

Once every week I saw the shepherd come down to Mentone, and guide all his flock to the seabeach. I could see nothing for them there but big stones. Folks say that perhaps this is what makes the mutton so hard; but I have no doubt the poor creatures get a little taste of salt, or something that does them good. At any rate, they follow the shepherd, and away he goes up the steep hillsides, taking long steps, until he reaches points where the grass is growing on the sides of the hills. He knows the way, and the sheep have nothing to do but to follow him wherever he goes. Theirs is not to make the way; theirs is not to choose the path; but theirs is to keep close to his heel.

Do you not see our blessed Shepherd leading your own pilgrimage? Can you not see him guiding your way? Do you not say, "Yes, he leadeth me, and it is my joy to follow"? Lead on, O blessed Lord; lead on, and we will follow the traces of your feet!

The shepherd in the East has also to be *the defender* of the flock, for wolves still prowl in those regions. All sorts of wild beasts attack the flock, and he must be at the front. Thus it is with our Shepherd. No wolf can attack us without finding our Lord in arms against him. No lion can roar upon the flock without arousing a greater than David. *He that keepeth Israel shall neither slumber nor sleep* (Psalm 121:4).

He is a shepherd, then, and he completely fills the character – much more completely than I can show you just now.

Notice that the text puts an adjective upon the shepherd, decorating him with a chain of gold. The Lord Jesus Christ himself says, *I am the **good** shepherd* (emphasis added). *The **good** shepherd* – that is, he is not a thief that steals, and only deals with the sheep as he bears them from the fold to the slaughter. He is not a hireling: he does not do merely what he is paid to do, or commanded to do; but he does everything *con amore,* with a willing heart. He throws his soul into it. There is a goodness, a tenderness, a willingness, a powerfulness, a force, and an energy in all that Jesus does that makes him to be the best possible shepherd that can be. He is no hireling; neither is he an idler.

Even shepherds that have had their own flocks have neglected them, as there are farmers who do not well cultivate their own farms; but it is never so with Christ. He is the Good Shepherd: good up to the highest point of goodness, good in all that is tender, good in all that is kind, good in all the directions in which a shepherd can be needed. He is good at fight, and good at rule; good in watchful oversight, and good in prudent leadership; good in every way most exceedingly.

And then notice he puts it: *I am **the** good shepherd* (emphasis added). That is the point I want to bring out. Of other shepherds we can say, he is *a* shepherd, but this is *the* Shepherd. All others in the world are shadows of the true Shepherd; and Jesus is the substance of them all. That which we see in the world with these eyes is after all not the substance, but the type, the shadow. That which we do not see with our eyes, that which only our faith perceives, is after all the real thing. I have seen shepherds, but they were only pictures to me.

The Shepherd, the real, the truest, the best, the most sure example of shepherdy is the Christ himself; and you and I are the sheep. Those sheep we see on yonder mountainside are just types of ourselves; but we are the true sheep, and Jesus is the true Shepherd. If an angel were to fly over the earth to find out the real sheep and the real Shepherd, he would say, "The sheep of God's pasture are men; and Jehovah is their Shepherd. He is the true, the real Shepherd of the true and real sheep." All the possibilities that lie in a shepherd are found in Christ. Every good thing that you can imagine to be, or that should be, in a shepherd, you find in the Lord Jesus Christ.

Now, I want you to notice that, according to the text, the Lord Jesus Christ greatly rejoices in this. He says, *I am the good shepherd.* He does not confess that fact as if he were ashamed of it, but he repeats it in this chapter so many times that it almost reads like the refrain of a song. *I am the good shepherd:* he evidently rejoices in it. He rolls it under his tongue as a sweet morsel. Evidently it is to his heart's content. He does not say, "I am the Son of God, I am the Son of Man, I am the Redeemer"; but this he does say, and he congratulates himself upon it: *I am the good shepherd.*

This should encourage you and me to get a full hold of the word. If Jesus is so pleased to be my Shepherd, let me be equally pleased to be his sheep; and let me avail myself of all the privileges that are wrapped up in his being my Shepherd, and in my being his sheep. I see that it will not worry him for me to be his sheep. I see that my needs will cause him no perplexity. I see that he will not consider it going out of his way to attend to my weakness and trouble. He delights to dwell on the fact: *I am the good shepherd.* He invites me, as it were, to come and bring my needs and woes to him, and then look up to him, and be fed by him. Therefore, I will do it.

Does it not make you feel truly happy to hear your own Lord say himself, and say it to you out of this precious Book, *I am the good shepherd*? Do you not reply, "Indeed you are a good Shepherd. You are a good Shepherd to me. My heart lays emphasis upon the word *good,* and says of you, 'There is none good but One, but you are that good One.' You are the Good Shepherd of the sheep."

So much, then, concerning the complete character.

May the Holy Spirit bless the Word still more, while I speak in my broken way upon the next point: the complete knowledge.

The knowledge of Christ towards his sheep, and of the sheep towards him, is wonderfully complete. I must read the text again – *I know mine own, and mine own know me, even as the Father knoweth me, and I know the Father* (RV).

First, then, consider *Christ's knowledge of his own, and the comparison by which he sets it forth: As the Father knoweth me.* I cannot imagine a stronger comparison. Do you know how much the Father knows the Son, who is his glory, his darling, his *alter ego,* his other self – yes, one God with him? Do you know how intimate the knowledge of the Father must be of his Son, who is his own wisdom, alas, who is his own self? The Father and the Son are one spirit. We cannot tell how intimate is that knowledge; and yet so intimately, so perfectly does the Great Shepherd know his sheep.

He knows their *number.* He will never lose one. He will count them all again in that day when the sheep shall pass again under the hand of him that counts them, and then he will make full tally of them. *Of them which thou gavest me,* says he, *have I lost none* (John 18:9). He knows the number of those for whom he paid the ransom price.

He knows their *persons.* He knows the age and character of every one of his own. He assures us that the very hairs of our head are all numbered. Christ does not have an unknown sheep. It is not possible that he would have overlooked or forgotten one of them. He has such an intimate knowledge of all who are redeemed with his most precious blood that he never mistakes one of them for another, nor misjudges one of them. He knows their constitutions – those that are weak and feeble, those that are nervous and frightened, those that are strong, those that have a tendency to presumption, those that are sleepy, those that are brave, those that are sick, sorry, worried, or wounded. He knows those that are hunted by the devil, those that are caught up between the jaws of the lion, and shaken until the very life is almost driven out of them. He knows their feelings, fears, and frights. He knows the secret ins and outs of every one of us better than any one of us knows himself.

He knows our *trials* – the particular trial under which you are now bowed down, my sister; our difficulties – that special difficulty that seems to block up your way, my brother, at this very time. All the ingredients of our life-cup are known to him. *I know mine own, . . . even as the Father knoweth me* (RV). It is impossible to imagine a completer knowledge than that which the Father has of his only begotten Son; and it is equally impossible to imagine a completer knowledge than that which Jesus Christ has of every one of his chosen.

He knows our *sins*. I often feel glad to think that he always did know our evil natures, and what would come of them. When he chose us, he knew what we were, and what we would be. He did not buy his sheep in the dark. He did not choose us without knowing all the devious ways of our past and future lives.

> He saw us ruined in the fall,
> Yet loved us notwithstanding all.

Herein lies the splendor of his grace. *Whom he did foreknow, he also did predestinate.* His election implies foreknowledge of all our ill manners. They say of human love that it is blind; but Christ's love has many eyes, and all its eyes are open, and yet he loves us still.

I need not enlarge upon this. It ought, however, to be very full of comfort to you that you are so known of your Lord, especially as he knows you not merely with the cold, clear knowledge of the intellect, but also with the knowledge of love and of affection. He knows you in his heart. You are uniquely dear to him. You are approved of him. You are accepted of him. He knows you by acquaintance with you, not by hearsay. He knows you by communion with you; he has been with you in sweet fellowship. He has read you as a man reads his book, and remembers what he reads. He knows you by sympathy with you: he is a man like yourself.

> He knows what sore temptations mean,
> For he has felt the same.

He knows your weaknesses. He knows the points wherein you suffer most, for

> In every pang that rends the heart
> The Man of Sorrows had a part.

He gained this knowledge in the school of sympathetic suffering. *Though he were a Son, yet learned he obedience by the things which he suffered* (Hebrews 5:8). *[He] was in all points tempted like as we are* (Hebrews 4:15); *it behoved him to be made like unto his brethren* (Hebrews 2:17); and by being made like us he has come to know us, and he does know us in a very practical and tender way.

You have a watch, and it will not go, or it goes very irregularly, and you give it into the hands of one who knows nothing about watches, and he says, "I will clean it for you." He will do it more harm than good. But here is the very person who made the watch. He says, "I put every wheel into its place; I made the whole of it, from beginning to end." You think to yourself, "I feel the utmost confidence in trusting that man with my watch; he can surely put it right, for he made it." It often cheers my heart to think that since the Lord made me, he can put me right, and keep me so to the end. My Maker is my Redeemer. He that first made me has made me again, and will make me perfect, to his own praise and glory. That is the first part of this complete knowledge.

The second part of the subject is *our knowledge of the Lord, and the fact by which it is illustrated. And mine own know me, . . . and I know the Father* (RV). I think I hear some of you say, "I do not see so much in that. I can see a great deal more in Christ's knowing us." Beloved, I see a great deal in our knowing Christ. That he should know me is great condescension, but it must be easy for him to know me. Being so divine, with such a piercing eye as his, it is amazingly condescending, as I say, but it is not difficult for him to know me. The marvel is that I should ever know him. That such a stupid, blind, deaf, and dead soul as mine should ever know him, and should know him as he knows the Father, is ten thousand miracles in one.

Oh sirs, this is a wonder so great that I do not think you and I have come at it yet to the full, or else we would sit down in glad surprise and say, "This proves him to be the Good Shepherd indeed, not only that he knows his flock, but also that he has taught them so well that they know him!" With such a flock as Christ has, that he should be able to train his sheep so that they should be able to know him, and to know him as he knows the Father, is miraculous.

O beloved, if this be true of us, that we know our Shepherd, we may clap our hands for extreme joy! And yet I think it is true even now. At any rate, I know so much of my Lord that nothing gives me so much joy as to hear of him. Brethren, there is no boasting in this personal assertion of mine; it is only the bare truth. You can say the same, can you not? If anybody were to preach to you the finest sermon that was ever delivered, would it charm you if there was no Christ in it? No. But you will come and hear me talk about Jesus Christ in words as simple as ever I can find, and you cry one to another, "It was good to be there."

Thou dear Redeemer, dying Lamb,
    We love to hear of thee:
No music's like thy charming name,
    Nor half so sweet can be.

Now mark that this is the way in which Jesus knows the Father. Jesus delights in his Father, and you delight in Jesus. I know you do; and herein the comparison holds good.

Moreover, does not the dear name of Jesus stir your very soul? What is it that makes you feel as if you wish to hasten away, so that you might be doing holy service for the Lord? What makes your very heart awake, and feel ready to leap out of your body? What but hearing of the glories of Jesus! Play on what string you please, and my ear is deaf to it; but when you once begin to tell of Calvary, and sing the song of free grace, and dying love, oh, then my soul opens all her ears, and drinks in the music, and then her blood begins to stir, and she is ready to shout for joy! Do you not even now sing,

> Oh, for this love let rocks and hills
>   Their lasting silence break,
> And all harmonious human tongues
>   The Savior's praises speak.

> "Yes, we will praise thee, dearest Lord,
>   Our souls are all on flame,
> Hosanna round the spacious earth
>   To thine adored name."

Yes, we know Jesus. We feel the power of our union with him. We know him, brethren, so that we are not to be deceived by false shepherds. There is a way nowadays of preaching Christ against Christ. It is a new device of the devil to set up Jesus against Jesus, his kingdom against his atonement, his precepts against his doctrines. The half-Christ in his example is put forth to frighten souls away from the whole Christ, who saves the souls of men from guilt as well as from sin, from hell as well as from folly.

But they cannot deceive us in that way. No, beloved, we know our Shepherd from all others. We know him from a statue covered with his clothes. We know the living Christ, for we have come into living contact with him, and we cannot be deceived any more than Jesus Christ himself can be deceived about the Father. *Mine own know me, . . . and I know the Father* (RV). We know him by union with him, and by communion with him. *We have seen the Lord* (John 20:25). *Truly our fellowship is with the Father, and with his Son Jesus Christ* (1 John 1:3).

We know him by love: our soul cleaves to him, even as the heart of Christ cleaves to the Father. We know him by trusting him – *[He] is all my salvation, and all my desire* (2 Samuel 23:5).

I remember once feeling many questions as to whether I was a child of God or not. I went into a little chapel, and I heard a good man preach. He was a simple workingman. I heard him preach, and I made my handkerchief wet with my tears as I heard him talk about Christ and the precious blood. When I was preaching the same things to others, I was wondering whether this truth was mine, but while I was hearing for myself, I knew it was mine, for my very soul lived upon it. I went to that good man and thanked him for the sermon. He asked me who I was. When I told him, he turned all manner of colors. "Why," he said, "sir, that was your own sermon." I said, "Yes, I knew it was, and it was good of the Lord to feed me with food that I had prepared for others." I perceived that I had a true taste for what I myself knew to be the gospel of Jesus Christ. Oh yes, we do love our Good Shepherd! We cannot help it.

And we know him also by a deep sympathy with him; for what Christ desires to do, we also long to do. He loves to save souls, and so do we. Would we not save all the people in a whole street if we could? Alas, in a whole city, and in the whole world? Nothing makes us so glad as that Jesus Christ is a Savior. "There is news in the paper," says one. That news is often of small importance to our hearts. I happened to hear that a poor servant girl had heard me preach the truth and found Christ; and I confess I felt more interest in that fact than in all the rise and falls of Whigs or Tories. What does it matter who is in parliament, so long as souls are saved?

That is the main thing. If the kingdom of Christ grows, all the other kingdoms are of small account. That is the one kingdom for which we live, and for which we would gladly die. As there is a boundless sympathy between the Father and the Son, so is there between Jesus and ourselves.

We know Christ as he knows the Father, because we are one with him. The union between Christ and his people is as real and as mysterious as the union between the Son and the Father.

We have a beautiful picture before us. Can you realize it for a minute? The Lord Jesus here among us – picture him! He is the Shepherd. Then, around him are his own people, and wherever he goes they go. He leads them into green pastures and beside the still waters. And there is this peculiarity about them: he knows them as he looks upon every one of them, and they every one of them knows him. There is a deeply intimate and mutual knowledge between them. As surely as he knows them, they know him. The world knows neither the Shepherd nor the sheep, but they know each other.

As surely as truly and as deeply as God the Father knows the Son, so does this Shepherd know his sheep; and as God the Son knows his Father, so do these sheep know their Shepherd. Thus in one band, united by mutual interaction, they travel through the world to heaven. *I know mine own, and mine own know me, even as the Father knoweth me, and I know the Father* (RV). Is not that a blessed picture? God help us to figure in it!

The last subject is complete sacrifice. The complete sacrifice is thus described – *I lay down my life for the sheep.*

These words are repeated in this chapter in different forms some four times. The Savior keeps on saying, *I lay down my life for the sheep.* Read the eleventh verse: *The good shepherd layeth down his life for the sheep* (RV). Read the fifteenth verse again: *I lay down my life for the sheep* (RV). Read the seventeenth verse: *I lay down my life, that I may take it again* (RV). Read the eighteenth verse: *I have power to lay it down, and I have power to take it again* (RV). It looks as if this were another refrain of our Lord's personal hymn. I call this passage his pastoral song. The Good Shepherd with his pipe sings to himself and to his flock, and this comes in at the end of each stanza: *I lay down my life for the sheep.*

Did it not mean, first, that he was always doing so? All his life long he was, as it were, laying it down for them; he was divesting himself of the garments of life until he came to be fully disrobed on the cross. All the life he had, all the power he had, he was always laying it out for his sheep. It means that, to begin with.

And then it means that the sacrifice was actively performed. It was ever in the doing as long as he lived; but he did it actively. He did not die for the sheep merely, but he also laid down his life, which is another thing. Many a man has died for Christ: it was all that he could do. But we cannot lay down our lives, because they are due already as a debt of nature to God, and we are not permitted to die at our own wills. That would be suicidal and improper. With the Lord Christ it was totally different. He was, as it were, actively passive. *I lay down my life for the sheep. . . . I have power to lay it down, and I have power to take it again. This commandment received I from my Father* (John 10:15, 18 RV).

I like to think of our Good Shepherd not merely as dying for us, but also as willingly dying – laying down his life – while he had that life, using it for us; and when the time came, putting off that life on our behalf. This has now been actually done. When he spoke these words, it had not been done. At this time it has been done. *I lay down my life for the sheep* may now be read: I have laid down my life for the sheep." For you, beloved, he has given his hands to the nails, and his feet to the cruel iron. For you he has borne the fever and the bloody sweat; for you he has cried, *Eloi, Eloi, lama sabachthani* (Mark 15:34). For you he has given up the ghost.

And the beauty of it is that he is not ashamed to acknowledge the object of it. *I lay down my life for the sheep* (emphasis added). Whatever Christ did for the world – and I am not one of those who would limit the relevancy of the death of Christ upon the world – yet his peculiar glory is, *I lay down my life for the sheep.*

Great Shepherd, do you mean to say that you have died for such as these? What! For these sheep? Died for them? What! Die for sheep, Shepherd? Surely you have other objects for which to live besides sheep. Have you not other loves, other joys? We know that it would grieve you to see the sheep killed, torn by the wolf, or scattered; but have you really gone so far in love for them that for the sake of those poor creatures you would lay down your life? "Ah, yes," he says, "I would; I have!"

Carry your wondering thoughts to Christ Jesus. What! What! What! Son of God, infinitely great and inconceivably glorious Jehovah, would you lay your life down for men and women? They are no more in comparison with you than so many ants and wasps, pitiful and obnoxious creatures. You could make ten thousand millions of them with a word, or crush them out of existence at one blow of your hand. They are poor things; make the most you can of them. They have hard hearts, and wandering wills; and the best of them are no better than they should be. Savior, did you die for such? He looks around and says, "Yes, I did. I did. I laid down my life for the sheep. I am not ashamed of them, and I am not ashamed to say that I died for them."

No, beloved, he is not ashamed of his dying love. He has told it to his brethren up yonder, and made it known to all the servants in his Father's house, and this has become the song of that house: *Worthy is the Lamb that was slain* (Revelation 5:12)! Shall we not take it up and say, *For thou wast slain, and hast redeemed us to God by thy blood* (Revelation 5:9)?

Whatever men may say about particular redemption, Christ is not ashamed of it. He glories that he laid down his life for the sheep. *For the sheep,* mark you. He does not say *for the world.* There is a relevancy of the death of Christ towards the world; but here he boasts and glories in the specialty of his sacrifice. *I lay down my life **for the sheep;*** "instead of the sheep" it might be read. He glories in substitution for his people. He makes it his boast, when he speaks of his chosen, that he suffered in their stead – that he bore, that they might never bear, the wrath of God on account of sin. What he glories in, we also glory in. *God forbid that I should glory, save in the cross of our Lord Jesus Christ, by whom the world is crucified unto me, and I unto the world* (Galatians 6:14).

O beloved, what a blessed Christ we have who loves us so, who knows us so – whom we also know and love! May others be taught to know him and to love him! Yes, at this hour may they come and put their trust in him, as the sheep trust in the shepherd! We ask it for Jesus' sake. Amen.

Chapter 14

Other Sheep and One Flock

And other sheep I have, which are not of this fold: them also I must bring, and they shall hear my voice; and they shall be one fold [flock], *and one shepherd.* (John 10:16)

This verse is guarded before and behind by two notable statements. Before it we hear the Master say, *I lay down my life for the sheep,* and immediately after it we meet with another grand sentence: *I lay down my life, that I might take it again* (John 10:17). The first statement, *I lay down my life for the sheep* is the sheet anchor of our confidence when storms attack the vessel of the church. The Lord Jesus has by his death proved his love for his people; and his determination to save them is made clear by his laying down his life for them; therefore, doubt and fear should be banished, and the very name of despair should be unknown among the Israel of God. Now we are sure of the love of the Son of God for his chosen flock, for we have an infallible proof of it in the laying down of his life for them.

Now also we are absolutely certain that Christ's purpose is perpetual; it cannot change. The Lord Jesus has committed himself to that purpose beyond recall, for the price is paid and the deed is done by which the purpose is to be chosen. Beyond this we are hereby assured beyond a shadow of a doubt that the divine purpose will be carried out, for it cannot be that Christ should die in vain. We think it a kind of blasphemy to suppose that his blood should be spilt for nothing. Whatever was proposed to be accomplished by the laying down of the life of the Son of God, we feel absolutely certain that it will be fully performed in the teeth of all adversaries; for we are not now speaking of man's design, but of the purpose of God, to which he devoted the heart's blood of his only begotten Son.

We both patiently hope and quietly wait to see the salvation of God, and the performance of all his designs of love; for that death upon the cross is a cause that will surely produce its effect. Christ did not die by chance. The assumption of a Savior disappointed in the results of his blood-shedding is not to be tolerated for a moment. In darkest times that glorious cross flames with light. No evil event can prevent its effectualness. Still, in that sign we conquer. If Jesus has laid down his life for the sheep, then all is well. Rest assured of the Father's love to those sheep; rest assured of the unchangeableness of the divine purpose concerning them, and rest assured of its ultimate achievement.

It must not, shall not, be that God's own Son shall lay down his life in vain. Though heaven and earth should pass away, the precious heart's blood of the Son of God shall accomplish the end for which it was so freely poured forth. Jesus says, *I lay down my life for the sheep;* therefore, the sheep must live who have been redeemed at such a price as this, and the Shepherd in them shall see the labor of his soul and shall be satisfied. So far, we are cheered by the vanguard that marches in advance of our text.

But as if the poor, timid people of God would, nevertheless, at times imagine that the purpose of Christ would not be achieved, behold in the rear another sentence: *I lay down my life, that I might take it again.* He that died, and so redeemed his people by price, lives that he may himself personally see that they are also redeemed by power. If a man dies to achieve a purpose, you feel sure that his very soul must have been in it; but if that man should rise again from the dead, and still pursue his purpose, you would see how resolutely he was set on his plan. If he rose with greater power, clothed with higher rank, and elevated to a more prominent position, and if he still pursued his great object, you would then be more than certain of his never-ending determination to perform his strategy.

In the risen life of Jesus, assurance is made doubly sure. Now are we sure that his plan must be carried out; nothing can hinder it. We dare not dream that the Son of God can be disappointed with the object for which he died, and for which he lives again. If Jesus died for a purpose, he will accomplish it; if Jesus rose for a purpose, he will accomplish it; if Jesus lives forever for a purpose, he will accomplish it. To me this conclusion seems to be beyond question; and if it be so, it puts the destiny of the sheep beyond all hazard. Did not Paul argue much in the same way when he said, *For if, when we were enemies, we were reconciled to God by the death of his Son, much more, being reconciled, we shall be saved by his life* (Romans 5:10)?

If any of you have been cast down by reason of present difficulties, let these two grand texts sound their silver trumpets in your ears. If you have been looking forth from the windows, and the outlook has seemed to be exceedingly dark, take courage, I pray you, from what your Lord has done: his death and resurrection are prophetic of good things to come. You dare not think that Christ will miss the end of his death; you dare not think that he will miss the purpose of his glory-life; why, then, are you cast down?

His will shall be done on earth as it is in heaven, as surely as he came from heaven to earth, and has returned from earth to heaven. His purpose shall be carried out as surely as he died and lives again. Is not this the secret reason why, when the Lord appeared to his sorrowing servant John, he said to him, *I am he that liveth, and was dead; and, behold, I am alive for evermore, Amen; and have the keys of death and of hell* (Revelation 1:18)? Is not the dying and then living Shepherd the safety and the glory of the flock? Therefore comfort one another with these words of your Lord: *I lay down my life for the sheep; I lay down my life, that I might take it again.*

There are four things in the text itself that deserve your attention, for they are full of consolation to minds troubled by the evils of these perilous times. The first is this – our Lord Jesus Christ had a people under the worst circumstances. When he speaks of *other sheep*, it is implied that he had certain sheep at the time; and when he says, *Other sheep I have, which are not of this fold*, it is manifest that even then the Good Shepherd had a fold. The times were grievously dark and evil, but a few true hearts clustered around the Savior and by his divine power were protected as in a *fold*.

It has been supposed that our Lord here alludes to the Jews as *this fold;* but the Jews, as such, were never Christ's fold. He could not have meant to call the Jews around him his fold, for a little further on he exclaims, *Ye believe not, because ye are not of my sheep, as I said unto you* (John 10:26). His fold was that little handful of disciples whom by his personal ministry he had gathered, and who stood folded, as it were, around their Good Shepherd. They might be sneered at as a little company, but he says to his enemies who are standing outside the fold foaming with wrath, "Other sheep I have that are not of this little fold: these you cannot see, but I have them nonetheless for that; these I must in due time lead, and then there shall be one flock and one Shepherd."

See, then, that the Lord Jesus had a people in the worst times. Doubtless these days are exceedingly dangerous, and I have certain brethren around me who never allow me to forget it, for they play well in the minor key, and dwell most judiciously upon the necessary topic of the general decline of the church and the growing depravity of the world. I would not stop them from their faithful warnings, although I can assure them that, with slight variations, I have heard the same tune for years. *Many a time have they afflicted me from my youth [up]* (Psalm 129:1), and it has been good for me. I recollect hearing some thirty years ago that we lived in awful times; and, as nearly as I can recollect, the times have been awful ever since; and I suppose they always will be.

The watchmen of the night see everything except the coming of the morning. Our pilots perceive dangers ahead and steer with caution. Perhaps this is as it should be; at any rate, it is better than sleeping in a fool's paradise. Be this as it may, it is clear that the days of our Lord Jesus Christ were emphatically terrible times. No age can be worse than that age that literally crucified the Son of God, crying, *Away with him, away with him* (John 19:15). Whether the present days are better than those I will not determine, but they cannot be worse. The day of our Lord's first advent was the culmination and the crisis of the world's career of sin; and yet the Good Shepherd had a fold among men in the midnight of history.

There was *a sad lack of vital godliness* in those days. A few godly ones watched for the coming of the Messiah; but they were very few, such as good old Simeon and Anna. A small remnant sighed and cried for the abounding sin of the nation; but the salt was almost gone: Israel was becoming like Sodom and Gomorrah. The choice band of mourners in Zion had not quite died out, but their number was so few that a child might write them.

Speaking generally, when the Savior came to his own, his own received him not. The mass of professing Christians in that day was rotten throughout; the life of God was gone; it could not dwell with the Pharisees nor the Sadducees, nor any of the sects of the times, for they were altogether gone out of the way. The Lord looked, and there was no man to help or to uphold his righteous cause: those who professed to be its champions had altogether become unprofitable.

As for the religious teachers, their mouths had become open sepulchers, and the poison of vipers was under their tongues; and yet the Lord had a people in Judaea even then. On earth there was still a fold for sheep whom he had chosen who knew the Shepherd's voice and gathered to his call and followed him faithfully.

It was a time when *will-worship abounded.* Men had given up worshipping God according to the Scriptures, and they worshipped according to their own notions. Then you might hear the trumpet in every corner of the street, for Pharisees were distributing their charity. You could see fathers and mothers neglected, and families broken up because the scribes had taught the people that if they should say *Corban,* they were free from all obligation to help father or mother.

They taught as doctrines the commandments of men, and the commandments of God were laid aside. To wear broad-bordered garments and phylacteries was exalted into a matter of first importance, while to lie and cheat were mere trifles. To eat with unwashed hands was thought to be a crime, but to devour widow's houses was a thing that to the most self-righteous Pharisee caused no qualm of conscience. The land was filled with will-worship, and that is one great and growing hindrance nowadays; but for all that, Christ had a fold of his own, and in it were those who knew his voice, and these, following at his heel, were enabled to go in and out and find pasture.

It was a day when there was the most *fierce opposition* to the real truth of God. Our Lord Jesus could hardly open his mouth but they took up stones to stone him. It was said that he had a devil and was mad; and that he was *a gluttonous man, and a winebibber, a friend of publicans and sinners* (Luke 7:34). The rage of men against Christ was then boiling at its greatest heat, until at last they took him and nailed him to the cross because they could not endure that he should live among them.

And yet he had his own in those dreadful times. Even then he had his chosen company for whom he laid down his life, of whom he said to the Father, *Thine they were, and thou gavest them me; and they have kept thy word* (John 17:6). To those he spoke, saying, *Ye are they which have continued with me in my temptations. And I appoint unto you a kingdom, as my Father hath appointed unto me* (Luke 22:28-29). Therefore, beloved, I gather that though at this time there is a sad decline in vital godliness, and though will-worship sweeps over the land with its tumultuous waves, and though opposition to the pure truth of Christ is more fierce than ever, nevertheless, even at this present time there is a remnant according to the election of grace. Even today the answer of God says to the complaining prophet, *Yet have I left me seven thousand in Israel, all the knees which have not bowed unto Baal* (1 Kings 19:18). Therefore, my brethren, in confidence possess you your souls.

Now, it is to be noticed that this little company of Christ's people he calls a *fold.* Afterwards they were to be a *flock,* but while his bodily presence was with them, they were preeminently a *fold.* They were few in number, all of one race, mostly in one place, and so compact that they could properly be said to be a *fold.* One glance of the Shepherd's bodily eye saw them all. Fortunately, also, they were so thoroughly distinct from the rest of the world that they were very evidently folded.

Our Lord said of them, *[Ye] are not of the world, even as I am not of the world* (John 17:16). He had shut them in to himself, and had shut the world out. Within this blessed seclusion they were perfectly safe, so that their Lord said to the Father, *While I was with them in the world, I kept them in thy name: those that thou gavest me I have kept, and none of them is lost, but the son of perdition; that the scripture might be fulfilled* (John 17:12).

Whatever their mistakes and faults, and they were many, yet they did not conform themselves to the generation among which they dwelt, but they were kept apart as in a fold while Jesus was with them. In that fold they were protected from all ill weathers, and from the wolf, and the thief. The Lord's presence with them was like a wall of fire round about them: they had only to run to him and he answered all their adversaries, and defended them from reproach.

Like another David, the Lord Jesus guarded his flock from all the ravening lions that sought to devour them. True, even in that little fold there were goats, for he himself said, *Have not I chosen you twelve, and one of you is a devil?* (John 6:70). Even then they were not absolutely pure, but they were wonderfully so; and they were marvelously separated from the world, preserved from false doctrine, and kept from dividing and scattering.

Within that fold they were being strengthened for the future following of their Great Shepherd. They were learning a thousand things that would be useful to them when afterwards he sent them forth as lambs among wolves, so that they would be *wise as serpents, and harmless as doves* because of what they had learned from their Lord. Thus, you see that in the worst times the Lord had a church; I might almost say the best church. May I not call it so? For that apostolic church upon which the Holy Spirit descended was not a bit behind the church of any era that succeeded it. It was the choice flock of all the flocks of the ages, even that feeble company of which Jesus said, *Fear not, little flock; for it is your Father's good pleasure to give you the kingdom* (Luke 12:32).

Yet you see one thing is notable here, that when Jesus had thus shut them all in, he would not allow them to become exclusive and glide into a state of selfish satisfaction. No, he opens wide the door of the sheepfold and cries to them, *Other sheep I have.* Thus, he restrains a tendency so common in the church to be forgetful of those outside the fold, and to make one's own personal salvation the sum and substance of religion. I do not think it wrong to sing,

> We are a garden wall'd around,
>   Chosen, and made peculiar ground;
> A little spot, enclosed by grace
>   Out of the world's wide wilderness.

On the contrary, I judge that the verse is true, and sweet, and ought to be sung; but then there are other truths besides this one. To us also the

Shepherd opens the door of the enclosed garden and says, *The wilderness and the solitary place shall be glad for them; and the desert shall rejoice, and blossom as the rose* (Isaiah 35:1). The fold is our abode, but it is not our sole sphere of action; for we are to go forth from it into all the world seeking our brethren. Seeing that our Lord has other sheep that are not of this fold, and these are to be found by him through his faithful people, let us arouse ourselves to the holy enterprise.

> O, come, let us go and find them
>> In the paths of death they roam;
> At the close of the day 'twill be sweet to say,
>> "I have brought some lost one home."

Beloved, I shall leave this point when I have said to you, Never despair! The Lord of Hosts is with his people. They may be few and poor, but they are Christ's, and that makes them precious. A common sheepfold is not a thing of glory and beauty, for rough walls compose it, and it is but a shack for sheep; even so the church may appear inferior and contemptible in men's eyes, but then it is the sheepfold of the Shepherd King, and the sheep belong to the Lord God Almighty. There is a glory about this that angels do not fail to see. Here is human weakness, but also divine power. We do not, I fear, estimate the strength of a church correctly.

I read of three brethren who had to carry on a college when funds were running short. One of them complained that they had no helpers, and could not hope to succeed; but another who had more faith said to his brother, "Do you ask what we can do? Do you say that we are so few? I do not see that we are few, for we are a thousand at the least."

"A thousand of us!" said the other. "How is that?"

"Why," replied the first, "I am a nothing, and you are a nothing, and our brother is a nothing; so we have three nothings to begin with. Then I am sure the Lord Jesus is one. Put him down before the three nothings and we have a thousand directly." Was not this bravely spoken?

What power we have when we do but set the great One in the front. You are nothing, brother; you are nothing, sister; I am nothing; we are all nothing when we are put together without our Lord. But oh, if he stands in front of us, then we are thousands; and again it is as true on earth as in heaven: the chariots of the Lord are twenty thousand, even thousands of messengers, and the Lord is among them as in the Holy Place.

Therefore, my friends, be not cast down at any time, but say unto yourselves, We have not even now come to so dark a night as once fell on this world. We are not at this painful moment in such a desperate condition as the church of Christ was in his own day; and if the Lord be spiritually in the midst of us, we need not fear *though the earth be removed, and though the mountains be carried into the midst of the sea* (Psalm 46:2), for there is a city that abides forever, and *there is a river, the streams whereof shall make glad the city of God. . . . God is in the midst of her; she shall not be moved: God shall help her, and that right early* (Psalm 46:4-5). Therefore, my fellow believers, *be strong and of good courage* (Joshua 10:25)!

But now, secondly, it is clear, for the text teaches it in so many words, that our Lord has other sheep not yet known to us. He says, *Other sheep I have.* I want you to notice that strong expression, *Other sheep **I have*** (emphasis added) – not "I shall have," but "I have other sheep." Many of these sheep were not even in the thoughts of the apostles. I do not think it had crossed the mind of Peter, James, or John that their Lord had any sheep in this poor savage island, then scarcely regarded as being within the borders of the earth; I do not suppose the apostles at that time even dreamed that their Lord Jesus had sheep in Rome.

No, their most liberal notion was that the Hebrew nation might be converted, and the scattered of the seed of Abraham gathered together into one. Our Shepherd King has greater thoughts than the most large-hearted of his servants. He delights to enlarge the area of our love. *Other sheep I have.* You do not know them, but the Shepherd does. Unknown to ministers, unknown to the warmest-hearted Christians, there are many in the world whom Jesus claims for his own through the covenant of grace.

Who are these? Well, these *other sheep* were, first, *his chosen;* for he has a people whom he has chosen out of the world, and ordained unto eternal life. *Ye have not chosen me,* said he, *but I have chosen you* (John 15:16) – there is a people upon whom his sovereignty has fixed its loving choice from before the foundation of the world. And of these elect ones he says, "I have them." His election of them is the basis of his property in them. These are also *those whom his Father gave him,* of whom he says in another place, *All that the Father giveth me shall come to me* (John 6:37); and again, *Of them which thou gavest me have I lost none* (John 18:9).

His Father's eternal donation of them seals his title to them. These are the people for whom he peculiarly and especially laid down his life, that they might be *the redeemed of the Lord* (Isaiah 62:12). *Christ also loved the church, and gave himself for it* (Ephesians 5:25). These are they that are redeemed from among men, of whom we read: *Know ye not that . . . ye are not your own? For ye are bought with a price* (1 Corinthians 6:19-20).

The Lord Jesus laid down his life for his sheep: he tells us so himself, and none can question his own statement. These are those of whom Jesus says, "I have them," for on account of these he entered into *suretyship engagements,* even as Jacob undertook the flock of Laban and watched day and night so that he would not lose them, and if one had been torn, he would have had to make it good.

These sheep represent a people for whom Christ has entered into suretyship engagements with his Father that he will deliver each one of them safely at the last day of account, not one of them being absent when the sheep shall pass again under the hand of him who counts them as they will at the last great day. *Other sheep I have,* says Christ. How wonderful that he would say, "I have them," though as yet they were far off by wicked works.

What was their state? They were a people without shepherd, without fold, without pasture, lost on the mountains, wandering in the woods, lying down to die, ready to be devoured by the wolf; yet Jesus says, *Other sheep I have, which are not of this fold.* They were sheep that had wandered exceedingly far, even into the most shameful iniquity, and yet he says, "I have them."

Bad as this world is today, it must have been far worse in the cruel Roman age as to open vices and unmentionable abominations; and yet these wanderers were the sheep of Christ, and in due time they were delivered from their sins, and fetched away from all the superstition and idolatry and filthiness into which they had wandered. They were Christ's even while they were afar off; he had chosen them, the Father had given them to him, he had bought them, and he determined to have them; no, he says, "I *have* them," and he calls them his own even while they are transgressing and running headlong into destruction.

It seems to me that these were as well known to Christ as those that were in his fold. I think I see him, the divine Man, standing there confronting his adversaries, and when he has cast his glance upon his foes, I see his eyes going to and fro throughout the whole earth to gaze upon a sight far more pleasant to him. While he speaks, his eyes flash with joyous fire as they light upon thousands out of every kindred and people and tongue, and while he quotes to himself the words of the twenty-second psalm: *All the ends of the world shall remember and turn unto the Lord: and all the kindreds of the nations shall worship before thee. For the kingdom is the Lord's: and he is the governor among the nations. A seed shall serve him; it shall be accounted to the Lord for a generation* (Psalm 22:27-28, 30). He spies out the myriads that are his, and he rejoices before his scornful foes as he sees his growing kingdom that they are powerless to overthrow.

Proud, self-righteous men may blindly refuse the leadership of the Lord's anointed Shepherd, but he shall not be without a flock to be his honor and reward. Did not the Lord at that time rejoice in his inmost heart and soliloquize within himself thus – *Though Israel be not gathered, yet shall I be glorious in the eyes of the Lord, and my God shall be my strength* (Isaiah 49:5)? This led him to say, *Other sheep I have.*

In this there is great comfort for God's people who love the souls of their fellow man. The Lord has a people in London, and he knows them. *I have much people in this city* (Acts 18:10) was said to the apostle when as yet nobody was converted there. "I have them," says Christ, though as yet they had not sought him. Our Lord Jesus has an elect redeemed people all over the world at this time, though as yet they are not called by grace. I know not where they are, nor where they are not; but for certain he has them somewhere, since still it stands true: *Other sheep I have, which are not of this fold.*

This is a part of our authority for going out to find the lost sheep; for we brethren have a right to go anywhere to seek after our Master's sheep. I have no business to go hunting after other people's sheep; but if they are my Master's sheep, who shall stop me from inquiring over hill and dale, "Have you seen my Master's sheep?" If any say, "You are intruding in this land," let the answer be: "We are seeking our Master's sheep that have strayed here! Excuse our pushing further than politeness might allow, but we are in haste to find a lost sheep."

This is your excuse for going into a house where you are not wanted, to try and leave your tract and speak a word for Christ: say, "I think my Master has one of his sheep here, and I am coming after it." You have received a search warrant from the King of Kings, and therefore you have a right to enter and search after your Lord's stolen property. If men belonged to the devil, we would not rob the Enemy himself; but they do not belong to him; he neither made them nor bought them, and therefore we seize them in the King's name whenever we can lay hands on them. I doubt not but what there are some here this morning who neither know nor love the Savior as yet, who nevertheless belong to the Redeemer, and he will yet bring them to himself and to his flock.

Therefore, it is that we preach with confidence. I do not come into this pulpit hoping that perhaps somebody will of his own free will return to Christ; that may be so or not, but my hope lies in another quarter. I hope that my Master will lay hold of some of them and say, "You are mine, and you shall be mine; I claim you for myself." My hope arises from the freeness of grace, and not from the freedom of the will. A poor haul of fish will any gospel fisherman make if he takes none except those who are eager to leap into the net.

Oh, for an hour of Jesus among this crowd! Oh, for five minutes of the Great Shepherd's handiwork! When the Good Shepherd overtakes his lost sheep, he has not much to say to it. According to the parable he says nothing; but he lays hold of it, lays it on his shoulders and carries it home, and that is what I want the Lord to do this morning with some of you whose will is all the other way, whose wishes and desires are all contrary to him. I want him to come with sacred violence and mighty love to restore you to your Father and your God. Not that you will be saved against your will, but that your consent will be sweetly gained. Oh, that the Lord Jesus would take you in hand and never let you go again. May he sweetly say to you, *Yea, I have loved thee with an everlasting love: therefore with lovingkindness have I drawn thee* (Jeremiah 31:3).

Our third topic contains in it much delight. Our Lord must bring or lead those other sheep. *Them also I must bring* – read it, and it will be more accurate thus: "Them also I must lead:" Christ must be at the head of these other sheep, and they must follow his lead – "Them also I must lead, *and they shall hear my voice.*" Those who belong to Christ secretly must be openly led to follow him.

First, it is Christ that has to do it, even as he has done it up to this time. The text says, *Them **also** I must bring* (emphasis added), and this language implies that those who have already come, he has brought. All that were in the fold Christ had brought there, and all that are to be in the fold he must lead there. All of us who are saved have been saved by the mighty power of God in Christ Jesus. Is it not so? Is there anyone among us that came to Jesus without Jesus first coming to him? Surely, no. Without exception we all admit that it was his love that sought us out and brought us to be the sheep of his pasture. Now, as the Lord Jesus has done this for us, he must do it for others; for they will never come except he fetch them.

Here comes in that emphatic, urgent *must* the proverb that *must* is for the king, and the king may say *must* to all of us. But did you ever hear of a *must* that bound the king himself and constrained him? Kings generally do not care to have it said to them, "You *must*"; but there is a king, the like of which king there never was nor shall be for glory and for dominion, and yet he is bound by a *must*. The Prince Immanuel says, *Them also I **must** bring* (emphasis added). Whenever Jesus says *must,* something comes of it. Who can resist the omnipotent *must*? Clear out, devils! Clear out, wicked men! Flee, darkness! Die, O death! If Jesus says *must,* we know what is going to happen: difficulties vanish, impossibilities are achieved. Glory, glory, the Lord shall get the victory! Jesus says of his chosen, his redeemed, his espoused, his covenanted ones, *Them also I **must** bring,* and therefore it must be done.

Furthermore, he tells us how he must do it. He says, *They shall hear my voice.* So our Lord is going to save people still by the gospel. I do not look for any other means of converting men beyond the simple preaching of the gospel and the opening of men's ears to hear it – *They shall hear my voice.* The old methods are to be followed to the end of the chapter. Our standing orders are, *Go ye into all the world, and preach the gospel to every creature.* We are not commissioned to do anything else but continue to preach the gospel, the selfsame gospel that saved us and that was delivered to us at the beginning. We know of no alterations, enlargements, or amendments to the gospel. We obey and follow one voice, not many voices. One gospel of salvation is to be proclaimed everywhere, and no other work is in our commission.

Then it is added, *They shall hear my voice.* It is promised that they shall first lend an attentive ear and then that they shall yield a willing heart to the voice of divine love, and follow Jesus where he leads. "What then?" says one. "Suppose I speak in Christ's name, and they will not hear?" Do not suppose what cannot be! The Scripture says of the chosen sheep, *They shall hear my voice.* The rest remain in their blindness, but the redeemed will hear and see. Do not again say, "Suppose they will not?" You must not suppose anything that is contrary to what Jesus promises when he says, *They shall hear my voice.*

The graceless may stop their ears if they will, and perish with Christ's voice as a witness against them; but his own redeemed shall hear the heavenly voice and obey it. There is no resisting this divine necessity: Jesus says – *Them also I **must** bring, and they **shall** hear my voice* (emphasis added). It was with this that Paul turned to the Gentiles, and said to the Jews, *Be it known therefore unto you, that the salvation of God is sent unto the Gentiles, and that they will hear it* (Acts 28:28). He had no fear about the reception the word would meet with; neither ought we to entertain any fear, since Christ has a people who must be led, and shall hear the voice of the Bishop and Shepherd of souls.

We have heard it said that if Christ *must* have his people, what is the good of preaching? What would be the good of preaching if it were otherwise? Why, dear sir, this fact is one great reason why we preach. That which you suppose to be a motive for inaction is the strongest motive for energetic movement.

Because the Lord has a people that must be saved, we feel an urgent necessity laid upon us to join with him in bringing this people to himself. They *must* come, and we *must* fetch them. Christian brethren, do you not feel that you *must* help in compelling them to come to the wedding feast? Is it not laid upon you that you *must* go after lost souls, that you *must* speak to them, seeing that you *must* have a hand in bringing these blood-bought ones to Christ by his Holy Spirit?

And again, are there not some in this place who feel a necessity laid upon them also that they *must* come? Do I not hear some of you saying, "I have stood out a long while, but I *must* come. I have resisted divine grace long enough, and now Christ has laid his hand on me; I *must* come." How I wish that a heavenly *must,* a blessed necessity of omnipotent decree, may overshadow you and bear you as a sheep to the fold.

Oh, that you may now yield yourselves unto God because the love of Christ constrains you. Submit yourselves unto God, acknowledging the supreme authority of his grace, which shall lead every thought into captivity, that henceforth Christ may reign in your hearts, and put every enemy under his feet. He says, *Him that cometh to me I will in no wise cast out.* "I will trust him," says one; "I feel I must." Just so; and that trust is a mark of your election of God, for *he that believeth on the Son hath everlasting life* (John 3:36). *Whom he did predestinate, them he also called* (Romans 8:30). If he is calling you, it is because he did predestinate you; and you may rest quite sure of it, and yield to him with holy joy and delight.

As for me, I feel so happy in preaching the gospel because I am not fishing with a *chance* and a *perhaps* that some may come. *The Lord knoweth them that are his* (2 Timothy 2:19), and they shall come. Every congregation is, in this sense, a picked assembly. I felt this morning when I came here that there were so many friends out in the country for the holidays that we would very likely have a meager house. I rejoice that I was altogether out in my reckoning, but even then I thought, God has a people that he will bring whom he means to bless. Here they are, and now while standing here I know that God's Word shall not return to him void: *So shall my word be that goeth forth out of my mouth: it shall not return unto me void, but it shall accomplish that which I please, and it shall prosper in the thing whereto I sent it.* (Isaiah 55:11).

But now, lastly, our Lord guarantees the unity of his church. *Them also I must bring, and they shall hear my voice; and there shall be one fold and one shepherd.* We hear a great deal about the unity of the church, and notions upon this subject are rather wild. We are to have the Roman and the Greek and the Anglican churches all joined together in one. If they were, the result would not be worth twopence, but much evil would come of it. God has, I doubt not, a chosen people among all these three great corporations, but the union of such questionable organizations would be a dire omen of mischief to the world: the Dark Ages, and a worse popedom than ever, would soon be upon us. The more those three quarrel with each other the better for truth and righteousness.

I would like to see the Anglican Church standing at drawn daggers with the Roman, and coming into a more and more open opposition to its superstitions. I would to God that the national church would in all things be delivered from the pope of Rome and his anti-Christian enormities.

Truly, this has been carried out as a matter of fact; there never was but one Shepherd of the sheep, even Christ Jesus; and there never was but one flock of God, and there never will be. There is one spiritual church of God, and there never were two. All the visible churches up and down the world contain within themselves parts of the one church of Jesus Christ, but there were never two bodies of Christ, and there cannot be. There is one church, and there is one head of the church. The motto of Christianity is – one flock and one Shepherd.

As a matter of experience this is carried out in believers. I do not care who the man is, if he is a truly spiritually minded man he is one with all other spiritually minded men. Those people in any visible church who have no grace are usually the greatest sticklers for every point of difference and ever particle of rite and form. Nominal professing Christians are soon at war, invigorated believers follow after peace. Of course, when a man has nothing else but the outside, he fights for it tooth and nail; but a man who loves the Lord, and lives near him, perceives the inner life in others, and has fellowship with that. That inner life is one in all the energized family, and compels them to be one in heart.

Set two brethren at prayer, the one a Calvinist and the other an Arminian, and they pray alike. Get a real work of the Spirit in a district and see how Baptists and Pedobaptists pull together. Tell of your inward experience and speak of the Spirit's work in the soul, and see how we are all moved by that.

Here is a brother, a member of the Society of Friends, and he likes silent worship; and here is another who enjoys hearty singing; but when they get near to God, they do not quarrel over this, but agree to differ. The one says, "The Lord be with you in your holy silence," and the other prays that the Lord may accept his brother's psalm. All who are one with Christ have a certain family feeling, a higher form of clannishness, and they cannot shake it off.

I have found myself reading a gracious book that has drawn me near to God, and though I know that it was written by a man with whose opinions I had little agreement, I have not therefore refused to be edified by him in points that are unquestionably revealed. No, but I have blessed the Lord that, with all his blunders, he knew so much of precious vital truth, and lived so near his Lord. What Protestant can refuse to love the humble Bernard? Was there ever a more consecrated servant of God or a dearer lover of Christ than he? Yet he was most sorrowfully in bondage to the superstitions of his age and of the Roman Catholic Church. Are you not all one with him who sang,

> Jesus, the very thought of thee
>> With sweetness fills my breast;
> But sweeter far thy face to see,
>> And in Thy presence rest.

The external church is needful, but it is not *the one and indivisible church of Christ*. Jesus as the life binds his church together, and that life flows through all the born-again ones, even as the blood flows through all the veins of the body. Drop the external, and look by faith into the spiritual realm, and you will see one flock and one Shepherd.

The practical lesson is, let us belong to that one flock. How are they known? Answer: they are a hearing flock – they hear the Lord and follow his lead. Be you one of those who listen to Christ's voice and to none other. Keep to the one Shepherd! How do you know him? It is Jesus: in his feet and hands are nail prints, and his side bears yet the scar. He it is who leads the one and only flock. Follow Jesus and you are right. Follow him everywhere and you are happy. The best way to promote the unity of the church is for all the sheep to follow the Shepherd. If they all follow the Shepherd, they will all keep together. Let us go forth and try and do that, and let us long for that happy day when all disputed points shall be settled by all obeying the Lord.

Compromises would only mean an agreement to disobey the Lord.

Let no man yield a principle under claim of charity; it is not charity to call falsehood truth. We must follow Jesus fully, and we shall come together. First pure, then peaceable is the rule. Oh, when shall the triple banner again float over all – *One Lord, one faith, one baptism* (Ephesians 4:5)? Oh God the Holy Spirit, forgive us our errors, and bring us to your truth! Oh God the Son, forgive us our lack of holiness, and renew us in your own image! Oh God the Father, forgive us our lack of love, and melt us into one family. To the one God be glory, in the one church, forever and ever. Amen.

Chapter 15

The Sheep and Their Shepherd

My sheep hear my voice, and I know them, and they follow me. (John 10:27)

Christians are here compared to sheep. Not a very flattering comparison, you may say; but then we do not wish to be flattered, nor would our Lord deem it good to flatter us. While far from flattering, it is, however, very consoling, for of all creatures there are not any more surrounded with infirmity than sheep. In this frailty of their nature they are a suitable emblem of ourselves, or at least, of so many of us as have believed in Jesus and become his disciples. Let others boast about how strong they are; yet if there be strong ones anywhere, certainly we are weak. We have proved our weakness, and day by day we lament it. We do confess our weakness; yet may we not grumble at it, for, as Paul said, so we find, that when we are weak, then are we strong.

Sheep have many needs, yet they are very helpless, and quite unable to provide for themselves. Without the shepherd's care, they would soon perish. This, too, is our case. Our spiritual needs are numerous and pressing, yet we cannot supply any of them. We are travelers through a wilderness that yields us neither food nor water. Unless our bread drops down from heaven, and our water flows out of the living Rock, we must die. Our weakness and our need we keenly feel; still we have no cause to murmur, since the Lord knows our poor estate, and helps us with the most tender care. Sheep, too, are silly creatures, and in this respect likewise we are very sheepish. We meekly admit it to him who is ready to guide us.

We say, as David said, *O God, thou knowest my foolishness* (Psalm 69:5); and he says to us as he said to David, *I will instruct thee and teach thee in the way which thou shalt go* (Psalm 32:8). If Christ were not our wisdom, we would soon fall prey to the destroyer. Every grain of true wisdom that we possess we have derived from him; of ourselves we are dull and giddy; folly is bound up in our hearts.

The more conscious you are, dear brethren, of your own deficiencies – your lack of stamina, discretion, wisdom, and all the instincts of self-preservation – the more delighted you will be to see that the Lord accepts you under these conditions, and calls you the people of his pasture and the sheep of his hand. He discerns you as you are, claims you as his own, foresees all the ills to which you are exposed, yet tends you as his flock, sets store by every lamb of the fold, and so feeds you according to the integrity of his heart, and guides you by the skillfulness of his hands. *I will feed my flock, and I will cause them to lie down, saith the Lord God* (Ezekiel 34:15).

Oh, what sweet music there is to us in the name that is given to our Lord Jesus Christ of *the good shepherd*! It not only describes the office he holds, but it also sets forth the sympathy he feels, the readiness he shows, and the responsibility he bears to promote our well-being. If the sheep be weak, still is the shepherd strong to guard his flock from the prowling wolf or the roaring lion. If the sheep suffer privation because the soil is barren, still is the shepherd able to lead them into pasture suitable for them. If they be foolish, still he goes before them, cheers them with his voice, and rules them with the rod of his command. There cannot be a flock without a shepherd; neither is there a shepherd truly without a flock. The two must go together. They are the fullness of each other.

As the church is the fullness of him that fills all in all, so we rejoice to remember that *of his fulness have all we received, and grace for grace* (John 1:16). That I am like a sheep is a sorry reflection; but that I have a shepherd soothes away the sorrow and creates a new joy. It even becomes a cheerful thing to be weak, so that I may rely on his strength; to be full of need, so that I may draw from his fullness; to be shallow and often at my wit's end, so that I may be always regulated by his wisdom. Even so does my shame rebound to his praise.

Not to you, you great and mighty, who lift your heads high, and claim for yourselves honor – not to you is peace, not to you is rest; but unto you, you lowly ones, who delight in the valley of humiliation, and feel yourselves to be taken down in your own esteem – to you it is that the Shepherd becomes dear; and to you will he give to lie down in green pastures beside the still waters.

In a very simple way, we shall speak about the proprietor of the sheep. *My* sheep (emphasis added), says Christ. Then, we shall have a little to say about the marks of the sheep. After that I propose to talk awhile about the privileges of the sheep. *[I]* **know** *my sheep* (emphasis added): they are privileged to be known of Christ. *My sheep hear my voice.*

Who is the proprietor of the sheep? They are all Christ's. *My* sheep *hear my voice.* How did the saints come to be Christ's?

They are his, first of all, because he chose them. Before the worlds were made, out of all the rest of mankind he selected them. He knew the race would fall and become unworthy of the faculties with which he endowed them and the inheritance he had assigned them. To him belonged the sovereign prerogative that he might have mercy on whom he would have mercy; and he, out of his own absolute will, and according to the counsel of his own good pleasure, made the choice independently and individually of certain persons, and he said, "These are mine." Their names were written in his book; they became his portion and his heritage. Having chosen them of old so many ages ago, rest assured he will not lose them now. Men prize that which they have long had. If there is a thing that was mine but yesterday, and it is lost today, I might not fret about it; but if I have long possessed it, and called it my inheritance, I would not willingly part with it.

Sheep of Christ, you shall be his forever because you have been his from ever. They are Christ's sheep because his Father gave them to him. They were the gift of the Father to Christ. He often speaks of them in this way. *As many as thou hast given [me]* (John 17:2); *them which thou hast given me* (John 17:9), says he, over and over again. Of old, the Father gave his people to Christ. Separating them from among men, he presented them to him as a gift, committed them into his hand as a trust, and ordained them for him as the lot of his inheritance. Thus, they become a token of the Father's love to his only begotten Son, a proof of the confidence he placed in him, and a pledge of the honor that shall be done unto him.

Now, I suppose most of us know how to value a gift for the donor's sake. If presented to us by one whom we love, we set great store by it. If it has been designed to be a love token, it awakens in our minds many sweet memories. Though the intrinsic worth may be of small account, the associations make it exceedingly precious. We might be content to lose something of far greater value in itself rather than that which is the gift of a friend, the offering of his love. I like the delicate sentiment of the poet, as it is expressed in that pretty verse –

> I never cast a flower away,
> The gift of one who cared for me;
> A little flower – a faded flower,
> But it was done reluctantly.

Yet oh, how weak the words of human passion! But oh, how strong the expressions of divine enthusiasm, when Jesus speaks to the Father of *the men which thou gavest me out of the world: Thine they were,* he says, *and thou gavest them me* (John 17:6); and *those that thou gavest me I have kept* (John 17:12). You sheep of Christ, rest safely; let not your soul be disturbed with fear. The Father gave you to his Son, and he will not lightly lose what God himself has given him. The hellish lions shall not tear the lowliest lamb that is a love token from the Father to his best beloved. While Christ stands defending his own, he will protect them from the lion and the bear that would take the lambs of his flock; he will not permit the least of them to perish.

My sheep, says Christ. They are his, furthermore, because, in addition to his choice and to the gift, he has bought them with a price. They had sold themselves for nothing; but he has redeemed them, not with corruptible things as with silver and gold, but with his precious blood. A man always esteems that to be exceedingly valuable that he procured with risk – with risk of life and limb. David felt he could not drink the water that the brave warriors who broke through the host of the Philistines brought to him from the well at Bethlehem, because it seemed to him as though it were the blood of the men that went in jeopardy of their lives; and he poured it out before the Lord. It was too precious a burden for him, when men's lives had been hazarded for it.

But the Good Shepherd not only hazarded his life, but he also even laid it down for his sheep. Jacob exceedingly valued one part of his possessions, and he gave it to Joseph: he gave him one portion above his brethren. Now, you may be sure he would give Joseph that which he thought most precious. But why did he give him that particular portion? Because, he says, *I took [it] out of the hand of the Amorite with my sword and with my bow* (Genesis 48:22). Now, our blessed Shepherd esteems his sheep because they cost him his blood. They cost him his blood – I may say, he took them out of the hand of the Amorite with his sword and with his bow in bloody conflict, where he was the victor, but yet was slain.

There is not one sheep of all his flock but what he can see the mark of his blood on him. In the face of every saint the Savior sees, as in a glass, the memorial of his bloody sweat in Gethsemane, and his agonies at Golgotha. *Know ye not that . . . ye are not your own? For ye are bought with a price.* That stands as a call to duty, but it is at the same time a consolation, for if he has bought me, he will have me. Bought with such a price, he will not like to lose me, nor permit any foe to take me out of his hand. Think not that Christ will permit those to perish for whom he died. To me the very suggestion seems to draw near to the verge of blasphemy. If he has bought me with his blood, I cannot imagine that he cares nothing for me, that he will take no further concern about me, or that he will permit my soul to be cast into the pit. If he has suffered in my stead, where is justice gone that the Substitute should bear my guilt, and I should bear it too? and where is mercy fled, that God should execute twice the punishment for one offense? No, beloved, those whom he has bought with blood are his, and he will keep them.

My sheep, says Christ. They are his, or in due time they shall become so, through his capturing them by sacred power. As well by power are we redeemed as by price, for the blood-bought sheep had gone astray even as others. *All we like sheep have gone astray; we have turned every one to his own way* (Isaiah 53:6); but, my brethren, the Good Shepherd has brought many of us back with infinite condescension: with boundless mercy he followed us when we went astray.

Oh, what blind slaves we were when we frolicked with death! We did not know then what his love had ordained for us; it never entered our poor, silly heads that there was a crown for us; we did not know that the Father's love had settled itself on us, or that ever the morning star knew its place. We know it now, and it is he that has taught us; for he followed us over mountains of vanity, through bogs and miry places of foul transgression; he tracked our devious footsteps on and on, through youth and manhood, until at last, with mighty grace, he grasped us in his arms and laid us on his shoulder, and is this day carrying us home to the great fold above, rejoicing as he bears all our weight and finds us in all we need.

Oh, that blessed work of effective grace! He has made us his own, he has defeated the Enemy, the prey has been taken from the mighty, and the lawful captive has been delivered. *He hath broken the gates of brass, and cut the bars of iron in sunder* (Psalm 107:16), to set his people free. *Oh that men would praise the Lord for his goodness, and for his wonderful works to the children of men* (Psalm 107:8).

My sheep, says Christ, as he stands in the midst of his disciples. "My Shepherd," let us one and all reply. All the sheep of Christ who have been redeemed by his power become his by their own willing and cheerful surrender of themselves to him. We would not belong to another if we might; nor would we wish to belong to ourselves if we could; nor, I trust, do we want any part of ourselves to be our own property.

Judge whether this be true of you or not. In that day when I surrendered my soul to my Savior, I gave him my body, my soul, my spirit; I gave him all I had, and all I shall have for time and for eternity. I gave him all my talents, my powers, my faculties, my eyes, my ears, my limbs, my emotions, my judgment, my whole manhood, and all that could come of it, whatever fresh capacity or new capability I may be endowed with. If I were at this good hour to change the note of gladness for one of sadness, it would be to wail out my repentant confession of the times and circumstances in which I have failed to observe the strict and unwavering allegiance I owe to my Lord. So far from regretting, I would rather renew my vows and make them over again. In this I think every Christian would join me.

'Tis done! the great transaction's done:
    I am my Lord's, and he is mine:
He drew me, and I follow'd on,
    Charm'd to confess the voice divine.

Now rest, my long-divided heart;
    Fix'd on this blissful centre, rest:
With ashes who would grudge to part,
    When call'd on angels' bread to feast?

High heaven, that heard the solemn vow,
    That vow renew'd shall daily hear:
Till in life's latest hour I bow,
    And bless in death a bond so dear.

And yet, brethren, though our hearts may now be all in a glow, lest they should presently grow cold, or the bleak atmosphere of this evil world should chill our devotion, let us never cease to think of the Good Shepherd in that great, good act, which most of all showed his love when he laid down his life for the sheep. You have heard the story told by Francis de Sales. He saw a girl carrying a pail of water on her head, in the midst of which she had placed a piece of wood. On asking her why she did this, she told him it was to prevent the motion of the water, for fear it might be spilled. And so, said he, let us place the cross of Christ in the midst of our hearts to check the movement of our affections, that they may not be spilled in restless cares or grievous troubles.

My sheep, says Christ, and thus he describes his people. They are Christ's, his own, a peculiar property. May I hope that this truth will be henceforth treasured up in your soul! It is a common truth, certainly; but when it is laid home by the Holy Spirit it shines, it beams, not merely as a lamp in a dark chamber, but also as the morning star rising in your hearts.

Remember this is no more our shame that we are sheep, but it is our honor that we are Christ's sheep. To belong to a king carries some measure of distinction. We are the sheep of the imperial pastures. This is our safety: he will not permit the Enemy to destroy his sheep. This is our blessedness: we are separated, the sheep of the pasture of the Lord's Christ. This is sanctification in one aspect of it, for it is the making of us to be holy, by setting us apart to be the Lord's own portion forever. And this is the key to our duty: we are his sheep; then let us live for him, and consecrate ourselves to him who loved us and gave himself for us. Christ is the proprietor of the sheep, and we are the property of the Good Shepherd.

Now, let us commune together awhile upon the marks of the sheep. When there are so many flocks of sheep, it is necessary to mark them. Our Savior marks us. It has been very properly observed that there are two marks on Christ's sheep. One is on their ear, the other is on their foot. These are two marks of Christ's sheep not to be found on any other; but they are to be found on all of his own – the mark on the ear: *My sheep **hear** my voice* (emphasis added); the mark on the foot: *I know them, and they follow me.*

Think of this mark on their ear. *My sheep hear my voice.* They hear spiritually. A great many people in Christ's day heard his voice who did not hear it in the way and with the perception that is here intended. They would not hear; that is to say, they would not listen or give heed, neither would they obey his call or come unto him that they might have life. These were not always the worst sort of people; there were some of the best who would not hear Christ, of whom he said, according to the original, as translated by some, *[Ye] search the scriptures; for in them ye think ye have eternal life: and they are they which testify of me. And ye will not come to me, that ye might have life.* They would get as far as curiosity or criticism might allure them, but they would not go any further; they would not believe in Jesus.

Now, the spiritual ear listens to God. The opening of it is the work of the Holy Spirit, and this is a mark of Christ's chosen blood-bought people, that they hear not only the hollow sound, but also the hidden sense; not the bare letter, but the spiritual lesson; and that too not merely with the outward organ, but also with the inward heart. The chief point is that they hear *his* voice. Oh, if all that heard my voice heard Christ's voice, how would I wander down every street in this city to proclaim the gospel of Jesus Christ. But alas! the voice of the minister is utterly ineffective to save a soul, unless the voice of Christ reaches the conscience and rouses its dormant powers. *My sheep hear my voice* – the voice of Jesus, his counsel, his command, clothed with the authority of his own sacred, sovereign utterance.

When the gospel comes to you as Christ's gospel, with demonstration of the Spirit, the invitation is addressed to you by him. You can look upon it in no other light, so you must accept and receive it. When his princely power comes with it – being mighty to save, he puts saving power into the Word – then you hear Christ's voice as a decree that must be obeyed, as a summons that must be attended to, as a call to which there must be a quick response. O beloved, do not ever rest satisfied with hearing the voice of the preacher. We are only Christ's speaking trumpets, there is nothing in us; it is only his speaking through us that can do any good. O children of God, some of you do not always listen to Christ's voice in the preaching.

While we comment on the Word, you make your comments on us. Our style, or our tone, or even our gesture is enough to absorb – I might rather say, to distract – your thoughts. *Why look ye so earnestly on us?* (Acts 3:12). I beg you, give less heed to the garb of the servant, and give more care to the message of the Master. Listen warily, if you please; but judge wisely, if you can. See how much pure grain, and how much of Christ there is in the sermon. Use your sieve; put away all the chaff; take only the good wheat in hearing Christ's voice. Well would it be if we could obscure ourselves that we might manifest him. I could wish so to preach that you could not see even my little finger; might I but so preach that you could get a full view of Jesus only.

O that you could hear his voice drowning ours! This is the mark, the peculiar mark of those who are Christ's peculiar people: they hear his voice. Sometimes, truly, it sounds in the ministry; sometimes it thrills forth from that Book of books, which is often grossly neglected; sometimes it comes in the night watches. His voice may speak to us in the street. Silent as to vocal utterance, but like familiar tones that sometimes greet us in our dreams, the voice of Christ is distinctly audible to the soul. It will come to you in sweet or in bitter providences; yes, there is such a thing as hearing Christ's voice in the rustling of every leaf upon the tree, in the moaning of every wind, in the rippling of every wave.

And there be those that have learned to lean on Christ's bosom until they have looked for all the world as though they were a shell that lay in the ocean of Christ's love, listening forever to the thundering cadence of that deep, unfathomed, all-mysterious force. The billows of his love never cease to swell. The billowy anthem still peals on with solemn grandeur in the ear of the Christian. O may we hear Christ's voice each one of us for ourselves! I find that language fails me, and metaphors are weak to fully describe it.

One point is worth noticing, however. I think our Lord meant here that his sheep, when they hear his voice, know it so well that they can tell it at once from the voice of strangers. The true child of God knows the gospel from the law. It is not by learning catechisms, reading theological books, or listening to endless controversies that he finds this out. There is an instinct of his reborn nature far more trustworthy than any lessons he has been taught. The voice of Jesus! Why, there is no music like it. If you have once heard it, you cannot mistake it for another, or another for it. Some are babes in grace; others are of full age, and by reason of use, have their senses exercised; but one sense is quickly brought out – the sense of hearing. It is so easy to tell the joy bells of the gospel from the death knell of the law; *for the letter killeth, but the spirit giveth life* (2 Corinthians 3:6). "Do, or die," says Moses. "Believe, and live," says Christ; you must know which is which. Yes; and I think they are equally shrewd and quick to discriminate between the flesh and the Spirit.

Let some of the very feeblest of God's people sit down under a fluent ministry, with all the beauties of rhetoric, and let the minister preach up the dignity of human nature, and the sufficiency of man's reason to find out the way of righteousness, and you will hear them say, "It is very clever; but there is no food for me in it." Bring, however, the best and most instructed and most learned Christian man, and set him down under a ministry that is very faulty as to the gift of utterance, and incorrect even in grammar; but if it is full of Jesus Christ, then I know what he will say: "Ah! never mind the man, and never mind the platter on which he brought the meat; it was food to my soul that I fed upon with a hearty relish; it was marrow and fatness, for I could hear Christ's voice in it."

I am not going to follow out these tests; but certain it is, that the sheep know Christ's voice, and can easily distinguish it. I saw hundreds of lambs the other day together, and there were also their mothers; and I am sure that if I had had the task of allotting the proper lamb to each, or to any of them, it would have kept me until now to have done it. But somehow the lambs knew the mothers, and the mothers knew the lambs; and they were all happy enough in each other's company.

Every saint here, mixed up as he may be at times with parties and professors of all sorts, knows Christ, and Christ knows him, and he is therefore bound to his owner. That is the mark on the ear. You have seen sometimes in the country two flocks together on the road, and you say, "I wonder how the shepherds will manage to keep them distinct. They will get mixed up." They do not; they go this way and that way, and after a little commingling they separate, for they know their master's voice; *and a stranger will they not follow* (John 10:5). You will go tomorrow, many of you, out into the world, some to the exchange, others to the market, and others again into the factory; you are all mixed.

Yes, but the seeming confusion of your company is temporary, not real and permanent. You will come right again, and you will go to your own home and your own fellowship. And at the end, when we shall have ended our pilgrimage, the one shall travel his way to the glory land, and the other to the abyss of woe. There will be no mistake. You will hear the Master's call, and obey. There is a mark on the ear that identifies every saint.

Christ's sheep hear his voice obediently. This is an important proof of discipleship. Indeed, it may serve as a rebuke to many. Oh, I would that you were more careful about this! *He that hath my commandments, and keepeth them,* said Jesus, *he it is that loveth me* (John 14:21). *He that loveth me not keepeth not my sayings* (John 14:24). How does it come to pass, then, that there are certain commands of Christ that some Christians will permit to lay in suspension? They will say, "The Lord commands this, but it is not essential." Oh, unloving spirit, that can think anything unessential that your Bridegroom bids you to do! They that love, think little things to be of great importance, especially when they are looked upon as tokens of the strength or the tenderness of one's regard. It may not be essential – in order to prove the relation in which a wife stands to her husband – that she should study his tastes, consult his wishes, or attend to his comfort. But will she the less strive to please because love, not fear, constrains her?

And can it be that any of you, my brethren, would harbor such a thought as your negligence implies? Do you really suppose that after the choice of Christ has been fixed on you, and the love of Christ has been pledged to you, you may now be as remiss or careless as you like? No; rather, might we not expect that a sacred passion, an intense zeal, a touch of inspiration would stir you up, put you on the alert, make yon wake at the faintest sound of his voice, or keep you listening to do his will? Be it ours, then, to act out with fidelity that verse we have often sung with enthusiasm –

> In all my Lord's appointed ways
> My journey I'll pursue.

However little the precept may appear in the eyes of others; however insignificant as compared with our salvation, yet does the Lord command it? Then his sheep hear his voice, and they follow him.

Christ has marked his sheep on their feet as well as their ears. They follow him; they are gently led, not harshly driven. They follow him as the Captain of their salvation; they trust in the power of his arm to clear the way for them. All their trust on him is supported; all their hope on him they lean. They follow him as their teacher; they call no man "Rabbi" under heaven, but Christ alone. He is the infallible source of their creeds; neither will they allow their minds to be ruled by private meetings, councils, nor decrees. Has Christ said it? It is enough. If not, it is no more for me than the whistling of the wind. They follow Christ as their teacher.

And the sheep of Christ follow him as their example; they desire to be in this world as he was. It is one of their marks, that to a greater or lesser degree they have a Christlike spirit; and if they could, they would be altogether like their Lord.

They follow him, too, as their Commander, and Lawgiver, and Prince. *Whatsoever he saith unto you, do it* (John 2:5) was his mother's wise speech; and it is the children's wise rule as well: *Whatsoever he saith unto you, do it.* Oh, blessed shall they be above many of whom it shall be said, "These are they *which have not defiled their garments. These are they which follow the Lamb whithersoever he goeth*" (Revelation 3:4; 14:4).

Some of his followers are not very scrupulous. They love him. It is not for us to judge them. Rather, we place ourselves among them and share in the rebuke. But happiest of all the happy are they who see the footprint – the print of that foot that once was pierced with the nail – and put their foot down where he placed it, and then again, in the selfsame mark, follow where he trod, until they climb at last to the throne.

Keep close to Christ; take care of his little precepts unto the end. Remember, *Whosoever therefore shall break one of these least commandments, and shall teach men so, he shall be called the least in the kingdom of heaven* (Matthew 5:19). Do not risk being least in the heavenly kingdom, though it is better to be that than to be greatest in the kingdom of darkness. O seek to be very near him, to be a choice sheep in his chosen flock, and to have the mark distinctly upon your foot!

I will not stop to apply these truths, but leave each one of you to make such self-searching inquiries as the text suggests. Have I the ear mark? Have I the foot mark? *My sheep hear my voice, . . . and they follow me.* I hope that I am among the number.

The last point, with which we now proceed to close, is the privilege of Christ's sheep. It does not look very large, but if we open it we shall see an amazing degree of blessedness in it. *I know them, I know them.* What does it mean?

I have not time now to tell you all it means. *I know them.* What is the reverse of this but one of the most dreadful things that is reserved for the day of judgment. There will be some who will say, *Lord, Lord, have we not prophesied in thy name? and in thy name have cast out devils?* (Matthew 7:22). And he shall say, "Truly, truly, I say unto you, *I never knew you; depart from me, ye that work iniquity*" (Matthew 7:23). Now measure the height of that privilege by the depth of this misery. *I never knew you.* What a volume of scorn it implies! What a stigma of infamy it conveys!

Change the picture. The Redeemer says, *I know them, I know them.* How his eyes flash with kindness; how their cheeks burn with gratitude, as he says, *I know them!* Why, if a man had a friend and acquaintance that he used to know, and some years later he found him a disreputable, abandoned, wicked, and guilty criminal, I feel pretty sure he would not say much about having known such a fellow, though he might be driven to confess that he had some years ago a passing acquaintance with him. But our Lord Jesus Christ, though he knows what poor, unworthy ones we are, yet when we shall be brought up before the Lord, before the great white throne, he will confess he knew us. He does know us, we are old acquaintances of his, and he has known us from before the foundation of the world. *For whom he did foreknow, he also did predestinate to be conformed to the image of his Son, that he might be the firstborn among many brethren.*

Moreover whom he did predestinate, them he also called. There are riches of grace in this, but we will consider it in another way. Our Savior knows us, our Shepherd knows us. Beloved, he knows your person and all about you. You, with that sick body, that aching head, he knows you and he knows your soul with all its sensitiveness; that timidity, that anxiety, that inherent depression – he knows it all. A physician may come to see you and be unable to detect what the disease is that pains or prostrates you, but Christ knows you through and through; all the parts of your nature he understands. *I know them,* says he; he can therefore prescribe for you. He knows your sins. Do not let that dismay you, because he has blotted them all out; and he only knows them to forgive them, to cover them with his righteousness. He knows your corruptions; he will help you to overcome them; he will deal with you in providence and in grace, so that they shall be rooted up. He knows your temptations.

Perhaps you are living away from your parents and Christian friends, and you have had an extraordinary temptation, and you wish you could go home and tell your mother. Oh, he knows it, he knows it; he can help you better than your mother can. You say, "I wish the minister knew the temptation I have passed through." Do not tell it; God knows it.

As Daniel did not need Nebuchadnezzar to tell him the nature of his dream, but gave him the dream and the interpretation at the same time, so God can send you comfort. There will be a word as plainly suited to your case as though it were all printed and the preacher had known it all. It must be so. Depend upon it, the Lord knows your temptation, and watches your trial; or be it a sick child, or be it a bad matter of business that has lately occurred; or be it a slander that has wounded your heart, there is not a pang you feel but God as surely sees it as the weaver sees the shuttle that he throws with his own hand. He knows your trial, and he knows the meaning of your groans; he can read the secret desire of your heart. You need not write it nor speak it; he has understood it all. You were saying, "O that my child were converted! O that I grew in grace!" He knows it; he knows it every bit. There is not a word on your tongue nor a wish in your heart, but he knows it altogether. O dear heart, he knows your sincerity!

Perhaps you want to join the church, and your proposal has been declined because you could not give a satisfactory testimony. If you are sincere, he knows it; he knows, moreover, what your anxiety is. You cannot tell another what it is that is bitter to you – the heart knows its own bitterness – he knows it. As his secret is with you, so your secret is with him. He knows you; he knows what you have been trying to do. That secret gift – that offering dropped so quietly where none could see it – he knows it. And he knows that you love him. "Yes," you are saying in your soul, "if ever I loved thee, my Jesus, 'tis now." No, you cannot tell him, nor tell others; but he knows it all.

So now, in closing, let us say that in the text there is mutual knowledge. "*I know them*, but they also know me, because they hear my voice, and recognize it." Here is mutual confession. Christ speaks, or else there would be no voice; they hear, or else the voice would not be useful. *I know them;* that is, his thoughts go towards them. *They follow me;* that is, their thoughts go towards him. He leads the way, or else they could not follow. They follow, however, when he leads the way. Being the counterpart of each other, what the one does the other returns through grace; and what grace puts into the sheep the Shepherd recognizes, and makes a return to them. Christ and his church become an echo of each other: his is the voice, theirs is but a faint echo of it; still it is a true echo, and you shall know who are Christ's by this. Do they echo what Christ says?

Oh, how I wish we were all sheep! How my soul longs that we may many of us who are not of his fold be brought in. The Lord bring you in, my dear friends. The Lord give you his grace, and make you his own, comfort you, and make you to follow him. And if you are his, show it. These, dear brethren and sisters, here at this time, desire to confess Christ in your presence. If they are doing right, and you are not doing as they do, then you are doing wrong. If it is the duty of one, it is the duty of all; and if one Christian may neglect making a profession, all may do so, and then there will be no visible church whatever, and the visible ordinances must die out. If you know him, acknowledge him, for he has said, *Whosoever therefore shall confess me before men, him will I confess also before my Father which is in heaven. But whosoever shall deny me before men, him will I also deny before my Father which is in heaven* (Matthew 10:32-33). God bless you, in the Lord Jesus' name. Amen.

Charles H. Spurgeon
– A Brief Biography

Charles Haddon Spurgeon was born on June 19, 1834, in Kelvedon, Essex, England. He was one of seventeen children in his family (nine of whom died in infancy). His father and grandfather were Nonconformist ministers in England. Due to economic difficulties, eighteen-month-old Charles was sent to live with his grandfather, who helped teach Charles the ways of God. Later in life, Charles remembered looking at the pictures in *Pilgrim's Progress* and in *Foxe's Book of Martyrs* as a young boy.

Charles did not have much of a formal education and never went to college. He read much throughout his life though, especially books by Puritan authors.

Even with godly parents and grandparents, young Charles resisted giving in to God. It was not until he was fifteen years old that he was born again. He was on his way to his usual church, but when a heavy snowstorm prevented him from getting there, he turned in at a little Primitive Methodist chapel. Though there were only about fifteen people in attendance, the preacher spoke from Isaiah 45:22: *Look unto me, and be ye saved, all the ends of the earth.* Charles Spurgeon's eyes were opened and the Lord converted his soul.

He began attending a Baptist church and teaching Sunday school. He soon preached his first sermon, and then when he was sixteen years old, he became the pastor of a small Baptist church in Cambridge. The church soon grew to over four hundred people, and Charles Spurgeon, at the age of nineteen, moved on to become the pastor of the New Park Street Church in London. The church grew from a few hundred attenders to a few thousand. They built an addition to the church, but still needed more room to accommodate the congregation. The Metropolitan Tabernacle was built in London in 1861, seating more than 5,000 people. Pastor Spurgeon preached the simple message of the cross, and thereby attracted many people who wanted to hear God's Word preached in the power of the Holy Spirit.

On January 9, 1856, Charles married Susannah Thompson. They had twin boys, Charles and Thomas. Charles and Susannah loved each other deeply, even amidst the difficulties and troubles that they faced in life, including health problems. They helped each other spiritually, and often together read the writings of Jonathan Edwards, Richard Baxter, and other Puritan writers.

Charles Spurgeon was a friend of all Christians, but he stood firmly on the Scriptures, and it didn't please all who heard him. Spurgeon believed in and preached on the sovereignty of God, heaven and hell, repentance, revival, holiness, salvation through Jesus Christ alone, and the infallibility and necessity of the Word of God. He spoke against worldliness and hypocrisy among Christians, and against Roman Catholicism, ritualism, and modernism.

One of the biggest controversies in his life was known as the "Down-Grade Controversy." Charles Spurgeon believed that some pastors of his time were "down-grading" the faith by compromising with the world or the new ideas of the age. He said that some pastors were denying the inspiration of the Bible, salvation by faith alone, and the truth of the Bible in other areas, such as creation. Many pastors who believed what Spurgeon condemned were not happy about this, and Spurgeon eventually resigned from the Baptist Union.

Despite some difficulties, Spurgeon became known as the "Prince of Preachers." He opposed slavery, started a pastors' college, opened an orphanage, led in helping feed and clothe the poor, had a book fund for pastors who could not afford books, and more.

Charles Spurgeon remains one of the most published preachers in history. His sermons were printed each week (even in the newspapers), and then the sermons for the year were re-issued as a book at the end of the year. The first six volumes, from 1855-1860, are known as *The Park Street Pulpit*, while the next fifty-seven volumes, from 1861-1917 (his sermons continued to be published long after his death), are known as *The Metropolitan Tabernacle Pulpit*. He also oversaw a monthly magazine-type publication called *The Sword and the Trowel,* and Spurgeon wrote many books, including *Lectures to My Students, All of Grace, Around the Wicket Gate, Advice for Seekers, John Ploughman's Talks, The Soul Winner, Words of Counsel for Christian Workers, Cheque Book of the Bank of Faith, Morning and Evening*, his autobiography, and more, including some commentaries, such as his twenty-year study on the Psalms – *The Treasury of David.*

Charles Spurgeon often preached ten times a week, preaching to an estimated ten million people during his lifetime. He usually preached from only one page of notes, and often from just an outline. He read about six books each week. During his lifetime, he had read *The Pilgrim's Progress* through more than one hundred times. When he died, his personal library consisted of more than 12,000 books. However, the Bible always remained the most important book to him.

Spurgeon was able to do what he did in the power of God's Holy Spirit because he followed his own advice – he met with God every morning before meeting with others, and he continued in communion with God throughout the day.

Charles Spurgeon suffered from gout, rheumatism, and some depression, among other health problems. He often went to Menton, France, to recuperate and rest. He preached his final sermon at the Metropolitan Tabernacle on June 7, 1891, and died in France on January 31, 1892, at the age of fifty-seven. He was buried in Norwood Cemetery in London.

Charles Haddon Spurgeon lived a life devoted to God. His sermons and writings continue to influence Christians all over the world.

Other Similar Titles

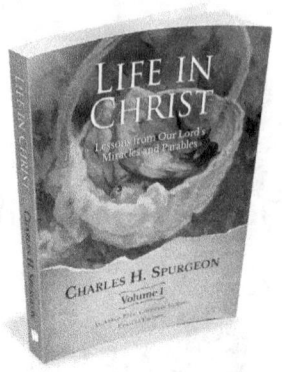

Life in Christ (Vol. 1 - 12),
by Charles H. Spurgeon

Men who were led by the hand or groped their way along the wall to reach Jesus were touched by his finger and went home without a guide, rejoicing that Jesus Christ had opened their eyes. Jesus is still able to perform such miracles. And, with the power of the Holy Spirit, his Word will be expounded and we'll watch for the signs to follow, expecting to see them at once. Why shouldn't those who read this be blessed with the light of heaven? This is my heart's inmost desire.

– Charles H. Spurgeon

Available where books are sold.

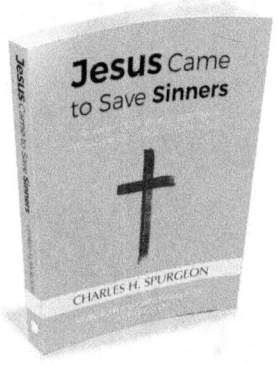

Jesus Came to Save Sinners,
by Charles H. Spurgeon

This is a heart-level conversation with you, the reader. Every excuse, reason, and roadblock for not coming to Christ is examined and duly dealt with. If you think you may be too bad, or if perhaps you really are bad and you sin either openly or behind closed doors, you will discover that life in Christ is for you too. You can reject the message of salvation by faith, or you can choose to live a life of sin after professing faith in Christ, but you cannot change the truth as it is, either for yourself or for others. As such, it behooves you and your family to embrace truth, claim it for your own, and be genuinely set free for now and eternity. Come and embrace this free gift of God, and live a victorious life for Him.

Available where books are sold.

Words of Warning,
by Charles H. Spurgeon

This book, *Words of Warning*, is an analysis of people and the gospel of Christ. Under inspiration of the Holy Spirit, Charles H. Spurgeon sheds light on the many ways people may refuse to come to Christ, but he also shines a brilliant light on how we can be saved. Unsaved or wavering individuals will be convicted, and if they allow it, they will be led to Christ. Sincere Christians will be happy and blessed as they consider the great salvation with which they have been saved.

Available where books are sold.

According to Promise,
by Charles H. Spurgeon

The first part of this book is meant to be a sieve to separate the chaff from the wheat. Use it on your own soul. It may be the most profitable and beneficial work you have ever done. He who looked into his accounts and found that his business was losing money was saved from bankruptcy.

The second part of this book examines God's promises to His children. The promises of God not only exceed all precedent, but they also exceed all imitation. No one has been able to compete with God in the language of liberality. The promises of God are as much above all other promises as the heavens are above the earth.

Available where books are sold.

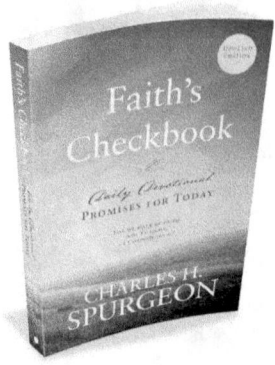

Faith's Checkbook, by Charles H. Spurgeon

Faith's Checkbook is a one-year devotional meant to encourage you to take God at His Word – to take hold of God's promises by faith. Each day you will be presented with a specific promise from the Bible, along with accompanying exhortation by Charles Spurgeon.

This is your "spiritual checkbook," if you will. God's bank account of provision is ample, and it cannot be overdrawn. Every situation you might face is equally met with a promise that, if accepted, will sufficiently see you through.

"God has given no promise that He will not redeem. He does not offer hope that He will not fulfill. To help my brethren believe this, I have prepared this little volume."
– Charles H. Spurgeon

Available where books are sold.

Morning by Morning, by Charles H. Spurgeon

Charles H. Spurgeon's devotionals *Morning by Morning* and *Evening by Evening* have inspired, encouraged, and challenged Christians for generations. Spurgeon, with his masterful hand, carefully selected his text from throughout the Bible and covered a broad range of topics, in order to present a well-balanced and fruitful daily devotional for readers both young and old.

Now updated into more-modern English for today's readers, and again separated into two volumes as originally published, with morning devotionals in one volume and evening devotionals in the second. We chose a 11-point font for the sake of legibility, and formatted the devotionals so each fits on a single page.

Available where books are sold.